GEORGE WOLLSTEN

EXPERT STOCK AND GRAIN TRADER

INVESTMENT GREATS

GEORGE WOLLSTEN

EXPERT STOCK AND GRAIN TRADER

By

George Bayer

Introduced and Edited by

Donald Mack

FINANCIAL TIMES
PRENTICE HALL

PEARSON EDUCATION LIMITED

Head Office:
Edinburgh Gate
Harlow CM20 2JE
Tel: +44 (0)1279 623623
Fax: +44 (0)1279 431059

London Office:
128 Long Acre, London WC2E 9AN
Tel: +44 (0)171 447 2000
Fax: +44 (0)171 240 5771

First published in the United States of America in 1946
First published in Great Britain 1999

ISBN 0 273 64314 2

British Library Cataloguing in Publication Data
A CIP catalogue record for this book can be obtained
from the British Library.

1 3 5 7 9 10 8 6 4 2

Typeset by M Rules
Printed and bound in Great Britain by
Biddles Ltd, Guildford & King's Lynn

The Publishers' policy is to use paper manufactured from sustainable forests.

ABOUT THE AUTHOR

George Bayer

When it comes to books dealing with generating the profits we all seek from the stock, futures and options markets, descriptions of the authors themselves more often than not tend to be skimpy or non-existent. Their writings speak for themselves, and as to who and what they are, we generally get only a few scanty details and that's about it. However, once in a while we are offered something which turns out to be richly different for a change. That's exactly what we get when it comes to George Bayer and this book *George Wollsten: Expert Stock and Grain Trader*. In it we handsomely receive a great deal to do with the man himself and, importantly, with explanations of the thinking and the rationale that lie behind many of his original creative concepts. Reading through this book, the reader is going to find out quite a bit about George Bayer because the George Wollsten in the book's title is George Bayer. George came to the USA from Germany just after the turn of the 20th century, and as will be seen he was soon attracted to the speculative markets that abounded in New York City and Chicago. Interweaving his life story with his innovative market achievements, there emerges for traders and investors a wealth of material to study and the choice to incorporate some, all, or even none of his ideas into their own trading and investing programs. Some of his other books are *The Egg of Columbus: or the Hidden Movements in Stocks and Commodities Markets*; *Gold Nuggets for Stock and Commodity Traders*; *The Time Factors in the Stock Market*; and *Stock and Commodity Traders' Handbook of Trend Determination*.

ABOUT THE SERIES EDITOR

Donald Mack

Collectors in their particular field of personal interest always seem to start with a few things that intrigue them, then as the years go by their collections, like Topsy, just grow and grow. Well, that's what happened to the editor of this classic book series. At first he acquired several books on the stock market. Then a collection started and it grew into some 200-plus books. Finally, it came down to gathering one copy of every book ever published on markets and on investment and trading. Before it ended, the collection was easily some 5,500-plus market books and a lot of bookshelves.

It all began when he bought a few New York Stock Exchange shares in his youthful exuberance, and wow! the profits just rolled in on those first few transactions (something not unusual for first-time investors to experience on their initial market forays). Then buying and selling more, he quickly discovered he wasn't quite the natural market genius that initial results had given him. Then from beyond the blue came that still, small voice whispering "Hey kiddo, if you're going to be serious about this trading and investing, you better do some studying (actually one heck of a lot more studying) or you ain't going nowhere."

So it was that he went from introductory general investment books to detailed general investment books to Fundamental Analysis books, and lastly to Technical Analysis books where he found a lifetime of study. Meanwhile the books continued piling up and piling up more and more. The answer – his Investment Centre Bookstore in the late 1970s and through the 1980s in Los Angeles, the only one in the USA that specialized in stock market and commodity books, both new and old. He discovered the greatest Technical Analysis books of all time were written 30 to 60 years ago, and the big surprise – they were just as good today and just as applicable as the day they were written. Since markets basically don't change (one buys on them, one sells on them, and prices are recorded with every transaction), price action charts don't change (prices go up, they go down, they go sideways), and investors and traders don't change either (they keep making the *same* mistakes since Adam and Eve first invested in Forbidden Fruit Inc.).

While he always stocked the bookstore with the market books in print at the time (ho-hum), it was those superb old market classics ranging all the way from the great general ones to the great technical ones of decades gone by that had his interest. Definitely *not every* book published during those decades was a great one, but Madame Greatness produced more than her fair share. The net result of his exposure to so many classic market books over the years, was that he gained an appreciation and a fair amount (and a bit more) of knowledge and expertise on these books. Then came a meeting of minds with our good publishers, the Financial Times Prentice Hall of London, England who saw the potential response there would be in bringing back from obscurity all the great classics that this editor suggested.

Working together, the American editor and the British publisher have inaugurated a marvelous series of great Technical Analysis classics which is still growing with new additions. For investors and traders far and wide they can now invest in the growing, not-yet-finished *Traders' Masterclass* series of classics which is now joined with this second now underway series named the *Investment Greats* series. The first series is the cream-of-cream in Technical Analysis writings; the second series ranges from classics, strong with technical content, all the way to no technical content at all. Every book will be found to be a gem in its own right and in the special investment area it covers. What a collection both series will eventually make together!

TABLE OF CONTENTS

ILLUSTRATIONS

THE INVESTMENT GREATS SERIES

What type of investor are you? Do you make choices or follow rules?

The greatest investors have always combined a strong awareness of guiding principles with a breadth of market vision that separates them from their peers. For the greats, schooled wisdom is elevated by instinctive imagination. Flair like this does not come easily, but through immersion in the inspiration of others, it can be encouraged and developed.

Selected and edited by experienced US trader and renowned investment book expert, Donald Mack, the *Investment Greats* series offers a glimpse into the psychology of the world's great investment minds, bringing together some of the classic investment literature of the past 100 years in a newly presented, modern format. For years these books have been hidden from all except a select few, but once again their secrets can be appreciated and absorbed by all. The *Investment Greats* series demonstrates the enduring power and quality of investment art.

This series will benefit and inspire investors at all levels with provocative ideas and timeless wisdom. It provides tools and techniques, but most of all, it offers a reader-friendly, literary style and a passion for investment which is as refreshing as it is infectious. These are unique classics with a personal voice.

If you appreciate the art of investment, the *Investment Greats* series will take you into the minds of the masters.

EDITOR'S INTRODUCTION

Considering all the many books on market analysis that have ever been published, this work by George Bayer has to be just about the most unusual book of them all, and that includes all of the genre of market books that have come our way decade after decade. And even temporarily setting aside its unusual contents, it will still be seen that just on the merits of its masterly classical technical material it could easily have been part of our now well-established *Traders' Masterclass* series. That series was designed to revolve around one core subject – classic Technical Analysis, that methodology of market analysis which is the analytical basis used by the greatest number of professional and individual traders and investors the world over. Yet, almost unbelievably, the fact is that many of the great Technical Analysis classics remain practically unknown to the mass of market people everywhere, and like Nature's rare and endangered animal species, they too face the very real threat of extinction.

Because these great technical works are full of material both similar (and in many ways superior) to much in this field that has been published, say, in the last ten to twenty years (in this writer's humble opinion), many are treasured gems worthy of being re-published. For this reason, along with several others, the publishers, Financial Times Prentice Hall of London, England, and the writer of this Introduction set in motion in 1997 just that re-publication goal. The result is that today we have under way what has been welcomed in so many quarters – the bringing back from the past a number of great and almost forgotten classical Technical Analysis works. If our initial expectations here were on the optimistic side, that could be forgiven if the expected reception for the first four classics had failed to materialize, but fortunately the response and acceptance has been as beautiful and more bountiful than we dared to predict. The original concept was that there would be a first Technical Analysis series of some twelve to fifteen books, and, if the reception by the investment public showed the kind of response we could at that stage only dream about, then a similar second series could follow. These were – no! the past tense is wrong here – these *are* superb works on their particular subjects which must and should be preserved not only in honor of the great minds that produced them, but for the equally great wisdom they possess. For serious students of speculative markets in the future (and these persons will exist, for markets will always demand their efforts and input), the opportunity to learn from, and to see how advanced these great market minds of the past were, should be available.

So, as pointed out, this George Bayer work could easily have been published by adding it to our first series of Technical Analysis classics and it would have fitted in very well indeed. But though it is full of great technical knowledge, it still in no way reads like any Technical Analysis book that I know of. With the excellent reception accorded the first four classic masterpieces in our Traders' Masterclass series, and knowing that there are a number of classics less technical, or not technical at all, we somehow just had to make these other great classics available too. The answer – start a new series to go with the more specialized first series.

As with practically all the great classics from what I call "The Golden Age of Market and Technical Analysis Literature – 1922 to 1957" that we are bringing back to the worldwide community of traders and investors, there is an old but familiar tale to do with books from the distant past. Time can be a friend to many books, but it has to be faced that, more often than not, it is a hard taskmaster for so many more. Generally speaking, Time's passage with respect to many of the great market books, and the lesser ones also, has mostly been a rough world of extreme cruelty to these works and it is not at all unusual for them to have lain almost unknown, even up to this time. And as there are many non-technical exceptional classic investment books that also need to be spared Time's fickle hand, the publishers and this editor have come up with this new second series, called the *Investment Greats* series. So in starting this new tack in the extension of our range of great market classics, this masterpiece of George Bayer's makes its contribution as the first in that new range. Here in the second series will be found books having a great deal of technical content, like this one, *George Wollsten: Expert Stock and Grain Trader*, to classics with little or even no technical content at all, but all very worthy and masterly works that, for the benefit of all market people, should not be allowed to perish.

To span the gap between the first more specialized series and this one, this work by George Bayer seemed the ideal choice to make the transition between the two camps represented here. The first series deals entirely with expositions of Technical Analysis as they are. They all present their readers with the opportunity to see afresh the myriad ways to deduce from charted action of any particular stock or futures contract its analytical prospects. *George Wollsten: Expert Stock and Grain Trader* more than fulfills this writer's belief that this book will stand the test of time, proving itself worthy of the attention it should receive and the market education it provides.

Before the more usual short introductory comments on what the reader can look forward to in the following material, there is a fascinating story to be told here to do with this book's background. It revolves around a few vital events of the type that Fate especially loves to spring on the unsuspecting. Thus Fate set the scene for this unique Bayer work to make its contribution to the market's stage and to the players who come to play on it. Those readers who have acquired a copy of the superb and acclaimed second book in our *Traders' Masterclass* series written by William Dunnigan and entitled *New Blueprints for Gains in Stocks and Grains*, combined with *The One-Way Formula for Trading in Stocks and*

Commodities, will possibly recall my several paragraphs to do with Mr Franklin Paul Jackson. Though this material can be found in the Introduction to the Dunnigan book, a repetition here for those who have not seen this Introduction will not be in the least bit out of place when the wondrous workings of Fate are brought out.

To begin this story of the events that took place and how they all fitted together, we have to start off by acknowledging Mr Jackson's standing, for he was a market giant whose writings in the 1940s and 1950s rank him as a member of that small unique band of the greatest of market masters. At the age of 86 he came into my bookshop after many years of retirement in Mexico, with a new vigor to get back into the market workings that he knew so well. This happened in 1984, as I recall, when I was working one day in one of the back rooms of my all-market bookstore. I heard my assistant talking with someone who had just entered the main salesroom, and though I didn't hear much, I did hear the visitor say that in the 1940s he had a market educational center in downtown Los Angeles called the Stock Market Institute. To someone such as myself who, day in and day out, was involved with very rare to not-so-rare market books as a dealer, a collector, a student of market movement, and constantly a seeker of rare market books that I knew about but had never seen, this visitor could only be one person. From one of his books, written in 1944 and inscribed to this same Stock Market Institute, I knew he had to be a certain market personage whose name was engraved in my memory for that name was that of the author of other books I had been seeking for years. And as it turned out, it was he!

My assistant said, when I came into the main book room, that my face was all colors of the rainbow, and he was right, for that was how I felt. My first words to this visitor were "Pardon me, but are you by any chance Franklin Paul Jackson?" And he answered "Yes! I'm Frank Jackson." To most in the investment community of the 1980s, and even more so now in the 1990s, I would have to say that his name, very understandably, wouldn't mean that much, if indeed anything. However, I knew from the few books of his that I had in my personal collection, and from the amount of time that had passed since they were published, that by all reckoning, I was in the presence of probably the last of the great market masters of the previously mentioned "Golden Age of Market and Technical Analysis Literature." An innocuous event (so it would seem on the surface), for here we have an elderly gentleman still retaining all his faculties and sharpness visiting a bookstore in Southern California. But this was no ordinary bookstore, and this, in market terms, was certainly no ordinary gentleman.

This bookstore was at the time the only one of its type in the USA, for it specialized solely in stock and commodity market books. As would be expected, it stocked just about everything in market literature that was newly published and current at the time (no big or difficult concept here). But much more importantly, where it was unique and where it really counted was that its inventory contained a much greater number of market books that were long out of print, including many that ranged from the rare, to the very rare, and on to the exceedingly rare.

These out-of-print books covered every category in terms of content that concerned Wall Street, stock markets, commodity markets, analysis and any other investment subject one could come up with. Some were very dated; many were not. Certainly the historical books, even though written as of a certain date, were a category greatly desired by very interested people. Then there were those books in the one extra-special area that always had much more demand than I could ever hope to meet. This was the area of original editions of the great works, or even (in consolation) the lesser great books, from the great masters on Technical Analysis. For those who may be new to, or even totally unaware of, this field and who are not at all clear as to what the word "Technical" applies to, it was always the area that reigned supreme in those bookstore days. Today, as the second millennium approaches, it does so still because it, unarguably, forms the backbone of almost every computer program of market and forecasting analysis, especially if we measure it by the number of traders it attracts to its thousands of analytical possibilities.

This field of Technical Analysis is unique in its make-up. First and foremost it has to be understood by the reader that *anything* written on it at *any* time can be and most times *is* eternal. Time need not ever see it die or fade away. The reason for this is simple. Good Technical Analysis writings will always be unlimited in their possible scope. They can have at their heart and in their market souls vast mental concepts for a field that knows absolutely no bounds, no limits, and no lack of practical application. This always showed up in the demand for the older great market classics. In my bookstore, great technical ideas, as most newcomers come eventually to learn in their own technical development, are both always wanted and always needed. That holds true whether these analytical concepts were conjured up as many as sixty years ago, or today, or might be at any time in the future.

Having learned of my specialized market bookstore, into it came Mr Jackson – out of the blue. To go into all the personal experiences, the inspirational techniques, and the overall market knowledge that Mr Jackson passed on both to this writer and to many visitors to the bookstore would require more pages than this Introduction is allotted. That he was an analytical market master of the highest order goes almost without saying. The knowledge he displayed in the several years that followed saw my respect for his market stature increase and increase, and that stature began at a level that only a few, a very few in any speculative marketplace anywhere could ever hope to reach in the first place. But having briefed you thus far on this remarkable man, you the reader may well at this point interject that the Introduction you are presently reading is in a book authored by George Bayer, so what does that have to do with Franklin Paul Jackson? Well, a great deal! For you see one day he came on one of his regular visits to the bookstore with a number of papers in his possession and among them was a handwritten letter that he had received in the late 1940s. It was from an old farmer in Illinois who from the ten or so pages in the letter revealed to me that here was a market mind so well steeped in market knowledge that he had to be a better market analyst than many of the great Wall Street and City of London analysts then and now. In this letter he drew Mr Jackson's attention to "this feller in Northern California, George Bayer, who was doing some extremely worthwhile work in market and technical analysis, and had written several books on his work."

Well, that mention of George Bayer alone was a bit of a shock to me. I knew that there was no way I could possibly know about every market book ever written or every author that wrote them. However, I knew or knew about so many of these books, relatively speaking, that anything on any unknown book and/or author coming my way was always a very welcome surprise. Well, George Bayer was definitely in that category for he had written about seven or eight books and yet I had not heard even a mention of him; to me he really was that unknown. Obviously my curiosity was aroused and I began to track down his output which soon led me to the conclusion that most of his books, if not all of them, must have been self-published and in very small numbers, making them rarities of rarities. The very first Bayer book that I managed to track down was a copy of this book *George Wollsten,* and to say that I found it extremely intriguing would be the understatement of the decade. For on first sight of its contents it was not the least bit difficult to recognize that here was a market gem that was going to make an impression on many in the analytical world. The result was that I first introduced him to all my regular book buyers, and then I went on to further publicize the man and his works in the numerous writings and catalogs that I sent out to my mailing list from time to time. So thanks to the fortuitous circumspect introduction that came through Mr Jackson, I was able to bring the Bayer name to the attention of a number of interested parties, but relatively speaking again, really only to a comparative few. One of those few was an old ("old" that is only in terms of visits to my bookstore) customer Larry Pesavento who has gone on to author several books during the past ten years or so that have included a great deal of material based on his perusal of all the Bayer writings.*

Leaving off any extensive delving into the contents of *George Wollsten* at this time, an initial perusal will probably find the reader coming to a stop at the illustration of one or all of the three "Ellipses" in this book. This was my initial experience, for they stood out so starkly that the uniqueness of his use of these "Ellipses" for market analysis and forecasting immediately grabbed my attention. Here was something strange that I had never seen before and haven't seen since. That no one had ever publicized this unusual technique (not an easy one to master fully) in some publication is only further proof that this Bayer concept has long been unrecognized. Certainly if it had been recognized, it would have been picked up by at least a few market letter writers, some of whom would have quickly latched on to it by presenting it as their own original product and thinking. But none to my knowledge has, so practically everyone reading about them here will be receiving their personal introduction to the "Bayer Ellipses" and how to work with them through the medium of his words in this book.

To get a sense of what may be behind this elliptical concept, we must first journey along with Mr Bayer to get an understanding just wherein lies the rationale for his use of this form, which is much better known in another field – Astronomy. Certainly it would not be improper at this point for anyone to inquire as to this rationale, for as surely as the Sun rises in the East there just has to be some principle behind it to give it its substance. There are

*See Larry Pesavento's *Harmonic Vibrations* and *Planetary Harmonics Of Speculative Markets*.

no surprises here, however, and we have only to look to the Universe surrounding us to find our explanation. There also has to be an accompanying question that if universal forms are of any value, why have others not uncovered them and why have they been so long in coming to our attention? Taking the second question first, the reasons behind technical analysts everywhere not having even the slightest inkling of the use of the "Ellipse" over the years have to remain unexplained. As to the question of rationale, the first place to look is in the writings of that greatest of market masters, William D. Gann. Gann was a firm believer in a great many aspects of the "Circle" for chart analysis and this, in turn, draws our attention to the three most important, almost perfectly formed, circles that affect our lives immensely – the Sun, the Moon, and the Earth. This has to mean that the Circle is one of the great forms of Nature, and as such it can and does figure a great deal when it is used as a tool for chart analysis. Another of the forms on our charts that should not go unnoticed, but does, is again a highly evolved natural form of Nature, the "Spiral," the greatest example of which can be found in the shape of all or almost all of the Galaxies. Going from the truly gigantic spirals to just about as small as we can think of, just consider every human that has ever lived or will live. Every person, bar none, owes a great debt to the Spiral (actually to a pair of them), for are not DNA and RNA in the form of intertwining spiral shapes without which we could not exist in our physical life forms?

Ah, you say, come on, let's face it, we can look over our charts till the cows come home and nowhere are there any spirals to be found on any of them. On the surface you would be right, or so it would seem. Just take a good look at your charts and, if you see any spirals, raise your hand. No hands will probably go up. Fine! For here we are talking of some of the highest orders of market analysis, which means analysis that goes back to what Technical Analysis in its truest form is basically about – excellent chart reading, superb chart reading, and out-of-this-world chart reading.

On this point we would quickly beg to differ by signifying that spirals are there even though one has to use one's mental faculties beyond the norm to see them. In a way this goes back to the old market premise that what is known by the many or can easily be seen by the same "many" is *hardly worth knowing*.

To see at least some form of spirals we would draw the attention of everyone who would raise the point about their absence to first read about "Coils" (a form of spirals) which Financial Times Prentice Hall recently re-published in their classic *Traders' Masterclass* series if they should have it – *A Course in Trading* by The Wetsel Market Bureau, 1934. Then, if you still think spirals are not applicable to charts, we would ask you to consider the Fibonacci Spiral that has attracted at least some attention in the past several years to its measuring potentials. And should more references be needed, we would advise you to look at the work of Christopher Carolan and his usage of the spiral form and Technical Analysis in his calendar research.*

For the third universal form, we have to consider that, contrary to what we initially learned in our younger years, the Earth and the Planets *do not* go around the Sun in circles, but they do so in elliptical paths. Thus, here we have another of the universal shapes of Nature, a natural shape that also could be important in playing a part in our chart analyses, if one so chooses to work with it after reading this book. This unique and unknown concept from the mind of George Bayer brings the thought to this editor that there is something more that needs to be said at this point. With many readers of this Introduction not having the chance to come in to contact with much of the great Technical Analysis thinking of past years, perhaps they may have fallen into some present-day thinking and a very well-conditioned trap. The trap is one of taking it for granted that the advanced mighty computerized

*See Christopher Carolan's *The Spiral Calendar and its Effect on Financial Markets and Human Events*.

Technical Analysis of today, some fifty years on, puts the great market minds of the past well into a distant secondary place in the scheme of things. Well, not only have the greats of the past not been left behind, but a case could be made that in some ways they were so far ahead of us today that we are the ones who need to do the catching up. Perhaps some new thinking needs to be considered.

Let's face it, computers are totally stupid, they are not capable of thought or any form of thinking, even with today's well-publicized Artificial Intelligence thrown in. The market masters of forty to sixty years ago were absolutely outstanding in their contributions to this unending field of analysis that we and those who follow us have to pursue to greater lengths the same struggle which they had to find those bigger and better answers. Here in this Bayer book we all can and should benefit by having our minds opened to new and creative ideas that, as mentioned, we would be hard put in the past decade (and further back) to find anything to equal. Not only are his "Ellipses" brilliant concepts; they are indicative of the real work of a Master Technician (and these are not his only contributions by any means, but read on).

Referring again to what Bayer writes, it has always been my impression that this book is in reality as close to the genre as anything that I have ever seen to the greatest market book of them all – *Reminiscences of a Stock Operator* by Edwin Lefevre and the fabled market operator, Jesse Livermore. While the Bayer book is not as beautifully or cleverly written as the work of the very professional Lefevre, I still think and feel that, style aside, it is much more technically oriented and more interesting. George Bayer was, as we know, German-born and, after being in the USA for over forty years, the English language was no problem for him. But to write in another language other than a writer's native tongue still takes some doing, and Bayer did it well, even if his writing is not always perfect English. So direct comparisons with the beautifully finished style of Lefevre are not really called for and would not be fair, but for technical worth, Bayer shows he really is a master in his own right.

As readers make their way through passages of the book, they will find it very unlike other market books. Written in the form of a story, we find the author intertwining his personal life in his new country with extensive passages that deal with his market experiences and developmental thinking, all in all giving a natural flow to the whole book. I would question his inclusion of the first two chapters that tell in great detail of his brother Jim Wollsten and his path and experiences in making his way from south Germany, through Italy to the USA. There are no market connections associated with Jim and with his chosen field, which for him was to be a very good farmer, and it is only when George follows him to the New World soon after Jim's arrival that we get into market investment and analysis.

There is something special to be gained from reading this book that easily escapes notice as it is not all that apparent. And that is that George Bayer was also of the W. D. Gann school that combines the highest degree of technical market knowledge with strong elements of mysticism. Strange as the joining of these two elements in the field of speculation may seem, if two of the greatest of analytical market minds show similar paths, then this is something that should not escape our consideration. At least, that is, not without a great deal of open-minded searching. Dealing in books as I did, and in the supplying of market knowledge of all kinds, I was not at all hesitant to make known in my catalogs a listing of some eighty books that Mr Gann had published. They were books that he found of interest in the field of the mystical. For me they turned out to be a natural addition and one that satisfied good numbers of requests that came my way. As I observed, the buyers were mostly those with many years of investment experience under their belts, and this interest was not too far removed from the norm at this level of development. That I can call it some sort of a "norm" is not really out of line, for it can be seen in the works of many of the great market writers and with many market-involved persons over the whole of the world.

Interestingly, and also very unusually, we find the author compelled to insert a few words of preliminary wisdom at the very beginning of the book under the heading which he labels "Foreward to First Edition." It's less than a page long and yet it really should be read, and several times too, to get its fuller meaning. If the reader after several attempts still misses what market analysis is really all about and where the real answers are to be found, then we shall be glad to help engrave it *for ever* in their psyche. For it is on this page that the author gives away the secret of all market mastery – Cycles and Time. The "Cycle" concept must absolutely be understood as being far removed from the commonly accepted stylized usage and presentation of "Cycles." Here we refer to sine waves and the like in economics, in mathematics and in all the superficial market connections as portrayed by the mathematically inclined, and others in many market books. The great market masters who took great interest in cycles were more than able to surmount the mathematical handicaps of their times and those of the equally backward 1990s. The mixed-up past and current concepts to do with cycles in the markets are fine for the majority that use them. For those seeking market success, there has to be an abrupt turn from the seemingly logical scientific cycle types and shapes to where the true market cycle lies – irregular ups and downs where *not one* resembles those before and those after. Sounds illogical, doesn't it? To the great Golden Age market greats, it wouldn't. From the totally discredited Ph.D.s and their higher mathematical-type thinking, as exemplified by the mighty fall of Long Term Capital Management in 1998, it would. What I am advocating to many readers is to make a start and activate some of those brain cells. Once this is faced, then one can start looking at cycles in market analysis as an entirely new animal, far removed from the useless idealized and stylized higher mathematical cycle thinking that has been prevalent for much too long.

Regarding the Time element to which Bayer repeatedly refers, what can we say? We can only *cry*. Here we have what is the great stated key (and stated over and over again in his books and his courses) by the greatest of market masters, William D. Gann. Seeing that this same Time element is hardly considered at all by the mass of technical analysts, we cry again! Similarly, in surveying just about all of the books on market analysis that have been in print during the last forty years or so, not to over-stress the issue, but relatively speaking it can be said that they are totally obsessed with price and its component usage (in indicators, that is). The ignoring of time factors and time measuring everywhere is almost universal and unqualified proof that they are beautiful tools to work with (based on the ultimate market truth that the majority are generally on the wrong side in the marketplace, especially at major turning points). Bayer's ultimate statement here, that Time along with Cycles are the real keys to analysing and forecasting market movements, makes them "the Ultimate." It is this recognition that makes so many of the great classics in the two Financial Times Prentice Hall series what they are. To this end we are dedicated to bringing back into the mainstream of Technical Analysis these very rare and worthy books. The great masters (long gone, unfortunately) knew what Time and Cycles meant; most of today's great masters of Wall Street and the City of London possess barely a clue compared to Bayer's well-put words on the subject.

The preceding paragraph expresses, in a nutshell, what makes this Bayer book such a masterpiece, in words that should be retained, at all costs, in the reader's memory and truly serve as the challenge they are. Additionally, there are numerous strong references in the book centering on looking at the "astrological." In today's language this would translate as "astronomical" (a point that the author also makes) and there is a big, big difference here. In this book the author shows only one application of the astronomical, which involves easy-to-acquire figures and simple-to-draw lines, in this case Mercury travelling across the paths of Jupiter and Saturn, which, when they cross, reflect movements in some markets. It is such a simple methodology that even I, who have no interest in the planets, astrology (nothing to do with today's newspaper versions), and other related things can easily understand and set the thing up. When I first began making this book available to my customers, one bright spark computerized the whole thing (which he reported as not being hard to do) and informed me that it had forecasting results with about a 75% success rate which in market terms is not only "not bad", it is very, very good.

The use of what the author refers to as the six-inch and the nine-inch Ellipses has already been covered, and in addition to these two Ellipses he also refers to the third one he discovered that he named the "Polish Ellipse." All three of the Ellipses can be quickly produced on a photocopier using clear plastic sheets that the market student can place in all directions on their charts. Another of the author's conceptualized ideas is the "Jiggle line" (a variation of the advance/decline concept) which he created and is unlike anything seen in other books, something else for readers to play with if they so desire. Then as a final dessert to finish off the book in puzzlement and wonder, he shows us how the circle can be squared, something thought impossible by many mathematicians. The use of this creation is left for readers to develop in whatever way they might feel inclined.

All in all and in many ways this certainly is a very unusual book, as mentioned before. It has a great deal of original, creative, and innovative thought to add to our technical knowledge which can only be most welcomed by investors and traders everywhere. It should serve very well indeed as a fine and intriguing book to begin this new *Investment Greats* series.

DONALD MACK
Series Editor
E-mail: DMack144@aol.com

FOREWORD TO FIRST EDITION

Since 1932 the author has published four books at intervals dealing with trading of Stocks and Commodities.

Unfortunately much of their contents have been found somewhat hard and difficult to the average man, even to those with a college education.

This time the entire problem has been remodeled, many parts eliminated as "too complicated," three new ideas added which so far have never been alluded to anywhere. It is those three ways which are bound to give confidence to any trader, that put him far ahead of all others who just buy or sell on statistics, economic or other bases.

Everything brought into this book is "home-grown."

The charts supplied for checking commitments as well as those produced with the aid of certain rules explained therein cover the period of 1909–1911 inclusive. The previous books covered periods of 1928 to 1944. Therefore a period of more than 30 years has been used to show that the rules work in any period, past or present; they should work in the future in the same way.

Hints are given to delve into ancient books of the dark ages after the study of this book has been completed to discover that they have all been written on the same subject – cycles and time.

Carmel, Calif.
November 24, 1945

INTRODUCTION TO FIRST EDITION

Two brothers, Jim and George Wollsten and their wives, Grete and Gusty play the major roles in the story.

Both had immigrated from Europe.

Jim takes up farming. George in the beginning helps him on the farm, but gradually shifts into trading wheat. An Agricultural Year Book brings him on this idea. A neighbor supplied valuable hints to encourage him in studies of economics.

In rapid succession, to everybody's surprise, he finds important rules for use in practical trading of wheat, as well as of stocks. For each trade commitment he explains carefully why he makes it, why he enters it and why he closes the deal at this time and at no other.

Traders and Customers' Men* are carefully analyzed. Many mistakes made by traders are brought forth to show how to avoid them.

Two full years of trading are gone through. His original capital had increased from $750 to several thousand in spite of a few errors of judgment that were bound to creep in until rectified by additional useful rules discovered in the course of time.

Among the unusual side issues he discovered was how to square the circle, something that even Encyclopedias state "is impossible." He shows how he did it . . .

While the story itself is interesting, the main subject "how to trade and avoid all the pitfalls of the Pit and of Wall Street" is developed slowly without complicated explanations. Everything is worked up naturally, just like a normal person would go about taking a walk up a mountain – to success in Wall Street and in the Pit.

*Customer's Men: a quaint term used many years back for those we today call "Stockbrokers."

CHAPTER I

JIM WOLLSTEN EMIGRATES TO THE UNITED STATES

Country Scene

The morning mist had just begun to lift around the sleeping village of Upper Red Hook, New York. Quiet reigned. Here and there the sound of an early Churchgoer's feet would echo through the streets. Ice and snow of a heavy December snowfall had almost melted away again because of an unprecedentedly warm Christmas week. The mist was almost a fog – a natural condensation of the humidity in the air.

For several months the croaking of frogs in the village pond had come to an end. There were no more flowers in the yards and pastures. Apple orchards, whose fruit represented the main income of the community, were barren and desolate. Cattle that used to graze on land not planted in orchards had been taken to their warm stables to await Spring, even more than Spring, since it takes grass and herbs some time to grow after Spring has arrived. Just plain barrenness became visible as day came forth through the mist. Some sort of greens peeped out in patches where the snow had melted again. Of course, something had to survive that heavy snowfall; even the rest of a winter which had given the inhabitants a foretaste of things to come had to be survived.

Nothing showed signs of life. It existed, but that is all that can be said. The trees on the highway, mostly sugar maples, led the way through and out of the village. Some distance away evergreen trees had assembled to form a contrast. Hemlocks and cedars, tall and slender, had curiously mixed together; in front of them barren maples and a few elms became a screen in summer.

The village stream was silent. A solid crust of ice had formed a month before. It had not yielded to the warm spell.

Here and there a sparrow would squeak; a squirrel would jump through the branches. They were looking for their breakfast of nuts; the sparrows were looking for some seed that had been overlooked by them so far. A brother sparrow had found a seed of corn. Another came rushing on, trying to talk him out of it. A regular fight ensued, which caused Jim Wollsten's rooster to put out a general alarm to his flock of chickens.

The pair could not as yet pay a visit to the chicken yard, since it was too early in the day. Paula had not yet fed the flock. No doubt they had such a visit in their minds for later in the day. How could they otherwise live when Nature was barren, seemingly lifeless and frozen? During the summer months there was never any question about food for anything that had wings. Seeds and tiny grasses grew in abundance at all places. A bug or a fly, in case they desired a change of diet, was always available. Pure water was to be had at fountains, from the stream, out of little rain puddles, which served them as bath tubs at the same time. Rain was no rarity in those parts, especially when thunder storms relieved the hot days and cleared the roads of dust.

Paula and Robert, the couple that helped at Wollsten's, were already up. So was Jim Wollsten, because lights in the two houses betrayed them. Jim and Robert were already in the barn, airing it to avoid overheating. Last Fall they had stored the best of their apple crop in it to hold for better market prices.

"I plumb forgot to ask George about the egg prices for the next few months. I'm sure he had the chart kept up," said Jim Wollsten to Robert. "He told me to hold the apples into February, anyhow, so that's something," he continued.

"Why not write and ask him?" said Robert, as he looked at the thermometer in the middle of the barn. "It's 38 degrees now. We'd better shut the windows before it gets too cold."

"I think I'll have to write two letters – one to New York and the other to San Francisco. Maybe I can locate him," said Jim Wollsten. "I don't know how long he intends to stay in New York. You didn't stay so very long at home either after you got married, did you? And he can afford to travel and see the world, you know."

Grete was still in bed with the baby, Jim Junior, nearby in the crib. Paula, Robert's wife, was preparing breakfast for the family, whose chief, for the past months, had been little Jim. Everybody in the family attended to him. The oatmeal had to be just so, the milk also.

Paula was about twenty-five, her husband a year younger. Grete, the mistress of the house, might have been two or three years younger, but that did not make much difference. They got along fine, even though there was no relationship existing whatever. Robert and Paula had been with them only about ten months.

"Don't you use any of that fresh milk again when Robert brings it in. It acts like castor oil on all of us," said Grete from her bedroom.

"I have never done it before, Mrs Wollsten," Paula answered. "Only yesterday we had used all the other milk when your honeymoon couple was here and the rest was sold. I thought it would be all right for once."

Pretty soon we see the family assembled in the kitchen to have breakfast. Robert had in the meanwhile milked the lone cow that was on the farm, Jim Wollsten had gathered a dozen eggs from the coops. Paula had been taught how to make hotcakes, a favorite of Jim's. The breakfast was simple and healthful. Since the couple had been taken on, Grete and Jim could take life a little easier. Before she would have to attend to everything herself – to the household, the cooking, and to the chickens as well as the many other things a woman on a farm must look after. Jim also had worked hard for the last three years to get a good start in America.

Jim Wollsten

Jim Wollsten had left his old country of Bavaria three years before. He was the youngest son of a farmer and had heard that in the New World there would be a chance to own a farm himself. He had saved up all the nickels and dimes he could obtain. It took at that time but twenty-five dollars to cross the big pond when a regular immigrant boat was used. Besides, it was just at the time when Jim was to be taken into the army there, as happened to all boys of twenty. He had the feeling that he was fit for the army. He preferred to see how the New World looked first. There would be still time to serve a few years later, in case the New World did not offer him a better future.

Farmers, even when grown up in a foreign country, have knowledge of many things, though when they come here they may appear to be "yokels." It usually takes them a few years to get used to the ways of our country, and to the language especially. Jim was doubtful whether he would be permitted to get on the steamers that leave Hamburg or Bremen because of the military service before him. He decided to go another way. First he went to Munich to change his marks into American money. He sewed fifty dollars inside his coat. One day an agent of a Western railroad who had stayed at the local inn explained to the men there in their own language the opportunities offered to settle in Western America. From him he heard that it would cost but twenty-five dollars, plus ten dollars for some tax, to get to America. In addition the railroad fare would be needed.

He knew from his geography at school that from Genoa, Italy, boats also sail away to America. A few days later he packed his belongings, consisting of an old suit, two shirts, a few pairs of socks, collars, a stiletto, a piece of soap, a comb, a razor, also a special ointment that would make his moustache grow. A moustache brush, bought in Munich, a pair of sturdy shoes, together with a bottle of ink and a pen, also went into the suitcase. His Sunday suit, shoes, and hat, he wore, and he said goodbye to his folks.

Jim Wollsten Emigrates to the United States

He once had been in Austria, at the first town across the border, and therefore he knew that no one would stop him from getting to that place. He bought a ticket for Kufstein, the town he had visited in Austria to climb mountains. Approaching Kiefersfelden, the last station in Bavaria, cold sweat formed on his forehead, and he anxiously watched the fields through the train window as he thought of what might happen at the border. The train pulled in. A few passengers got off. It pulled out without anything having happened. Five minutes later the station of Kufstein in Austria was reached. Jim was in a daze because nothing had happened. The customs inspection at that place took but a few minutes. The official quickly saw that no duty could be raised from the contents of his suitcase.

From there he took a train for Ala, which was the southernmost town of old Austria. South of the city limits was Italian territory. Nobody bothered him as he got off the train. The trip had been very pleasant, as it brought him through mountain territory throughout, even through a big, long tunnel – the Brenner Tunnel.

Only one little difficulty occurred to him. About an hour or so before he reached Ala, the new passengers talked another language. The lower part of old Austria spoke Italian. It was the "Trentino Italian" spoken south of Bozen. After sitting around the old station for a while, he heard one fellow talk German and timidly approached him to ask whether there was a place to stay overnight.

"Why, I'm a stranger here myself," replied the man with an accent that sounded to him more like Prussian than Bavarian German. And for these fellows a true Bavarian has never had much use since the revolution of 1848. With an "Excuse me," he sat down again beside his suitcase. After a while he began to walk into town. All the store signs had words that meant nothing to him. At one place he noticed a sign: "Birra." Some intuition made him read "Beer also," or "Bier a (auch)," as he would say in his own language. Jim entered with his suitcase to get a glass of beer, and especially to see whether or not some sleeping quarters could be obtained. He was able to get the glass of beer. They even accepted German money from him, although they used different currency there. Somehow or other he could not explain that he wanted a place to sleep. Plenty of "Alberghi," hotels, or inns had rooms at Ala, but how was he to know that word when they call such alberghi "Wirtschaft" in his own language?

He knew that the next village on the Italian side was about three miles south. He had seen it from the time table. The ride had given him sufficient time to figure out how to proceed to get out of Austria without being sent back to Bavaria. He had the idea that luck was not always to be counted on, especially when one is supposed to become a soldier and wants instead to settle in America. He knew a passport was not needed to go into Italy, because nowhere was it necessary to have passports at that time. Even to go to America none was required.

The Adige river ran southward through the town. If he were three miles below, in Italy, things would look much rosier. In desperation he picked up his suitcase and simply headed south on the old highway, that would be considered a back country road in America and which led along the river. Half an hour out of town he saw to his left a small house with a flag on top. There a wooden barrier ran across the road. A small gate for pedestrians was to one side. A couple of donkeys loaded with sacks came up from the Italian side to cross the border with their driver. Jim waited to see what would happen to them. While sitting on his suitcase, he watched.

First the driver walked into the little house and reappeared a few moments later. Another man now came out and opened the gates. Driver and donkeys moved on toward Ala.

"Well," thought Jim to himself, "eventually I will have to do the same if I ever want to get through that barrier." On top of the building was a sign, "Duane." Whatever that meant Jim did not know. He was sure, however, that it was the customs house.

When things are at their darkest the light sometimes appears, and so it was now. Jim went into the building with a show of more confidence than he felt.

"I want to go through to see something in Italy," he declared.

To his surprise the customs official answered in Jim's own language, saying, "All right. Keep going if you want to get there."

Jim smiled. He had not grasped the answer immediately. With his suitcase he walked through the gate, but about 50 feet beyond he saw another of those gates with a building close by. A big sign read "Italia," and informed all travelers that this was the border. A red, white, and green flag flew from the roof. Jim entered the building with a much different feeling from what he had felt before. Then his main worry had been to get out of Austria, and now it was how to get into Italy. Here, too, it was a matter of showing the contents of the suitcase before he could keep going. But within a couple of minutes he was through the last barrier that he was to meet until he was to reach the boat that would bring him to the New World.

It was getting late. Since leaving Munich Jim had had no regular meals, and that had been nearly two days ago. During the night he had slept a few hours in the train after it grew dark. The rest of the time was spent dreaming of how the New World might look should he ever reach there. "Is the rye there like ours? Have they cows and horses like us? Can the boat be trusted to find the harbor on the other side of the pond?" In between he would nibble on a piece of smoked ham, and continue to wonder.

He was thirsty, immensely thirsty. In his excitement at passing from Austria into Italy he had had no time to think about it, but now his senses began to function again. Finally he could stand it no longer. He left his suitcase on the road to go down to the river for a drink. He even washed himself, face and hands. Back on the road he ate another piece of ham and then continued his march southward.

The mountains on both sides approached the river more and more, and finally a gorge was formed. Beyond was the big valley of the Po. It was not long thereafter that he reached the first Italian town, Rovereto. Opposite the railroad station he found a place which looked to Jim like a hotel. He entered. It proved to be one Although nobody could speak his language, he had no trouble getting a room. As soon as he had a room he went to bed and slept soundly through the night.

Grete, His Sweetheart

"So far, so good," remarked Jim to himself when he awoke. His morning prayers took up considerable time, because he had much to be thankful for. He had to offer an additional prayer that he might reach the New World in safety – the place he wished to have for his new home. And besides, there was Grete. Grete, for whom he especially carried pen and ink, the sweetheart he had left behind. She was so sweet and beautiful. Everything and anything would make her happy. She loved country life, although brought up in the city of Munich. She used to visit her grandparents each summer in the country, where she would help pitch hay and load it. During the late Easter vacation she would climb with the boys into the trees to shake off cockchafers. She could walk along fences without falling. During the summer vacations she would go along to swipe carrots for Jim from neighboring vegetable patches. While Jim watched, Grete, the smaller, would crawl on all fours to reach the precious roots. She liked to watch the blacksmith with Jim, but both made a wide detour around the butcher's shop. Once, when they were looking curiously into the butcher's shop, the big butcher took his knife and sharpened it and approached the door. Both had felt that there was a significance in his action that boded them no good.

Many of the boys had their eyes on her. She would not give them any attention. Of his present plans Jim had told her nothing, fearing she might betray his intentions without meaning to. She might even ask the priest for his counsel, and in seeking to help him she might multiply his difficulties. Only a few hints had he ever given her of the thoughts that were first in his mind, and these had been enough to convince him that he had better leave well enough alone. He would have her come to him in the New World as soon as possible. He had faith in himself that he could succeed there. He would work hard, he would earn money, he would buy his own farm, and he would have Grete, too.

After his prayers were said he wrote Grete a letter in which he revealed that he was now in Italy and would leave soon for the New World, that is what he called America. He also told her of his love – something he had never dared do before. He also described his trip to Rovereto. Only with much difficulty was he able to secure a stamp to paste on the envelope.

The hotel clerk directed him to a nearby restaurant where he obtained a glass of black coffee, without cream. Instead of cream he had a small glass of cognac. Something that looked like our cornmeal bread was served with the coffee. The man, enveloped in a big white apron, who delivered it said, "Polenta," and a few other words. Had he heard right? Was there a roast duck to appear for breakfast? He remembered from school a tongue twister which they said when kids: "Leni dradantum, procenta" – that last word, was that the word the man had used? The three words were supposed to represent the language of a priest which nobody could understand but himself. They meant, "Helen, turn the duck around and roast it on the other side."

In Italy

He was the only guest. It was already ten o'clock. He ate the polenta, which had a queer, somewhat bitter taste, but no duck appeared. He called the man after a while and, to show that he meant to have that, he ordered, "Polenta." The manager, waiter, handy-man, and, apparently, the breakfast cook, disappeared to return before long with the same yellowish squared cuts that tasted so bitter. He was hungry enough to eat two ducks, but could not explain. Jim had decided it was best to eat this portion too, since he did not know when and where his next meal would be. He paid him with Italian money received from the hotel keeper, who changed one of his five-mark bills. He had received silver pieces, several big coppers with the King's head on them. He did not know just what all this money was worth, but he knew it must be equal to five marks less his room rent and the postage stamp.

The way he felt as he walked with his suitcase to the station is not easy to describe. His hunger had disappeared, but he was among strange people who spoke another language. He was on his own, full of expectancy, and eager to discover what was to await him in the New World. He wondered how that boat which was to carry him there would look. Everything was quiet as he entered the depot to buy his ticket for Genoa. He consulted the time tables that decorated the walls, selecting the one which had the longest grease line smeared over the stations' names. There he was: Rovereto, Ala; a few stations below he read: Verona in larger letters; and following that were the names of Rome, Bologna. Napoli, Genoa. The next train was to leave at noon. Jim decided to sit out the time at the station to be sure he would not get lost and miss the train. He felt for his money sewn into his coat. It was there. He had no overcoat with him. It was Spring, and in Italy it was already warm.

About half an hour before the train was due, some people entered the station. Another couple with baskets entered, and others with bags, some with children, all of them chatting at high speed. He understood absolutely nothing of what they said. Fortunately they were of demonstrative manner, moving their arms while talking and making him conscious that he himself had been working his own hands and arms last evening while trying to get a room at the hotel. In their case it was for emphasis: in his case it was a necessity. A few minutes before the train time the ticket seller suddenly pushed open his window. Everyone ran towards it to secure tickets. He asked for a ticket for Genoa. The train from Austria arrived; the morning local had stopped at all stations for the last five hours and had still another hour to go to reach its destination, Verona. It was a mixed train; freight cars, passenger cars, just as they could be put together. The cars were not like ours, but each car had all single compartments, with about twelve doors to the car. Some doors were marked first class, others second class, but the biggest part was marked third class. He chose the first compartment. The passengers surveyed the newcomer for a moment as he sought to seat himself among the men, bundles, and suitcases. By that time the train had resumed its journey southward. Conversations started again. Short Italian stogies were kept burning by long drafts between sentences. As they approached Verona, the passengers arranged their belongings. Some began to stand up in the narrow space that separated the two benches of the long compartment. Jim had not spoken a word all the while. He did not even listen. "I hope," he thought to himself, "it will be better than this in America!"

At Verona Station he was fortunate enough to notice a man in a booth outside of which several names had been painted. One of these names said, "Auskunft." Oh boy! Could he use "Information." He made his way directly to the man to ask him which train would get him to Genoa. The man at the information window might have had two years of high school at some Italian town. Perhaps he had taken a course in German, but he had difficulties in understanding what Jim said, since Jim used his Bavarian dialect and not the language of the northern part of the country, and there are marked differences between the two in accent and pronunciation though the words may be the same.

Jim finally understood that a fast train was to leave within the next fifteen minutes for Genoa. He learned, too, from which track the train would leave. The train was to reach Genoa by seven o'clock.

The trip was very interesting, leading through fertile, rolling land.

At Genoa

Promptly at seven, the train pulled into Genoa, the point from which Jim was to begin his great adventure. Things seemed to become easier for him. He knew that outside the hotel there would be the name "Albergho." He knew that at a place marked "Birra," there would be nothing to be had but beer or wine. A restaurant, he knew, would look much different, but he knew he could recognize one when he saw it. As for the food, he did not know what to choose, but by pointing with his finger he knew he could get something, whatever it might be. He had had nothing to eat since ten o'clock except a small cut of the ham and a piece of the stale bread he had brought with him. After the train had left, he ate swiftly. He recognized the name of a station. Andreas Hofer, he remembered from his school days, had once been there.

Jim went to the "Albergo Chiave d'Oro," the Golden Key Hotel, whose sign he saw in a street near the depot. After washing up in the big porcelain bowl and drinking from the huge water container which sat within the bowl, he went out in search of a restaurant. The streets were narrow, the stores were poorly lit. As he continued his way, he was made aware of many unpleasant odors. He looked about him, but not until he passed a bake shop, its window filled with cakes, tarts, and rolls, did he see a huge hose, nearly ten inches in diameter, running from the shop to a well known wagon. Two men operated an old-fashioned suction pump on top of the wagon. Nobody seemed to mind, but Jim moved on swiftly. Shortly after he came upon a restaurant which had nothing connected with it which would spoil his appetite.

Of the meal Jim can still recall that wonderful "Risotto Palermonese," as the dish was called on the bill of fare. First he thought it was some sort of hash, but it was too yellow. It looked, too, something like oatmeal mush without milk or cream. Served in an elongated dish and decorated with brown branches which had no name, it resembled many things but could be identified as none. His empty stomach was too hungry to permit delay. The first forkful told him it was rice; the second proved that it was good. It was not long before the platter was empty.

Not long ago he had asked the foreman of a cheese factory this side of Pine Plains, a man who was an Italian, whether he knew anything about this special dish served him so long ago and so far away. "Why," said he, "the real Risotto Palermonese is made in Sicily and takes about a week to make. It's very expensive to make a Risotto Palermonese. Rice is the cheapest part of it. The soup stock in which the rice is cooked several times to make it soggy costs time and money. Saffron is also hard to get. Then other spices are added. Mushrooms go with it, and truffles, too. We had it in Italy only when a child was baptised."

"I always thought it was curry powder," said Jim. "The whole dish was yellow."

"No, you mistake. They use no curry powder for Risotto. They use Saffron. That's why they call it Palermonese," he declared.

This information satisfied Jim about his first dinner in Italy.

A bottle of red wine was brought. There was half a loaf of white bread. Payment was asked in advance, something Jim didn't mind. The effect of the wine was soon evident. It was "suffig;" he longed for more. But reasoning that he was going to be up early in the morning to find out about a boat for the New World, he left as soon as he had finished eating. He was satisfied until he got out into the street. The cool night, in addition to the loss of regular sleep and the general nervousness created by the uncertainty of the time, kept him uneasy. He made his way to his hotel, reached his room, went to bed and dropped off to sleep.

The Long Sleep

What happened to him that night may sound strange to most readers, but many stranger things do happen in life which science cannot explain though men know they have lived through them.

Some time during the night he awoke and found himself wide awake. Everything was quiet and dark. He felt for the night table that was somewhere near the bed and lit the candle. His watch had stopped, although he recalled that he had wound it during the train ride from Verona. Hmmmmmm. Had luck changed just before he was to leave for the New World? He hadn't overwound the watch, because when he tried to wind it now it ticked. He listened again. No sound. Yes, this was the room he had taken. There was his suitcase. On the chair. as he had left them, were his trousers, neatly folded. He felt for his shoes and found them where he had put them. He leaped from his bed and within three minutes rushed down the old wooden stairs to find out what? He didn't know. In the small, dusty lobby, poorly lit, he could see nobody. On the far wall he made out an old clock that must have decorated the lobby for a hundred years. He went nearer to it to make out the time. Did he see alright? Or was the wine still working on him? It showed ten-thirty. Ten-thirty, but that was about the time he had gone to bed, and he had slept.

Just then a small side-door opened. A man who looked as if he belonged to the place entered the lobby. Jim rushed to him and asked him what time it was. The little man stared at him, not understanding a word of Jim's dialect. If he could only say in Italian, "What time is it?" Of course a hotel man, be he manager, porter, waiter, or clerk, provided he has been in the business for some years, sees a great deal that other men never see. They know how to handle drunks, how to stop fights, how to size up bluffers. They know how normal and abnormal people act. The little man was an old timer in the game. The look he gave Jim was one of surprise at seeing the young Tedesco (as they call the German there) at this hour. He quietly walked behind his desk and brought forth an old German–Italian dictionary which became the interpreter there and then. Jim had seen such dictionaries when his brother George was studying Italian and had even thought of buying one before he left home. The clerk handed it to him to find out what he really wanted. Jim thumbed the pages, saw German words on one side and Italian on the other. There, there was the word: time, tiempo, Zeit. To make a long story short, it took Jim just about two hours to find out that it was going to be Friday when morning came and not Thursday. He had slept the clock round! As soon as he became conscious of this fact his stomach verified the situation. Prior to this, his digestive organs were inactive. Jim went back to his room, ate a piece of the remaining ham, and took the now empty water jug downstairs to obtain water. The rest of the night he used to write his parents, his sweetheart, Grete, and a few of his chums in his native village.

At dawn he was already out in the streets of Genoa, surveying the situation. He found the harbor from which he hoped to sail. He saw big sail boats, one after another, tied to iron posts. Other boats, which must have been freighters and steamers, lay at anchor or were roped tight to the piers. For an hour he walked up and down, admiring everything. Then he decided to walk more into the center of the city to find out about getting passage to America. There, look. "Hamburg-Amerika-Line," read the sign. Quickly he crossed the avenue to inquire of them, even though, on second thoughts, he hesitated because, well, we won't talk about that. But next door he saw a sign reading "Lloyd Sabaudo," which also seemed to run ships. On the outside, in small letters, he read a sign, "Man spricht deutsch."

The "Gloria"

"Oh, yeah?" questioned Jim. "That's just what I want." He entered the door, approached a desk and said, "Ich will eine Fahrkarte nach Amerika" (I want a ticket to America). After explaining to Jim that the steamer "Gloria" would sail for New York on Monday and that their boats had every conceivable convenience, the man handed Jim some circulars. In those days transportation companies brought immigrants by the hundred thousand to America as cheaply as possible. All transportation then was a matter of mass production at low cost.

In the circulars Jim read descriptions of several boats. America, too, was pictured, especially the Golden West. Jim was not choosy about boats. To him one looked like another. All were big, monstrous, with masts and chimney. The inside, naturally, had to be the same, thought Jim. Beautiful, gorgeous, he pictured it. But all he longed for, after all, was to get to America. The man helped Jim get the money out of his coat by cutting open the lower seam with a pair of scissors. Out came forty dollars in fives and a single ten-dollar bill with a gold back. Jim paid down twenty-five dollars for the cheapest possible accommodation. The rest he put in his handkerchief and tied a farmer's knot around it.

That was done. He had the ticket. On his way again to the harbor he had breakfast of black coffee and cognac and a piece of bread. He was now going to inspect his ship, the one for which he had bought his ticket.

There she was! A chimney, port holes, masts, flag flying at the after deck. Ropes as thick as his arms held her to the pier. Loading and unloading was going on from both sides. A few sailors were sitting halfway down the ship painting. As he came closer, the name of the boat could be read at the back: Gloria, and below it Genoa. That was it, the ship which was to take him to America! Jim did not listen to the chatter and talk that went on around him. He knew he wouldn't understand it anyway. At the far side he could see a sort of a chicken ladder leading up to the upper deck. A man in uniform stopped him, saying: "Billietto." Oh, yes, he had a "Billet," thinking at the same time about getting a German–Italian dictionary so that he could at least look up a word now and then. The word for "ticket" happened to be the same in both languages, which was why, for a moment, even a German fellow could understand. But from now on, he realized, he must become acquainted with a little Italian. He realized, however, that English was the language of the New World, a thought which led him to get an English dictionary before he left.

Jim showed his ticket and went up the narrow gangway, a rope ladder. These are used while the boat is in the harbor. On the day of sailing or of arrival wider ladders are used, the narrow ones being primarily for personnel. Few people visit a boat before actual sailing time. At other times it is but the few curious ones who come. These are especially young people who just cannot wait until they have put their noses into every pie.

Once aboard, Jim felt as though he were on the dance floor of the Hirschbrau at Bruck, the name of the village he came from.

The ship was leaning slightly towards the pier side. It was only partly unloaded. Jim was never used to such leaning and at first thought something was wrong with the ship, but said nothing; he couldn't anyhow, so far as that was concerned. A young chap was assigned to him to show him his home for the next fortnight. He was led to the rear of the ship, where the crew during the voyage had all the work to do. Down they went below decks. The air became thick. Odors of cigars, garlic, and other pungent matter were many. He thought the stairs would never end, but at last a wide space, dark and full of bedsteads, appeared. All had a sort of covering over them like the four-posters of father and mother's day. Otherwise Jim felt as if he had entered a barracks. He started a conversation with the assistant who showed him around. He tried to mimick things by holding his arms to the side of his face and by pointing to himself in his efforts to discover which bed would be his for the trip. He had no success. As they walked slowly through this forest of bedsteads, Jim noticed that instead of a tarpaulin the cover was another bedstead. Pillars which supported the superstructures abounded. They became visible as his eyes became accustomed to the darkness. Bull's eyes at regular intervals allowed light to enter the dormitory. They appeared much larger to him now compared to when he saw them from the side as he approached the ship. Who will be my fellow passengers? he wondered. If only his brother George, two years older, were out of the army. Surely he would have come.

George Wollsten

George was in the army with the light cavalry at Dillingen, where he had been stationed since September to do his one year's service for the country. War or no war, every able-bodied boy of twenty had to join the army. Infantry men served two years, cavalry and artillery served three years. The boys knew nothing else. This was a necessity. Just as for seven years they had to be at school before being released, unless they went to a higher school, so did they have to do their period of service in the army. At thirteen years of age boys were usually apprenticed to a tradesman or began to work on a farm. This apprenticeship lasted three years, and for it their parents had to pay. Twice a week they were required to attend a trade school segregated into groups so that, for example, cobblers, saddlers, or allied trades had theoretical instruction on certain days while those learning to be carpenters or cabinetmakers had school on other days.

After their apprenticeship was over, the youngsters would usually stay an extra year with their original boss before going on the "Walz;" this meant traveling on foot from one town to another to work here a while and there a while to gain experience and see something of the world besides. The more courageous boys would even penetrate into other parts of Europe. Most of them stayed within the limits of their own tongue. In that way it would happen that a Bavarian boy might be found at any place up the shores of the North Sea. The immediate attraction might be the work itself, some female magnet, or whatever else attracts a man to a place. There he would stay, then, and from there he would be taken into the army to return to this place when his time was up.

George, who had been in Munich at a higher school for eight or nine years, had been given special privileges in the army service and was required to do but one year's service instead of the usual two or three. He could also select his own branch in the army. He had learned French, English, and some Italian as well as many other things of which Jim had never heard. George would come home for the summer vacation with two or three suitcases full of books. Even though Jim liked books, George's were a little too hard for him. Jim was a farmer, not a book worm. And yet, both would get along fine. George had occasionally mentioned that he would go away to some foreign country as soon as he was finished with his training, but never had he mentioned which country he had in mind. George didn't know himself. While he had apparently laid out a well defined plan as to how he might put his know]edge to practical use, he would nevertheless need a push to get started. When first the idea had come to Jim to see the New World, he didn't even think of George because, after all, though brothers, they were far apart in mind.

"Well, two weeks will soon pass," thought Jim. After a while he found himself back at the office of Lloyd Sabaudo, where he could at least talk his own language.

Farming was hard work. He knew all about it. He had seen fields and forests, towns and villages of Italy now, plenty of people, too; but he could not get over why those people should speak another language. Why should they call an inn an albergo, or a ship a piroscafo? That word he had heard the steamship men use several times when he spoke of the "Gloria."

He could retain this word rather easily, since it must have some relation to "Bier saufen," which means to drink beer. But how such a relationship could be he didn't know. It might have to do with "ersaufen," meaning to drown. That sounded more logical to him. He even asked the agent whether many of his boats went down. The agent said no and asked how Jim liked the "Gloria."

"Swell," he declared. "Some boat. Much bigger than the ones on Lake Starnberg."

Other people arrived who were also probably ready to emigrate. Jim was about to leave when he was told to be at the boat by eight o'clock on Monday morning. Saturday and Sunday passed quickly. To make sure he would not miss the boat, he stayed up that night. The steamship agent had given him an address where he could buy a dictionary. He found the bookstore and bought himself a German–English dictionary as well as an Italian. His funds had declined rapidly, but according to the description of conditions in America given by the agent at Bruck, there was nothing to worry about. Work could be quickly found in the New World, provided one wanted to work. What helped Jim much, though unknown to him, was the panic of 1907, which had then run its course. Just before Christmas of that year there was a turn for the better. The rapid expansion of business from early 1904 until the end of 1906 had apparently been too much for America's economic health. There was a period of retrenchment, otherwise matters might have become serious.

Economic Conditions in 1907

Such was the case with the decline of business all over the country early in the summer of 1907. Nobody paid much attention to it. Stock markets had sagged in the Spring. Around the middle of the year prices had rallied, and so did business. Jobs also increased. But this was only temporary. The real plunge started a few weeks later that shook business houses not only in America, but all over the world. The United States seem to be a barometer for the world at large. At any time business is poor with us, we can take it for granted that conditions are worse somewhere else. The average man has nothing to do with high finance. All he is interested in is his job. If he is a farmer, he is interested in prices of produce, for that is the basis of his livelihood. He is well aware that commodity prices are subject to wide fluctuation. Some years wheat may be worth 40 cents: in other years it may be worth two dollars. The cause for such wide swings is well known. They call it supply and demand. When there is a scarcity of wheat, prices are high; when there is plenty, wheat goes begging.

The main reason in Jim's mind for buying an Italian dictionary also was that, so far, his finger never seemed to hit upon any eggs on the bill of fare. He was tired of black coffee and cognac, which he got without difficulty in the morning. He was tired of the spaghetti and ravioli. He longed for eggs. The two days left to him in Genoa he spent checking words he needed badly. They were all in the book, but trying to pronounce them was another thing. That same evening he selected "Uove da sorbire." To make sure he got them, he carried his dictionary in his pocket. He intended to have his soft-boiled eggs, and he checked the phrase again on his way to a restaurant.

Waiters, as a rule, are willing to help strangers unless they are busy with a crowd. Even though Jim asked for "Uove da sorbire," the waiter could not understand what he said. Jim pulled out the dictionary, found the word "Ei" and a little farther down discovered "weich;" to this he pointed. The waiter looked at it carefully. He himself was not much of a master of reading and writing. His face seemed to brighten, however. He said a lot of words and slipped into the kitchen. After a short time two eggs appeared in front of Jim. It was his first victory over the Italian language. "I'm learning," he congratulated himself.

During Sunday he also investigated his English dictionary, but those words looked worse to him than the Italian. Twice he had to take a walk for fear his tongue would unhook somewhere near the throat. He might get lock-jaw, he thought. How do they do it? For a while he thought he'd rather try to learn Italian. Italian and German did have many words in common. However in English "Bread" equals "Brot," but "Brett" equals "Board." There were complications. Into the suitcase with you! For the time being, at least. Jim had to admit that some people spoke a hard and confusing language.

The Emigrants

The natives of our country, the United States, those of the third and fourth generations, can hardly put themselves into the frame of mind of the actual emigrant. Neither can they imagine what goes on in the emigrant's mind before he reaches these shores. An

Englishman usually goes to his colonies; so does a Frenchman. Their problems are comparatively simple. But among Germans, Italians, Poles, Greeks, and many other nationalities, there is a certain number who have the idea that they can improve their lot by emigrating to some other country. They themselves do not call such a change emigration. They are not even conscious of what the word implies. They leave home, friends, relatives, sweethearts – all things dear to them. Most of them leave with the plan of working hard and later returning home. They are young, enterprising, hard-working individuals. There can be no love in their souls for the new country to which they go. How could there be? They don't even know it. Whatever they hear of it at some place or somewhere is always highly colored. Unfavorable things are never mentioned. The things they like to hear are exaggerated. It takes them time to become accustomed to the people, to the language. They have to learn to love the new country and its methods, in short, its life. It takes nerve to leave a country, to go out into the dark unknown.

There are possibly a hundred thousand people or more born in Brooklyn, New York, or the Bronx who never in their lives get any farther than Coney Island or Van Courtlandt Park. Many of those shrug at the immigrants as representing the overflow of Europe. True, they do represent a certain type of the overflow, but they are by no means scum. Not many dare to undertake such great adventure; they fear hardship. We might just as well call immigrants the cream, or top of the milk, which goes into a special bottle. In this instance it is the New World.

Few seem to remember that in America we have another important country, the Argentine, which also has been built up by immigrants and which seems to prosper as we do.

There are people who like to live in warmer countries. Others like cool climates. Some are fond of coffee: others of beer or whiskey. Animal man always goes to a place where he thinks he can find what he wants. Only secondarily does he try to satisfy his ambitions and desires.

Jim, at Genoa, could have taken a boat to the Argentine just as well, because right next to the "Gloria" was the "Pantellaria," of the same Lloyd Sabaudo line, which would have brought him to Buenos Aires at the same price. The agent even said to him that farming and cattle growing were specialties down there, and that men were waiting to take immigrants right to the farms in the interior without expense. For a moment this advantage made a small dent on his mind. It would cost him nothing to get his first job. But he was man enough not to want or expect something for nothing. In short, he said: "No. I want to go to America, not to the Argentine."

The Trip to New York

Monday, at seven in the morning, Jim was already at the pier looking at his boat. Billows of smoke came out of the funnel. Other people arrived. Some carried big bundles wrapped in bedsheets. Others had dilapidated suitcases that must have contained their belongings. Big ladders had now taken the place of the small one of Friday, so that passengers could board the boat. He was one of the first to be allowed to go on deck. Someone handed him a number printed on a green card. He knew already where his sleeping quarters were, and to them he directed his steps. Activity was high all over the ship. The loading of goods still went on. The hatches, wherein goods disappeared, were open. Passing them, he peeped in as a net filled with goods was lowered. Below decks he parked his suitcase on one of the bedsteads which had now been made into a regular bed with a pillow, a black blanket, and clean, white sheets.

People came in. All looked alike to him. He did not hear a word of German. All the passengers seemed to be Italians. He suddenly felt lonely, *so* all alone by himself. He had nobody to talk with. He watched the people. Further back, among the bedsteads, someone began to play a mouth organ. There, some other fellow unpacked his violin. Others started smoking. He had tried one of the black stogies. He remembered the time when they once went, after the day of the Fair, to the Hirschbrau Beerkeller, to pick cigar butts from under the benches to smoke behind the dunghill of farmer Kemeter. He remembered how Karl had suddenly paled and disappeared. For a week the poor kid was in bed with nicotine poisoning. No, he didn't care for them.

No women. They had other quarters. About nine o'clock he felt very tired because he hadn't slept during the night. He had not even had any breakfast. He laid down on the bed for a while – the bed he had selected for himself. There was so much noise and so much walking around that he suddenly arose to leave the place and go up on deck for fresh air. In order that nobody should take his bed, he took out of his suitcase a sheet of writing paper and wrote on it in big German letters: "Jakob Wollsten." The script no one could read who had not learnt German writing. Of that he did not think. This piece of paper he pinned to the pillow with a safety pin which he discovered in the suitcase. That made it clear, at least to Jim, that this was his bed. Jim then asked a couple of other young fellows to watch his bed for him. One seemed to understand what Jim meant. He laughed, said a few words, and went back to his companions who called out "Va bene, va bene" – their way of saying "O. K."

Even though Jim did not understand what they said, the sound of the young voices was reassuring. He climbed the stairs and reached the clear light of day. Crowds of people were still on the Embarcadero, as they called the pier. Some mothers with crying babies, children of all ages, young fellows, older people – all waited their turn to gather their belongings and board the vessel. Where they came from Jim could not imagine. Where they would all go he could not imagine either. The dormitory in which he was to sleep for two weeks appeared to him nearly filled before he left it. Still there were hundreds of others waiting to go aboard. Of course Jim had never seen any boats before except those small steamers on Lake Starnberg which are filled up when fifty people get aboard. He did not know that those boats were geared for human freight. They had several decks forward and back. They could carry with ease from two to three thousand persons. He was not the only one whose destiny intended for him a new sphere, new surroundings, new ideas, a new way of life.

At eleven sharp the tow lines were dropped. Gangways, except one for late-comers, had been removed. Several long, deafening blasts of the steamer's whistle were heard, a new sensation for Jim. Several small tug-boats started to push the boat away from the pier. The trip to America had begun. In less than half an hour he could see Genoa in panorama, a city he had actually seen little of. Slowly mounting a hillside, the city sat there quietly as the vibration of the boat's huge engines rumbled in his ears.

Suddenly he heard a strange noise that came closer and closer to him. It was a boy with some contraption and a wooden hammer who struck a gong while proceeding at a steady pace. "Reveille," he thought. That must mean something, he decided. He rushed downstairs to his new home which lay in the direction in which the boy had disappeared. He saw his suitcase still on the bed, and the sign was there also. The three boys he had seen before were still chatting. He felt that they were congenial. He went to them slowly, hoping to become acquainted. They asked him a few questions in a language he could not understand, so he said "Tedesco," (German) to them to make known his reason for remaining silent. Hands, feet, fingers – each and every member of the body man has at his disposal can be used to aid expression. With the help of a sympathetic audience almost anything may be made known.

Jim's hunger acted upon him like a goad. He succeeded in making his companions realize how hungry he was. They quickly took him by the arm and carried him along to the big mess hall. It was located two floors above the dormitory. Long tables and benches, with a gangway through the middle, ran from one side of the ship to the other. Frames, forming squares, were around the tables, a novelty he had never seen before.

"What can these be intended for?" he asked himself.

The boys sat down with Jim. Big bowls of food were already set in front of them. All that was necessary was to help oneself to meat, spaghetti, and bread. For each man there was a bottle of wine. The food tasted wonderful to Jim. After they were filled, they walked around on deck. The land appeared far off by now. He knew the boat was to make a stop at Africa at the port of Algiers. He remembered from school that the people of Africa were black and that the climate was very hot. However, he was due for a shock when on Wednesday morning he saw no black faces at all in the crowd that swarmed about the docks at Algiers. Many Arabs were present, and Jim had thought they lived only in Arabia. Several Arabs had come aboard. Jim inspected them carefully, observing their appearance and their actions.

At noon the boat left Algiers, headed through the Straits of Gibraltar, and pushed into the Atlantic.

Jim's appetite was wonderful by this time. The movement of the boat did not bother him much. Only the noise of the screw pushing the boat forward was terrific. His bed lay rather near it. Young fellows soon adjust themselves to unusual noises, and soon it bothered him not at all. He still lunched with his friends. Following lunch he went back to lie in his bunk. He did not feel too well. For the next three days Jim could not brook the sight of food. Only once a day did he go to the mess hall, and then he ordered black coffee.

The crowd of passengers confined in his quarters was a jolly, happy lot. The men sang and danced, some played mouth organs, accordions, violins, and other instruments.

No storm or incident occurred to mar the trip. Two weeks to the day after leaving Genoa he saw the Statue of Liberty before him as the boat steamed up the Hudson river. A dense group of tall buildings became visible to his right. It was New York City.

Suddenly his skin chilled. He had never had such a sensation before in his life. And with it all there was a feeling of uncertainty.

"I hope I don't get sick now," he thought to himself, "just when I reach my destination."

"Of course, in a big city like New York there are no farms, but in the country there should be plenty," Jim conjectured. He would soon find out. His friends were going to the homes of relatives in New York. Where could Jim go? God only knew.

The pier was reached. People disembarked. For some reason Jim was not permitted to leave the boat. On the contrary they put him, with several others, into a small boat and headed away from the pier.

"What now?" thought Jim. "Has something gone wrong?"

After half an hour's ride the little boat put him in front of a big building. Everybody walked off the boat. They marched into the building, Jim with them. He was on Ellis Island, the big immigration station for New York harbor. They had brought him there because he knew nobody to whom he might go in the United States. They brought him there to help him and tell him where he might find employment. It was only a matter of half-an-hour before a man approached him.

Julius Holten

"Are you Mr Wollsten?" the man questioned in German.

"Yes," responded Jim.

"I am from the Young Men's Christian Association, and I want to help you," offered Jim's companion.

Wollsten's face brightened. He had not expected help from anyone.

"How did he know I was coming?" thought Jim, bewildered by the turn of events. Aloud he said he was a farmer and wanted to get to a farm. That is what he wanted. After a few questions whether he had relatives here and how much money he had left, the pair left the building. Jim lugged his suitcase all the while, of course, and the two got on another boat. Within ten minutes they landed in lower New York, took a train that ran high above the city streets, alighted after a while and went into a big house. There Jim got a room and food and was told to be ready to leave the next morning.

CHAPTER II

JIM WOLLSTEN'S FIRST YEAR ON THE FARM

The stranger knew of a job for Jim, that would give him a start. It was May 25, 1908, when he landed in New York – a red letter day for Jim. He was thankful to God that he had come to this strange land without mishap, and he was thankful, too, that he had met this stranger who had proved so helpful to him.

After a meal, Jim went to his room. It was two in the afternoon. Checking up on his funds, he found that he had just fifteen American dollars left. In addition he had a few German, Austrian, and Italian coins.

That day must have been a real, genuine, good-luck day for Jim.

The next morning he rose early. Jim's first American breakfast was quite different from the ones he had been used to in Italy and on the "Gloria." Boiled eggs, hotcakes, syrup, and coffee were there for him. What a meal! At home he usually had coffee and bread to start the day, a stew of tripe or boiled lights at ten o'clock, seasoned with spices and vinegar and cooked in a thick sauce.

Mr Schafer

The German-speaking friend came soon and introduced him to a Mr Schafer, a prosperous farmer of Upper Red Hook, who had found a way to get competent help for his farm by hiring immigrants such as Jim. Mr, Schafer happened to be in New York and had inquired regarding help since he needed a young man to work during the summer months. Mr Schafer had no thought of finding a steady man, but at times good fortune smiles upon us. Mr

Schafer was an American whose grandfather had come from the old country. He knew of Germany and could speak German only a little. For this reason Jim's part in the conversation was strictly limited. With the man acting as interpreter, Jim learned that he was being asked to work as a general farm hand for sixteen dollars a month and found. To this Jim readily agreed, too happy for words. Quickly he calculated the American money in terms of its equivalent, sixty four marks. "That's twice as much as I was paid over there!" he thought.

Upper Red Hook

Upper Red Hook was but three or four hours' train ride from New York up the Hudson Valley. Rolling country, mostly fruit orchards, usually apples of various kinds, made a pleasant appearance. Every farmer had a few cows, horses, bee hives, and lots of apples.

It did not take Jim a long time to get down to work, even though many of the details of his job were unknown to him. The language made it hard at first, but Mr Schafer quickly recognized in him a willing worker. In fact, he soon discovered that if he let the boy have his own way the work would be done better and faster. Mr Schafer had many irons in the fire. He was at the same time one of the local real estate men. This kept him on the go much of the time; and especially now, when many of his neighbors discovered that the prices of their products would not cover the payments on their loans, and foreclosures occurred frequently. He himself had acquired several good farms by taking over mortgages. Jim knew little about orchard culture. His family had had a few trees on their place in Germany. The main highways frequently had apple trees as shade trees, but he had never seen orchards of such size as were found here. During the summer a team was steadily at work keeping the weeds low and the ground cultivated. Jim saw for the first time the spraying outfits on wagons. One man would pump and another would spray with the hose like a fireman.

Jim took care of the cows and horses and picked up around the place. It was not very long before he began to learn a few words of English. He could not speak in complete sentences, but was able to make himself understood. After work he invariably studied, using his precious English dictionary. When he could not pronounce a word he was always able to find someone who would help him. In a year's time Jim underwent a complete transformation. He could scarcely recognize himself. Since he left his friend in New York, he had never heard a word of German spoken. He used the English language and now had a vocabulary superior to many people born at Red Hook. Through the use of the dictionary he even acquired words that were antiquated or rare, and they sometimes had a bizarre effect upon his speech. Mr Schafer was proud of him. Glowing letters went off to Europe, and George, who by this time had been released from the army, perused the contents carefully.

CHAPTER III

GEORGE WOLLSTEN ARRIVES AT NEW YORK

Who do you think landed in New York on June 20, 1909? It was George.

"If Jim can do it, so can I," he had decided one day early in April of that year. Jim had written him saying that he had had a long conversation with Mr Schafer on Lincoln's birthday and that Schafer had decided to let Jim take over a farm on a rental basis. By that time Jim had become acquainted with various properties held by Mr Schafer and had set his heart on the adjoining farm which Mr Schafer also owned.

Jim had saved practically all the money he had earned. His father had sent him a thousand marks, and this gave him some operating capital. The rental agreed upon was $350 a year. The crops would be Jim's. Jim would pay the normal costs of upkeep and Mr Schafer would pay the taxes. The bargain was sealed with a 50-dollar down payment, the rest to be paid when the crops were marketed.

This day marked a great stride for Jim on the road to success. He quit the job he held after giving Mr Schafer time to go to New York to find another man.

The farm house was in pretty good shape. Plainly furnished, it was still good enough for a bachelor. Jim was now twenty-one, still an early age at which to assume the responsibilities of an owner.

Tools and agricultural implements were on the farm. There were no livestock. Immediately he bought a cow, a horse, and a thousand baby chicks. Spring was at the door. He bought enough food for his animals to see them through the summer. Grain prices had risen ever since he became aware of them. Times were getting better again, just as after a long period of rain the sunshine comes again. At intervals he had heard from Mr Schafer and other farmers of that vicinity what a tough time they had had two years before.

The last apple crop had brought much better prices than the previous one, but it had been rather a small crop. Everything pointed toward an improvement in the general economic situation.

About Grain Prices

It may be said parenthetically that young men who grow up on a farm are usually better acquainted with the rise and fall of prices than are city-bred boys because the general welfare of a farming community depends upon these prices. A loaf of bread may cost a dime at the bakery whether wheat sells at 40 cents or at two dollars a bushel at Chicago. But there is a difference of at least a dollar to the farmer. The same apples may cost a nickel a pound or fifteen cents a pound. What is that to a city man? He may say, "Things are much more expensive than they used to be." Or, when the trend is downwards he may say, "I'm getting a lot for my money." But the weight in price changes makes itself felt more when it is a question of large quantities. The farmer with his crops notices them the most.

George had advised Jim of his coming immediately after he received the news that Jim had rented a farm. The day before George's arrival Jim went to New York to see his friend who had helped him so much. Jim obtained all the information possible about New York harbor so that he could not possibly miss him. Jim went to the pier of the "Lloyd;" this time it was the North German Lloyd which had its piers at Hoboken, across the river. There was not much difficulty, since he knew enough English to ask people along the way. The man who had befriended him before, Mr Jules Holten, explained what he should do to reach 23rd Street. There he crossed to Hoboken on the ferry, walked along the river a block or two, and was at the pier. The summer heat was intense just then.

The reunion of the brothers was a happy one. George, who usually led when it was a matter of action, had to run in second gear for once. He meekly followed Jim to the ferry and then through the streets of the big city, gaping and stopping here and there to see sights unknown to him. True, Jim himself had not seen anything of New York, but to him it was like any other big city – Munich or Genoa, for example. What of it? They can grow neither wheat nor apples here, he thought. George had other thoughts. He, too, knew that the city was not the country, but he also knew that there were many things to be done in the city. He didn't say it aloud. He didn't want to hurt his brother's feelings just then, though like other brothers they had quarreled.

In the evening, after the train had passed through Poughkeepsie, a heavy thunderstorm cooled the air considerably. By the time they reached Upper Red Hook the storm passed. They arrived at the farm without getting wet. They talked while on the train about matters of mutual interest – about father, mother, Grete, the other brother, George's trip, and Jim's own trip of a year ago. This continued when they reached home and lasted until two in the morning. Then Jim, who was farmer, cook, housekeeper and handy-man at once, turned the big, old-fashioned couch in the living room into a temporary bed for either of them. He broke three matches into different lengths to let George try and pick the longest one. He did, and won the right to choose the bed or the couch. George had the good sense to take the couch anyway.

For a while, it was agreed that George would help Jim with his work. He knew quite a bit of English, though it sounded much different from the regular American variety. George had a school accent. Besides, many of the common, everyday words were unknown to him. He was not handy with work, but was willing. He kept a careful account of the chickens, figured out with the aid of mathematics how many eggs the chickens would normally lay, and congratulated Jim on his foresight in buying so many chickens at one time.

"That was a swell idea," he declared frequently.

Jim had acquired a cat a week or two after the chicks had come. He noticed that mice had somehow survived the cold winter. They had been helping themselves to chicken feed. Peter, black as night, had a white neck. His four paws seemed to have dipped into white paint. Peter was a great hunter of mice. All he required was milk. Zenzi, the cow, provided enough for all.

Mr Schafer came over occasionally to see how Jim was getting along. He came over especially to meet his brother soon after George had arrived. In fact the other neighbors also learned of George's arrival and all had found excuses to drop by and get acquainted with the newcomer. Everyone began to like the pair because of their polite, unassuming ways. Everyone noticed how the farm had been improved through careful management. George had brought his meager savings with him, and this helped a long way toward buying certain necessary things. The big job of pruning the apple trees had been done long before by Jim alone, who had put in many a fourteen-hour day to finish the job. Schafer's orchard foreman had given him invaluable hints on how to do it. He especially taught him that when pruning he should cut all those branches which interfered with the growth of a heavier branch. He was also taught to cut the branches just above the bud and never to prune below the bud, since that would leave a dry piece of wood sticking out later on.

On Horticulture

"The bud sprouts forth the new growth from the branch," he had been told, and this he often repeated to himself. "The bud must be at the end."

About fertilizing Jim did not need instruction; nor had it been necessary to teach him to plough and harrow.

As to timing these operations for best results, he only could guess like all the other farmers, though he felt that some law exists which, when used, gives extraordinary results. He knew that some farmers used the moon to plan their work, but that idea, he thought, was absolutely wrong.

By the time George had arrived, everything was in full growth. Apples had formed in the trees and were laying on more body day after day. The chicks had grown in size. Prices also had gone up for eggs, for chickens, and for foodstuffs generally. Jim's crop of apples was sure to be in demand. A small vegetable patch had been planted. During those days of chicken raising, Jim was busy cooking potatoes twice a day in big pots to feed them, skin and all. Jim had to buy them, of course, so that his chickens might have a change of diet, but now a large part of his garden was planted to this feed.

Time passed rapidly. The two young men worked along harmoniously during the summer. Jim thought much of Grete. To her he had reported each week on his achievements. He wrote her now saying how he wished she were here so that they might be married and carry on together. If only she would have him! The Menharts, Grete's parents, liked Jim, so there was nothing to interfere from that quarter.

Jim was level-headed. He tried to use good judgment. He wanted to be sure of a fair income so that he could support a wife. Her coming would be just a matter of saying the word. Jim decided to wait for the crop to be marketed before finally deciding to ask her to come. He discussed the matter with George seriously many an evening.

They found little time to go to the village. True, once in a while they would visit here and there, discussing conditions of crops, talking about the country, and, in fact, almost any of those things farmers like to discuss.

The Agricultural Year Book

George, by chance, had one day got hold of an Agricultural Year Book, published by the government for farmers. It was not long before he had an entire string of them. He worked with them and studied the varieties of apples, their origins, and the prospects of the various types. He also discovered in those books statistics on eggs and chicken prices paid to farmers in years gone by. He began to plot them crudely on squared paper to see more plainly what sort of patterns would develop. For this purpose those back issues came in handy. He was fortunate. A neighbor mentioned that he'd go to Poughkeepsie where a second-hand store had many of them at a cheap price. He had seen them. Some went back to 1878. It was but a day later when George went into Poughkeepsie and returned with a suitcase filled with these books and a number of others that appeared worth-while to him.

About Graphs and Plotting Commodity Prices

In school George had been taught about graphs. Now was his first chance to employ that knowledge in any practical way. Several price graphs were constructed by him for wheat, rye, and oats. He quickly noticed that these commodities did not run alike from month to month. Some commodities would decline in price during periods when others advanced in price. He made this discovery as soon as he compared the graphs with one another. George and Jim would discuss these patterns. George would point out periods of high prices and periods of low prices, but Jim never did believe very much in figuring since as long as he farmed he would have to grow and sell at whatever the price might be when the crop was ready. He just simply would have to take that price.

He knew that his roosters, most of which he had sold by early September, brought him back the cost of the chicks and also the cost of the feed he had spent on the flock so far. The chickens were left as his profit. Jim expected them to lay soon. George had watched egg prices already. He saw that they had come up from around 20 cents in the early Spring to 34 cents by September. This was the price paid at the farm.

In order to forget about Grete during the harvesting of the apple crop, which he figured would keep both on the go he sent off a letter asking Grete to take the next boat. They would get married on the day of her arrival. He was sure she would love America, the farm, and everything that was on it. George had suggested that he add, "And go to the telegraph office when at Hamburg and send me a message saying when your boat leaves."

Fruit boxes had been delivered from a nearby mill. The apple picking began in earnest.

The Apple Harvest

George tinkered with an old grading machine for three days. He had never seen one of these machines in his life and was anxious to see it work. From Schafer's man he had already learned a lot about how the picking and packing of the fruit was done. He wanted to do things just right. The man had told them about the chemical solution through which the apples had to be put to kill off insect pests that might be on the apples. He explained the use of the machine, the various holes by which the apples were sized, the largest remaining on the top tray and the misfits dropping to lower trays. These were used to make cider. The picking ladders had all been gone over. Two extra helpers had been secured to aid with the work. They were local boys who had experienced several years of apple picking. The apples came in wonderfully. Jim had done some picking the year before, but he was still somewhat of a novice at the job. George, no farmer, was as green as he could be. It was a joke the way he climbed up the ladders. Awkward, he made matters much more complicated than was necessary. He watched the two boys and soon figured out how the work should be done.

In order to save time, a smoked ham had been boiled. Several pounds of potatoes were cooked ahead also. A big pot of coffee was prepared that would last them through several meals. The crop had first been picked into old boxes and brought to the barn. There the boxes were piled, up as high as one could reach. The weather favored them all along. It was still hot, but not quite as hot as it had been during mid-summer. Beneath the trees, however, there was a sweltering heat as soon as the sun approached the zenith. It would not cool off until late afternoon, when soft breezes came up from the Hudson. For two weeks they had picked. Now they were just ready to start all over to comb the trees once more for late-comers. A total of 1700 boxes had been picked when they were finished. It was a good crop. The various kinds were kept carefully apart. George consulted various Agricultural Year Books in an effort to get as much information of past years as possible. He tried to discover the best time to sell for a high price. In short, he tried to find when was the best time to effectuate their sale. He quickly saw that up to Christmas apples were usually fairly low in price. On the farm they brought in about 80 cents a bushel. He saw that after the New Year apple prices usually almost doubled. Jim and George one day both had a conference with Mr Schafer to talk over the original agreement Jim had made with the land owner. This had specified that Jim's rental payment was to be made upon the sale of the crop. However, it did not contain any clause specifying the time by which the crop must be sold. If they could keep their fruit back from the market until prices rose substantially, they would be in a position to make much more money than they would if they had to sell immediately.

Mr Schafer listened carefully to the arguments brought forth by the young men and paid particular attention to the statistics George showed him which indicated a rise in prices after the first of the year. George had a new idea, too. He wanted to spend some money to insulate the barn with straw. It satisfied Schafer that he had to deal with a man who had ideas that were safe and sound. In fact, he profited by this meeting himself.

An additional agreement was made postponing the payment of

the rental until Lincoln's birthday. George also asked Mr Schafer to grant Jim an option to buy the farm within the next three years. This was also given and a reasonable price was named. He was able to do this because he had bought the farm at a bottom price and he was glad to do it because he liked the way the two young men worked. He valued them as neighbors, too.

The Wire from Grete

On the twenty-first of the month a boy with a bicycle pedaled up just while everyone was busy picking apples. He was looking for Jim Wollsten. It was a wire for Jim.

Excited beyond measure, Jim ignored the boy's outstretched pencil and without signing for the telegram he rushed over to his brother.

"George! Grete must have left for America. It's a telegram." He had not opened the message yet, and before he could the boy was after him again to sign for it. This done, he opened the telegram and read: "I am on ship. Munchen arrives October 5 New York. Grete."

The first part made sense, and so did the last part. But what had that to do with "Munchen"? For many hours Jim had been in the apple trees picking. His right arm was pretty nearly lame. At times he was not sure whether he had an apple in his hand or not. His mind at the same time went over many different subjects. He thought of the apples and what a price he might get, about his chickens, about the work on the barn that would prevent the apples from freezing. He had not thought of Grete at all. He was far away from Grete. His thoughts could connect a wire with Grete and her departure from Hamburg. Munchen had come into his mind occasionally, especially when he was very thirsty. How fine that beer tasted! He could see himself in the Donisl consuming several steins of Pschorr beer along with a couple of "Weisswurst" (white boiled sausages with a thin skin). George, whose brain worked much faster than that of his brother, quickly told him that there was a ship by the name of Munchen. That must be the boat on which Grete was coming. The wire practically ended the work for the day. Jim just could not work any more. He went to the house, lay down, and asked himself "What next?"

Jim had to get a bed for Grete. George would have to get a bed. He had not minded the sofa as a bed for the past three months. "What else do I have to get?" he asked himself. "I might just as well get everything together right now." He had to get wedding rings to be married and a license, too.

Immediately he marched over to Mr Schafer, who was busy directing the fruit picking on his own farm. Jim quickly explained what had happened.

My future wife, Grete, is coming on the fifth of next month. I just got a telegram from her that she's on her way," he began. "Where can I get married in New York, and where can I buy some rings?" Jim also explained that he needed beds.

Quietly Mr Schafer considered the situation.

"Take it easy, Jim," he advised. "Come over tonight and we'll talk it over."

In a happy mood, even whistling a tune, Jim walked back to his farm. George had kept on working. The picking had to be done. Evenings were becoming cooler. After a hearty meal both brothers went over to Mr Schafer's to learn what he had to suggest.

Wedding Plans

"First of all, Jim," Schafer said, "you can marry your girl right away, as soon as she leaves the ship. I'll take a day off myself and we'll go to New York together. I have several other matters to look after down there. As for beds, I'm sure Dingle's have some in town. Rings you can buy in New York," Schafer explained. "George," he added, "what are you going to do? Do you plan to stay here permanently? What are your plans?"

George said he intended to remain for a while, but that he did not mean to remain a farmer all his life.

"I don't like to get up so early in the morning," George declared. "You folks seem to be used to it, but not me. Besides, I've learned things in school days which I am going to apply in a practical way in this country. What I have in mind has to do with farming a good deal."

George also asked about financial papers in New York, and Mr Schafer mentioned a number, including the "Times," the "Herald," and the "Evening Mail."

"That last one sounds good," thought George. "That could be here in the morning so that I could see how those commodity markets fluctuate from day to day." He had thought much while picking apples about the price patterns he had plotted on that squared paper on grain, eggs, and chicken prices. The information gleaned from the Agricultural Year Books had given him the price variations from month to month over a period of many years.

Market Quotations

George knew the markets were in operation every day. Quotations surely could be found in the financial newspapers every day. Such was the case in the "Munchener Neueste Nachrichten," which even printed the closing prices of several stocks of the New York Bourse each evening along with the prices from the local Exchange at Munich as well as the prices for grains, hides, and other commodities. Of course those things were rather vague in his mind. What would he do with those plottings? He was determined to plot some of those prices from day to day, just to see how those patterns would develop. He felt that later on he might be able to tell the farmers about planting much wheat or little, about substituting other crops in the event that his forecast showed better prices for them the next season.

George had known of a case in Germany when one year caraway seed was practically unobtainable. That year it had brought a big price to the lucky farmers who had grown caraway. Other farmers figured that such prices would keep on being paid, and many set out to grow caraway also. But they were wrong. There was too much of the commodity the next year and the price dropped away sharply and many farmers had to sell at a loss. He actually told this story to Schafer and Jim that evening, and Schafer explained to him that there existed regular markets for grains at Chicago, where traders would buy options on many thousands of bushels for delivery at a later date with the hope that the prices would yield a profit between the time of purchase of the option and the time for actual delivery of the grain.

"Most of these people are speculators," Mr Schafer said, "who do nothing but buy and sell rye, wheat, or some other grain. They never actually have the grain in their possession. Some have never seen a grain field. But they seem to have a feeling when prices are to move up or down. Of course," he continued "those manipulations," as he called them, "take ready cash and quite a bit of it. That is how some people make an awful lot of money. On the other hand, many seem to lose all they have."

"How do you recognize these fellows?" George asked.

Mr Schafer Explains Trading in Grains

"Oh, you can't tell them from the others. They look like you or me. I was over in Chicago at the pit, the place where they trade these options, some years ago. What a madhouse! You'd think a big fight was going on. Once in a while they would calm down, but as soon as you'd catch your breath they'd be off again. One or more of these fellows would start to bid. Others would shout or point with their fingers so as to complete a deal. Whatever happens there is sent by telegraph to most all big cities of the country immediately so that traders who sit in New York, Albany, or Philadelphia might know of it. But it's a complicated affair, I'm sure of that."

I was over in Chicago at the Pit. What a madhouse!

"How much would you say it takes to get started at such trading?" asked George.

"Oh, anywhere from two or three thousand dollars up," Schafer surmised. "That much would last a little while, anyway."

"Nothing less?" inquired George.

"Well, there are small quantities to be had also, from thousand bushel lots on up. Such a lot would take about $125 to handle on margin."

"Margin? What do you mean by margin?"

"Margin? What do you mean by margin?" George inquired.

Schafer tried to explain the meaning of the word by saying that margin was a sort of a security on a contract, whereby the trader agrees with some unknown farmer, somewhere in the United States, who at that time has wheat for sale for delivery, say, in July, to buy now at a stipulated price agreed upon at the pit.

If the price for this wheat should continue to move up during the time this trader was the legal owner, the difference would represent the trader's profit. He could sell this "paper agreement" to someone else through a broker at any time. In case the price should drop, however, his margin, or deposit money, would gradually be eaten up until about one half of it was gone. At that time the broker would call upon the margin operator for additional funds.

The former owner of the wheat was sure of his originally agreed price until such time as the trader should sell it to someone else or take delivery of it in July, the date agreed.

The explanations sounded fairly clear to George, but Jim could not follow too closely since many words had come into the conversation which he had never heard of. Besides, his mind wandered off to the boat on which Grete was probably sleeping by now. He made his own voyage over again in his mind until it was time to get some sleep.

"I may have to ask you a few more questions on the subject in a few days, Mr Schafer, after I've analyzed and clarified these things in my mind," George said as he was about to leave.

Dingle's Department Store

Dingle's, the department store of Upper Red Hook which carried all sorts of goods, from clothes to chinaware, was pretty well known to Jim. He had been there several times to buy work shoes, some shirts, and other things. He had never been up on the second floor, however, and there he found a special department devoted to houschold goods and furniture. It is strange how people can and will act. Some people can walk through streets for years and never notice certain stores which could supply them with goods they could use. They do not have to be small holes in the wall. Even big, sizable stores are oftentimes either not seen at all or the people have decided in their minds that these stores don't carry what they need.

Others do not investigate, as they should, and many do not like to enter a store unless they are ready to buy at once. Few store owners would object if one should visit their places just to get acquainted. If there should be one in a hundred set upon selling to anyone who enters his front door, he may make a sale once but not twice. True, in larger cities it may not matter much how they treat the "through traffic," but in smaller p]aces, unless the merchant uses discretion and patience and knows, besides, the details of the village gossip, he may soon have to move to a bigger town.

George and Jim went up that morning after chores had been done. Jim wanted to buy two beds, and George had an idea all his own.

After Jim had taken from the old woollen sock fifty dollars, leaving $324 still hidden, George seized the opportune moment to put the whole of the remaining hoard in his pocket. At Upper Red Hook he had seen some time before the sign reading "Upper Red Hook National Bank." He knew money was not safe kept at home in an old sock behind the pillows of the couch or sofa. It belonged in a bank, on deposit, where it could be withdrawn by writing a check. This much he had learned at school. The details of how this was done, he figured, the bank would gladly explain.

All the time he had been with Jim he had in mind to speak to him about that, but there had been so many other things for him to learn that he had even put his own money into the same sock. But that situation was to end that day.

As they came into town, George led Jim right into the bank. Jim followed by force of habit without looking to see where he was going.

"What the heck do you want in this place?" he asked when he realized where he was.

"You'll see in a minute," George replied and went to a desk which had on it a plate reading "President." There he was greeted by an elderly gentleman who invited them to sit down.

"I'm George Wollsten. This is my brother Jim," George began. "We want to open a checking account. Jim has rented a farm from Mr Schafer over toward Pine Plains. Can we open an account with $300?"

"Of course you can," the president replied. "I shall have the papers made out for you to sign so that we may have the signatures. Is this to be a joint account?"

"No," said George. "Make it for Jim alone. He is going to be married on October 5, and he'll have to be more business-like." Turning to Jim, George said, "Let me have the $50 you have in your pocket."

Dutifully, in a daze, thinking that there would be no beds, Jim handed over the money to George, who had emptied the contents of the woollen sock on the president's desk. Yes, $324 was there, and to this Jim's fifty was added. Jim received his check book and deposit book and the two left the bank.

"George, what's the matter with you? Are you not glad that Grete comes? Don't you want me to buy some beds?" Jim could hardly restrain his tears.

"Now Jim," George said, "take it easy. You are going over to Dingle's right now and get your beds, but you're going to pay for them with a check so that you'll have a record of the purchase and a record of the date of the purchase. This is the beginning of your married life, and so you might just as well start it right. I don't want any money – not just yet. I'll work with you for a while until I have found out certain things which are hard to explain. Right now I know just about what I want to learn. You can help me a little later on in getting over the first hill."

By this time they had reached Dingle's and had inquired of the first sales person about furniture, especially beds. They were directed upstairs where they discovered beds, sofas, tables, and other furniture. Jim had gone over several single beds and had about made up his mind to take a pair when George called him over to a couch which had some peculiar contraptions in it, though on the surface it appeared the same as any other. It could be turned into a double bed. Neither had ever seen anything like it before.

"That's nice, and it would be good and wide," Jim admitted, "but it probably will be pretty expensive and I would need two of them."

"What do you mean, two of them? Aren't you going to get married to Grete? Or does it mean that she will only cook and wash for you? If you're going to love one another you'd better sleep together. You'd better figure on only one bed. Read about Casanova and find out how many beds he bought when he got married!"

Jim blushed. He had never discussed such things with George. What would he say to Grete when she saw only one bed? He felt that she would like to have one bed with him, too, but he had never discussed such things with her. The few kisses he had stolen had been respectable in their nature. In fact, Jim hadn't yet grasped the real truth regarding the obligation of marriage besides supporting one's wife. Those things he would have to learn in time. He thought that Grete might teach him something if things came to the worst. But George, the monster, overawed him into buying that couch with the double bed. The price; with mattress and spring, was $23.75. A pair of pillows, a double blanket, and several sheets and pillow cases brought the price to $39.80. He gave the order with the understanding that it would be delivered the next day. George wrote out the check, marked it number 1, and passed it over to Jim for his signature.

The Barn Gets Insulated

The days went fast – too fast for Jim and George too. They wanted to do a lot yet before Grete came. While Jim now began grading the apples with his old machine, wrapping each in a small piece of tissue paper and selecting only the very best, George ordered a dozen bales of straw and a couple of thousand feet of lumber so that they could start insulating the barn against the frost. A keg of nails arrived with the lumber. Very little space was left in the barn. Several hundred boxes had to be stored temporarily in the wagon shed to keep them out of the rain that would be coming soon. By that time they figured that most of the grading and packing would be done. The second and third grade apples could be packed in barrels and sold at the current market price, leaving the best for sale later.

In the meantime Jim had ordered from New York the Evening Mail. At that time evening papers sold for a penny a copy, and a dollar brought it for three months and paid the postage to Upper Red Hook, too.

It was fortunate for Jim and George that a narrow side of the barn was facing north instead of a broad side. From the north came the winter winds out of the Berkshires. The west side was bad, too. George began insulating the north side. Straw was stuffed rather heavily and yet loosely between the two-by-four studs that formed the frame of the barn. Then he would nail the boards to them. For the first hour or two he hit his fingers more often than the nails, but he was determined to show Jim how things should be done.

In a week he had completed that entire side without any assistance whatever. The west side was next, but was only partly finished when October 4 arrived. Even Jim had only done part of his grading and packing by that time. The new handy-man of Mr Schafer's was to feed the chickens during the absence of the brothers.

On that Monday morning, George went into the village to make a long distance call to the North German Lloyd at New York to find out when the Munchen was due to dock. They told him that she would be at the pier by ten the next morning. On the way home he reported this to Mr Schafer, asking him at the same time whether or not he could find time to come to the wedding.

"Of course, I'll come along with you boys tomorrow morning," he responded. "You two come over to my house, though, this evening," he added.

That day everything else seemed to go wrong due to the nervousness caused by Grete's arrival. George had known Grete when she was a little child carrying around her "kafka," the doll which had lost most of its hair but which meant more to Grete than any other. Later on he remembered her in school with her spotless apron and her books on her shoulder. He often met her until he went to a higher school to study to become, as he thought, a teacher. He had stayed at Munich with an uncle and aunt all those years. Only during vacations did he come home. The oldest brother, Frank, who was to take over the farm, was already the right hand of the father. Jim was the youngest.

"How kids grow up," he thought to himself as he hammered on the boards and stuffed the straw between them. "Who would have thought only three years ago that I would be with Jim in America and that Grete would be marrying Jim in New York? This farm is far larger than ours at home and it won't be long before Jim and Grete will own it."

Outside the old grading machine kept on grading apples. Jim talked to the apples about Grete, telling them that she would be home in a day or two and that she was to rule the household. Some of the apples, Jim predicted, would enter the oven and become apple strudel.

CHAPTER IV

GEORGE'S APPROACH TO THE MARKETS

The early morning train from Albany came puffing around the corner on its way south. At Upper Red Hook it stopped abruptly as if it had forgotten for a moment to stop and then thought of it at the last moment. Three passengers had been waiting for ten minutes. They were Mr Schafer, Jim, and George. The last evening the brothers had called upon their neighbor who suggested that they leave by the first train.

The new double bed had arrived at Wollsten's together with the other paraphernalia that were ordered. The big room upstairs had been made ready to become the newly married couple's room. It looked more like a sitting room than a bed room. What a surprise Grete was to get when she looked for a bed. George took for himself the back room on the ground floor and had taken over Jim's old bed. The kitchen was cleaned up that night as well as two bachelors knew how to do it.

As the train ran down those three hours along the Hudson, the three of them spoke first about various things. George, however, was greatly interested in grain trading, and there the conversation was finally directed. Here was the chance to find out more about it. George had already prepared several questions which he had jotted down on paper.

Discussions During Train Ride Between George and Mr Schafer

"Mr Schafer," he asked, "can anyone buy or sell in those markets whether he is a citizen or not?"

"Anyone, as long as he has the money, can buy or sell grain in the markets" declared Mr Schafer, to whom the question of citizenship and trading had never occurred.

Foreigners are a queer bunch. Many of them have a feeling of fright within them, a fear that they might do something against the laws of the new country in which they desire to settle. Many things they hesitate to do because they are not sure of themselves and don't know whom to ask. Some associate with natives of their own country, but from them they can expect little. Those who happen to drift quickly into association with native Americans can call themselves lucky. They are the exceptions.

The old saying that water seeks its own level is only too true with immigrants. For years the majority will stick with the people with whom they became acquainted on the boat. Others similarly restrict their contacts. To get into American homes as a friend is just as difficult as it would be for an American to settle in France, Italy. or Germany and strike up friendships there.

Let us suppose that an American should set out for Paris. What then? Suppose he had only fifteen dollars in his pocket. How many days do you think this would last? He could not live, if in Rome, looking into the Vatican City, the Arena, or the Amphitheatre. In Paris he would become bored with looking at the Arc de Triomphe, the Tuileries, or la Tour Eiffel. Neither would he wish to look continuously upon the Glyptothek or the two Pinakotheks at Munich. When it is a matter of earning a piece of bread, those beautiful places mean little to the animal man.

George's next question was: "Through whom can the trader communicate in order to have his wishes executed?"

Mr Schafer told George that there were brokers in the larger cities throughout the country who had wire connections with the centers of trade. This meant direct connections with Chicago, New York, Winnipeg, and other trade centers. These brokers, Mr Schafer explained, charged a small commission for executing the orders of their clients. In New York the trade center was the Stock Exchange, while in Chicago or Winnipeg it was the Grain Exchange.

"Aside from New York's Stock Exchange," Schafer added, "there are also Coffee, Sugar, Hides, and Cotton Exchanges. There are many small Exchanges, too, in other cities such as Philadelphia, Baltimore, Cleveland, and New Orleans."

"What happens when the market declines? How can people trade then? When a person can see that he would lose if he bought, who would buy?"

Mr Schafer, a man who had gone through the wringer during the long depression of the early nineties told George some of his experiences.

"George," he said, "there are two kinds of traders in grains. The former can't see declines approaching; the latter never believes the sun will shine again once there is bad weather. The first type is called a 'bull,' and the second a 'bear.' Both are their own enemies. A good trader must see both sides of the market. He must buy when economic conditions are bad, which means when prices are low. These prices invariably will come up. Then prosperity develops all around like magic. After a while, when everybody believes in still further miracles, he must sell and go short, which means he must sell the same amount he originally held long without actually possessing it. He gambles that he can later buy that amount in the open market at a lower price. This gives a main trend up as well as a main trend down. It may be compared with spring, summer, and autumn up to the time of the first frost. That's the bull move. The rest, the decline or bear move, may be compared with the late fall and winter. Two and one half parts lead up, but only one and one half parts lead down. Thus the advances take a much longer period of time than the bear moves, which are wicked, fast, and destructive."

Bear moves are wicked, fast, and destructive.

This was a complicated statement, full of meaning. George was amazed to hear Mr Schafer come forth with such knowledge, some of which he had heard of in school but much of which had been clarified.

By nine o'clock the train pulled into the Grand Central Station. A Greenhut Sigel-Cooper bus was waiting outside the station which Mr Schafer knew would bring them down to 14th Street and Sixth Avenue. It was really meant to bring department store customers to the store, but outsiders used it often to get down and buy at the store later should they need something. They took seats right in front. The carriage went through Park Avenue and turned into 14th Street near Madison Square Garden. From there they continued by tramway to the piers, took a ferry for Hoboken, and by nine-forty they had reached the Hoboken side.

At Hoboken; the Boat

It took but a few minutes to bring them to the Lloyd Pier. The Munchen was just pushing into the dock. In a half hour's time the three men would be able to go on deck. Mr Schafer was able to present papers which got them aboard without any further formalities.

George observed the proceedings carefully. He felt that Mr Schafer was more than just an apple grower. George had noticed that Schafer knew about trading and about places the average farmer could not know about. But George kept this to himself as he followed along.

On deck Mr Schafer led. He went into the big dining room to see certain officials and shortly thereafter Grete appeared, laughing and crying as she ran toward George, whom she saw first. She ran to him, overcome by her emotions.

"Hello, Grete!" he exclaimed. "There's Jim; don't you see him?"

Grete hardly recognized Jim, who had grown taller and browner, and was now smooth shaven and dressed differently from anything she had seen before. He was a bit scared, too.

"Grete, wie gehts?" (Grete, how are you?) was all he could say.

In the meantime Mr Schafer had spoken a few words to the officials and all were permitted to leave the boat. Grete had two big suitcases besides a large trunk which had to be inspected at the pier by the customs officials, but this did not take very long. An express man was given orders to ship the trunk to Upper Red Hook and the suitcases were lugged over to New York on the ferry and up to the station. There they left them in the checking room of the depot at the suggestion of Mr Schafer.

While on deck George had introduced Grete to Mr Schafer. They shook hands as if they were acquaintances of long standing. It was seemingly just the time for people to make life-long friends. They did not understand each other's language. A plain, healthy girl, almost six feet tall, with blond hair, a sweet face, somewhat elongated, wiped a few remaining tears from her eyes, looked Mr Schafer straight in the eyes and said "Guten Tag."

Inquiries by Jim and George about the trip and about home were directed at Grete, who responded as fast as possible.

Finally Jim broke out, "Grete, dear, will you become my wife?"

"Would I have come otherwise?" she replied, giving him a kiss right in front of everybody. Passengers, however, are quite immune to such scenes. This can be readily understood when it is known that Hoboken is a town where many Germans and Hollanders live who never in their lives get farther than New York or Jersey City, even though they become loyal citizens of our country as soon as they have resided the required number of years here.

"What would you say," Jim suggested after catching his breath, "that we get married right away?"

"Today? Don't we have to wait for two weeks?" asked Grete. In Germany it was customary for any couple to apply for a license and have their intentions posted at the city hall where anyone might file objections. Two weeks had to elapse before the marriage.

"No," Jim replied. "Mr Schafer told me that this is not required here. He especially came down with us to see us get married. He knows where we have to go and . . ."

Without finishing his words Jim pulled Mr Schafer to the side and whispered into his ear about the rings.

"I won't forget," Mr Schafer promised, smilingly.

At the depot they had a bite to eat at a cafeteria which seemed to be a part of the station.

"Grete, stay close beside me," Jim said as they entered the place. "I don't want you to get lost," he explained.

This was quite unnecessary, since she had her arm in his. The little gazing which she did was directed at the huge buildings, the marble halls of the depot, and the other sights of the great city which seemed to her like a dream. She was happy. But she wasn't hungry, though she did have a bite with them just to be sociable. After a while Mr Schafer left with Jim for a few minutes, leaving George with Grete to talk about home. Jim and Mr Schafer went up to Fifth Avenue where they looked for a jewelry store to buy rings. Jim had observed the size of her ring finger. Incidently, Mr Schafer had done the very same thing. The two found a jewelry store on Forty-second Street before reaching the Avenue. Here they selected a pair of plain gold rings. In only a few minutes the initials were engraved, reading "J.W. to G.M., Oct. 5, '09." The other was marked "G.M. to J.W., Oct. 5, '09." Now Jim felt relieved. He had the rings. The rest would be easy.

The Ride to the Wedding

Soon they were back at the cafeteria. Schafer led the group to the station and down a maze of steps. Suddenly they found themselves in the subway and a train came clattering in with a deafening noise. Schafer took some tickets which he threw into an open box in front of a ticket taker. They passed through narrow gates and caught the train. None of them had been on a subway with the exception of Mr Schafer. They felt as if they were in a daze. They just sat down and waited for what was to happen next. They couldn't even talk. The noise was deafening. Other trains would pass in the opposite direction, giving each a feeling as if the world was going to crash right then. It didn't, though. After numerous stops the end of the hellish ride arrived. Suddenly the train appeared to make a long curve. Wheels squeaked and the train came to a stop. The station was well lit. It curved like the wall of an Italian arena. A sign read, "City Hall." They emerged into the fresh air.

There was no thought of marriage at all during the actual ride. Their minds were too much taken up with thoughts of how they were to get out of the devilish thing again. Schafer could have taken some other means of conveyance, but he enjoyed watching their expressions of happiness, fear, and worry. He also enjoyed the look of relief they all showed when finally they emerged from the underground railroad.

The City Hall was only a small building in the midst of a park which was bordered by tall buildings. Over yonder was a building which topped the others and bore a sign reading "Tribune." A small part of Brooklyn Bridge was visible, but they did not recognize it as such. They walked into the building, Mr Schafer in the lead. The clock outside showed twelve-thirty. So did the clock on the Tribune Tower. Mr Schafer made them wait in the lobby while he entered a room and came out with a piece of paper. Jim filled it out at one of the desks in a corner. It was an application blank for a marriage certificate.

All of them entered another room in which a gentleman was sitting. He read what Jim had written, and while the pair stood in front of him he rose and said something. Jim said, "Yes." The man said a few more words, apparently addressing himself to Grete, who didn't understand a word. Jim gave her a poke in the side and said, "Sag ja," so she obediently said, "Ja" (yes). A little more was said by the man, but it sounded like Greek to Grete. They received a certificate of marriage and shook hands all around.

"Have you got rings with you?" asked the man. He had to repeat the question because Jim didn't understand him.

"Give the man the rings," Mr Schafer instructed, and Jim fished through several pockets for them. It took George to locate them in the upper left vest pocket.

Who actually put on the rings, whether it was George, the man, or Mr Schafer, neither Jim nor Grete could ever recall. But they walked out of the room each with a ring on a finger.

George took the certificate out of Jim's hand to put in his pocket for safe keeping. The two newly-weds were too confused to be accountable for their actions. Too many things to which they were new and unaccustomed were passing in front of them. Usually Jim was very level-headed. Few things could excite him. We have seen this all along. He had now left his hat by mistake in the room, and had to go back to get it. He did not remember whether he had given his bride a kiss as the rings were put on or not.

"Well, you're married now!" exclaimed George. In the lobby Mr Schafer and George congratulated the pair. They wished them all the happiness they would desire for themselves. It was not quite two o'clock when the four came out of the City Hall.

Mr Schafer had several calls to make which prompted him to leave.

"You folks can take a carriage now. Drive down to Wall Street and afterwards ride up town to find our friend Holten. I'll meet you there at six. Tell the driver to let you off at Columbus Circle. The YMCA is close by."

"That was fine of Mr Schafer," thought Jim, relieved nevertheless to be able now to speak German.

George would have left the couple to themselves, but how could he? He had never been to New York himself except on the day his boat docked three months before. It was a risky thing to be all by oneself in such a big city. Not that he felt he would not be able to find his way back home to Upper Red Hook, and yet he had had many ideas while picking apples and working on the barn. First of all he wanted to find some book shops. He wanted certain types of books that would deal with markets, economics, and related subjects. That shop in Poughkeepsie had had a lot of Agricultural Year Books, but George still did not have enough of them. He did not exactly know what books he wanted, but he felt that if he saw them he would know immediately if they would answer his purpose.

At Wall Street

Wall Street, he knew, was the place where the Exchange was located and where shares were traded. That would be interesting to see. Outside the park George hailed a carriage. The three got in, Grete sitting in the middle. Jim, holding her tightly around the waist, was to the right of her. George sat at the left.

"Take us to Wall Street, where the Stock Exchange is."

"Take us to Wall Street, where the Stock Exchange is," George told the driver.

The carriage had to make a complete turn-about to set out in the right direction. They were on lower Broadway. The closer they came to Wall Street the higher the buildings were and the more people appeared on the streets.

"Where do all these people go?" asked Grete.

"Search me," said George. "That's what I'd like to know myself."

"They don't wear hats, either," remarked Grete, "so they can't be going very far."

There was a street sign, "Wall Street." The driver turned into the street. Part of the way down he stopped. This was the Exchange. They got out and paid him off. George led the party. They first surveyed the building from the outside, then, looking for an entrance, found a small door on the Wall Street side.

George could hear the noise of many voices toward the rear. As he walked in that direction he was stopped by a guard.

"Whom do you want?" asked the guard.

"Oh, I just want to see the Exchange," was his answer.

A swinging door opened and closed continuously as people

passed in and out of the Exchange. These were runners, floor traders, and other privileged persons. George had a glimpse at those moments of the big stands with people clustered around them, all men. To one side he could see numbers marked with chalk and letters at the top of each row. These made no sense to George whatever, but at least he had seen something, and he intended to find out more.

These were runners, floor traders, and other privileged persons.

"Where can I get a permit to look the Exchange over?" he asked the guard.

"You have to get an OK from a broker with whom you do business," was the reply.

George thought the matter over a moment and then withdrew to join Jim and Grete, who were standing on the corner looking fondly at one another and oblivious to passers-by.

"Let's get going, love birds," called out George.

They took another cab that brought them through narrow Nassau Street, crowded with people on both sides. There seemed to be a never-ending stream. Where they came from they could not figure out.

As they finally emerged near the City Hall, where an hour before Grete and Jim had been married, the cab proceeded at a fast pace taking them toward mid-town. Suddenly George spied a book store. There was, in fact, a whole series of them, lining both sides of the street. They had reached Fourth Avenue, the center for used books. He thought himself to be on the "Auer Dult," a trade fair held twice a year at an old church in Munich where the back was leased to second-hand book dealers who put thousands of books on display. That was where he was at home, buying all kinds of them which he thought might be valuable to him later. George had left all his books in Germany except for a few which he had considered indispensable.

"Driver, please stop a moment. I'll go over to that store to see what they have," George said. He thought a moment and then continued, "Maybe I'd better pay you now. How much do I owe you?" George paid off the driver and the three got out. "There's a restaurant. You eat something and by that time I'll be back." George walked across the street to view the books he saw on display outside the stores.

At the Old Book Store

There was nothing more pleasing to George than to browse around in an old book store. They contained for him unknown treasures at low cost. He asked for books on trading grains and was shown a special section containing books on economics. There was one titled "The Silver Panic of 1893." Another read "Sepharial's Key to Market Operations," and another "Successful Methods for Wall Street Speculation." There were many more, too, but he selected those three for preliminary study so that he'd learn a little more about trading and its intricacies.

He selected three for study so that he'd learn a little more about trading and its intricacies.

With a beaming face he left the store.

"Now I have something that will form a basis for later success," he thought to himself. He surely was not going to die a farmer up at Upper Red Hook, even though he got along with his brother and liked his brother's choice for a wife.

George found both drinking coffee at the restaurant and waiting for him. Half an hour passed quickly and Grete had been stretching her neck already looking for George to come back. George also had a cup of coffee and a piece of cake.

As they left the place they continued to walk for a while in the direction the carriage would have taken them had they continued in it. This brought them up to Union Square, with its wide plaza. They recognized the surroundings, having passed it in the morning. They kept on going, passing through the park. Soon they reached the Broadway side where they asked a passer-by how far it was to Columbus Circle and how long it would take to walk there.

"Half an hour or so. Just keep on Broadway." was the reply.

It was nearly four o'clock, early yet for the six o'clock appointment with Mr Schafer. They decided to keep on walking and to see something of the town. At Twenty-third Street they came to the Flat Iron Building and stood a long time at Twenty-fourth Street to admire it. Grete counted 29 stories in it.

"What a monster!" exclaimed Jim. "I'll bet you it makes one tired walking up and down a couple of times a day."

Gradually they approached Times Square. On the way a boy was selling the "Evening Mail," of which George bought a copy. He intended to read it on the way home on the train. At Times Square they admired the building, as do all newcomers to the city. Several men tried to talk them into a sight-seeing tour of the town, but they were determined to be at Columbus Circle at six o'clock.

As they walked along, Jim and Grete cooing like turtle doves, George saw a big newspaper stall. There was the "Munchener Neueste Nachrichten."

"Imagine that!" he said. "There's our home town paper, too!"

He bought a copy about two weeks old that may have come over on the boat carrying Grete.

Finally they reached Columbus Circle, tired and hungry from the long walk. They were not used to pavements. Grete would not admit that she was tired. She had the first night of marriage to live through yet. Besides, she had been resting for two weeks now. On the boat all she could do was walk up and down the deck. What excitement she had lived through since the boat had docked!

Wedding Dinner

Jim now took the lead in the direction of the YMCA. He knew it was on a side street. There was a big empty lot between the YMCA and a main thoroughfare. Soon he thought he recognized that thoroughfare, since he spied the iron structure with a little orange tower on top. It was the Sixth Avenue elevated at 53rd Street which he saw at the point where it crossed Eighth Avenue.

There was the empty lot he was looking for on 57th Street!

"We have to go back again," he admitted. "It's down there somewhere."

They took Eighth Avenue to 57th Street and soon the building came into view.

The weather was still warm at that time, but it began to get cooler towards evening.

They found Mr Holten, who was overjoyed at the success of his young friend whom he had helped and who had appreciated his help very much. Grete could talk in German to Mr Holten. She thanked him for what he had done for Jim. She knew all about him already from Jim's correspondence.

Mr Schafer appeared within the next ten minutes and all decided to have a good dinner before departing for home. The idea of leaving the couple for the wedding night at some New York hotel was dropped by Schafer because the crop of apples had to be packed before it became too cold. They'd simply have to take a honeymoon at some later date when the work was out of the way. All agreed with this suggestion. The group insisted that Mr Holten come along. It was he, in fact, who selected the place for the dinner. He chose "Luchow's" on Fourteenth Street below Fourth Avenue, a place known for many years for its excellent food. They specialized in wild fowl, venison roasts, and many other dishes for the gourmet.

There also were excellent beers from the old country. Beer from Pilsen in Bohemia, from Munich, and wines of every kind were to be had. The meal was so plentiful and tasty, the beer so good, that they all agreed it was well worth the trip. By eight o'clock they were at the Grand Central depot picking up the suitcases to catch the late train for home. Mr Holten, having said "Auf Wiedersehen," disappeared into the crowd. They caught their train for Upper Red Hook and reached home at midnight.

CHAPTER V

ACTIVITIES DURING THE WINTER OF 1909–10

George had quite a normal philosophy of life. He would see that right and justice would be set at their just places. Unfairness he just couldn't stand. He hated loafers as well as those who talked nonsense. He couldn't stand for animals to be hurt, even snakes, because, as he said, they are in the world for some purpose. In fact they live on insects, mice, or whatever comes to them as they sit quietly with their heads in the air, wiggling their tongues incessantly and keeping them oiled for instant use. With regular pests, however, such as mice or rats, he could be pitiless. They deserve to be rooted out, he thought, wherever they show themselves.

Homeward Bound

The monotonous night trip of nearly four hours produced a little dozing among the four passengers. Their stomachs, unusually overloaded, called for a resting period for digestion. Grete had begun to sleep, resting her head on Jim's lap, shortly after they passed Tarrytown station. Jim woke her as they pulled into the Upper Red Hook station. The walk home in the cool of the night revived her again. She even began to talk and laugh a happy girl's laugh. Mr Schafer, too, tried to make himself jolly and agreeable despite his language difficulties.

At Mr Schafer's farm they thanked him for the invaluable assistance he had given them and for the time he had spent with them. Then the three of them proceeded to their own farm. Everything was in good order. The two kerosene lamps, wicks up as far as possible, were carried all about to show Mrs Wollsten her new home.

"I can see, my dear Jim," she thought quietly to herself, "that you need a wife. I shall be a good wife to you, not only in love but also in work."

Grete was not one of those dancing damsels or one of those girls of the flirting variety that let mother wash a pile of dirty dishes while they gad about. She had learned from her mother all that a housewife should know before she was one herself. She could make tasty dishes without a cook book. Nothing was left on the plates after dinner, because her cooking, though plain was flavorful and good.

For a long time she had been in love with Jim, though she had never hinted at it. Now it had all happened as she had wished. She was his wife, and she was determined to prove that she deserved to be his wife.

As might be expected, when the newly-weds' room was reached Grete declared it looked very good, but where was the bed? Did they have to buy one first or go without for a while? That would be all right, too, as far as she was concerned. Then Jim began to pull apart the sofa which opened into a bed. Pillows, blankets, sheets – all were there. Grete emitted a slight gasp as she observed this, but so much had occurred during the last fourteen hours that she had grown almost immune to novelties and strange things.

"What humbug! What have planets to do with markets?"

George soon said good-night and disappeared downstairs to his own room, leaving the two by themselves to enjoy the night. He perused his three books for an hour to see what they had to say about trading. He had selected them solely because of their titles. He was tired, too, and could only remember that in Sepharial's "Key to Market Trading" there had been mention of planets at various places which were said to affect the trend of trading.

"What humbug!" thought George. "What have planets to do with markets?" He extinguished his lamp, turned around twice, noted the stars and the planets as he did so, and fell asleep.

Routine Work Resumed

A few days later Grete had become accustomed to her new surroundings and to being a wife. She had become acquainted with the cow and the horse, the chickens, the apple orchards, and with many of her neighbors. Mr Schafer had been accepted as more of a father who lived next door than a mere neighbor.

The regular routine of work was resumed. Jim continued to sort apples and Grete quickly learned how to pack them. George went ahead with the insulation of the barn. The chickens had begun to lay, producing an income to tide them over the next few months. While a dozen eggs brought 25c, theirs, which were small, brought only 20c. At least they brought something.

All told there were about 600 chickens. Diseases common among young chickens had fortunately not appeared. Since there were no diseases, no one thought of any. George used to say that a man was healthy as long as he didn't know he had hands, feet, ears, or eyes. But as soon as he noticed pain some place he became conscious of that part of his body. Only with one's head was it different. If one got that part out of order George would say, he was not often conscious of that.

When something is started at the right time it is bound to succeed, irrespective of whether someone else tries to put a crimp into it. Such a one is just out of luck and hurts himself more than he can harm the other man. Few people seem to be born at the right time. Most are born under only mediocre auspices, and some are born unfortunate. Even with these, however, hard work, study, and endurance can bring about a great improvement in their lot. In fact it is possible to produce good even out of evil. One can catch rattlesnakes if he goes carefully about it.

Grete took care of the cow and chickens all along and cooked and did the general house work too. This left the two boys free to attend to their special tasks. George closed shop two hours sooner and opened it two hours later, giving him a chance to devote some time to his own study. After all, he was only helping Jim and Grete get started.

George Approaches Markets

He had obtained some squared sheets for graph making, but as soon as he had reached into the book "Successful Methods for Wall Street Speculators" he saw that graphs printed therein were much different and should not be made upon such rough material as he had bought. The "Evening Mail" came regularly now, and he studied the price changes as they occurred from day to day in stocks, grains, and commodities. This required quiet and concentration. One could not work twelve or fourteen hours a day and then sit down and work again on things which need an entirely different approach. He had seen some advertisements of brokers offering their services, and for want of a better idea he wrote one of them as follows:

"Whereas I intend to become a market trader soon, after I finish studying a few books. I want you to tell me where graph paper can be obtained similar to that used in making graphs of the various stock and grain movements. Please send me this information and oblige . . ."

An answer came within two days saying that such graph paper can be bought from Keuffel & Esser and from Dietzgen & Co., both of New York. To them each he wrote a letter and received a variety of graph papers within a few days. From this he selected one that provided 366 spaces for the days of the year across the long side and had the months printed on the top and bottom. The color was green instead of orange, and he judged it would not harm the eyes as much as some other color. A drawing set, complete with triangles and a ruler, he had brought along with him from Europe. He also had a book of logarithms, something which was always handy in making rapid calculations. At the same time he bought the paper he had ordered six kinds of differently colored inks for a purpose not even clear to himself yet. He just wanted to have them.

The Agricultural Year Books (he had about eighteen which he had bought that time at Poughkeepsie) gave him the idea that there might be tables available which would show what markets had done from day to day for several years back. Instead of waiting for six months to see how his charts would develop from entries made from the tables printed in the newspaper, he might be able to see at a glance what had happened in the past.

George knew very well that when a thief comes to a house and finds something of value it isn't long before he returns. Also he knew that if one lies and another realizes it, that other person can be pretty sure the same fellow will lie again. Those are natural weaknesses in men. Why, George reasoned, shouldn't economic movements of commodities and stocks also follow predictable patterns?

At any rate he wrote the broker once more, thanking him for his recent information and saying that he needed more before he would be ready to come down and talk business. He asked if there were any more printed records available that would give grain prices for several years back, stock prices, and prices of other commodities.

Back Records

Promptly a reply arrived saying that the Board of Trade at Chicago publishes each year a complete daily record of all grain options traded there together with high, low, and closing prices. Cottonseed oil prices could be had from the Produce Exchange at New York upon application. Cotton prices too could be had from their statistical department provided he did not require the records of too many years back. Stock prices could be more easily obtained through the New York Financial Chronicle, which issues a magazine weekly containing the daily high and low prices for all stocks traded on the Exchange. These records, too, could be had for a number of years back.

"That letter was worth sending," George thought. He was practically overwhelmed with the wealth of information it had brought him. He scarcely knew where to start. In the meantime a hundred sheets of graph paper had arrived. He re-plotted chicken prices paid on the New York farms for the past several years on that very evening, using the information provided by the Agricultural Year Books. He used one square of the paper that had three small lines within it and called this four-line space one cent. The lowest registered price he could find was 10.2 cents a pound paid in the north Atlantic states. These prices rose as high as 18.8 cents. On the graph, or chart, as he preferred to call those specially prepared sheets, he ignored the monthly and daily divisions printed on the top and bottom margins of the graph sheets.

George's Analysis on Market Movements

Prices in the Agricultural Year Book had been given "per month," without any consideration of the fluctuations that had occurred between the first of the month and the first of the next. Nevertheless he was satisfied to find out even that much regarding chicken price fluctuations. It was a start, at least. The pattern which developed looked much different from that he had made on squared paper. He saw that the price picture showed waves running upward slowly and then declining slowly, but they were not running strictly according to the seasons of the year. Not only was this true, but he saw, too, that they varied from one year to the next. This made him realize this important fact: PRICE MOVEMENTS ARE INDEPENDENT OF THE SEASONS OF THE YEAR!

This made him realize: PRICE MOVEMENTS ARE INDEPENDENT OF THE SEASONS OF THE YEAR!

Something else, but not the sun, must have an influence upon price movements. This conclusion was arrived at more through hard thinking than from Sepharial's book which mentioned the stars and the planets. He had only looked through this book superficially and had not consulted it again.

George had never thought much about planets or stars. He knew that they existed. He knew something of their periods, but what he knew was limited to that taught in school. He had heard of "Planetenschlagerinen," meaning women who tell fortunes from the planets, but he had never seen one that he knew of. He had been brought up to believe that man's will and money makes the world and that God is the overseer of them all.

From the Bible he remembered that God had given free will to man to do good or to do evil as he may desire. How, then, could the planets affect anything? Still he remembered too that in the stories of the Greek and Roman Gods the number of their deities went up into the hundreds.

George Thinks of Greeks and Romans

Those Greeks and Romans, he was sure, had not been simple. Their literatures and architectures were enough to convince George of that. Could they have fooled us all by inventing a lot of gods whose names only a genius could remember while they were actually speaking of planets and stars all the time? And what about that enormous stretch of time between the fall of the Roman Empire and the time of Charlemagne? Five hundred years or more are there, over which teachers jump just as George used to jump across a brook without thinking anything of it. But history had been made in that time, too, though all we know of it is that it was the period of the Goths, the Visigoths, and other races which fought interminable wars with one another.

George closed Sepharial's book with the realization that there was something wrong somewhere. He determined to learn more about that ancient period. It was two o'clock before he put out the light. Grete and Jim had already been asleep for several hours. It was long since time for him to sleep also.

Jim used to start work by six in the morning. At times he was at work on the chores even earlier. George, however, habitually appeared about nine in the morning.

One lot of apples, the lower grade, had been sold off. Those which remained could be stored inside the barn, and even a killing frost could not affect them. The late vegetables were also hauled into the cellar where some were "heeled in" to insure longer life. Only kale was left out to freeze as much as it wished.

The First Frost

It was not any too soon. By October 18 the first killing frost knocked out all the beautiful dahlias, cockscombs, red hot pokers, and other beautiful summer flowers in one night. Even though warmer weather set in, the damage was done and could not be undone. They both redoubled their efforts to finish the insulation of the barn after additional lumber had been bought, along with another load of straw. The days grew visibly shorter. Before November arrived the work had been completed.

George had figured that insulation would keep the barn temperature above freezing point even though outside the temperature might drop as low as 20 below zero. He knew such a low temperature was possible because he found records of high and low temperatures throughout a period of years and knew that on January 18, 1899, the temperature for Poughkeepsie had been –18. He drew a chart of the temperature given for 1899 at Poughkeepsie, registering the high and low values. The high and low of each day he connected with a line day after day, and thus he had his first perfect chart of one type of movement. He was very proud of it. Grete and Jim, he insisted, should look it over and give their opinions.

"It may be so, but I don't know," remarked Jim as he sat down to read his Upper Red Hook Herald and search for an advertisement which might tell him where to buy wood, a matter which he considered of far greater importance than what the weather had been ten years ago.

Jim was the practical man who knew his way around a farm and who had learned a lot about apples in the short span of a year and a half. Of course he did not entirely ignore books. Many an evening he read those old Agricultural Year Books and had even written already for the one that was soon to appear. He even found in them something George had overlooked. He saw pictures of California orchards where orange trees were protected by smudge pots. He was keenly interested in this for reasons that were quite evident.

"See here, George," he had said, "they burn oil in those things to keep out the frost as much as possible whenever the temperature drops in the fields. Couldn't we prepare for an emergency in the barn in the same way in the event that the straw insulation did not prove to be sufficient?"

George thought it was a great idea. He patted Jim on the shoulder as a teacher does to a pupil who has given a good answer.

"That will have to be tried outside first to see what size of flame develops. Otherwise we might burn the whole barn down," declared George.

A few days later they ordered a small drum of crude oil from Poughkeepsie. A few old pots were also secured, and a period of experimentation began. No matter how many matches they put to the crude oil they could not make it burn. George thought of applying heat to the oil, and they carried one pot into the kitchen, heated it on the stove, and took it outside again to try once more. Now a slow flame started, very dark and sooty. Some heat was there, too. The flame never rose more than eight inches in height and the pot kept burning for almost eight hours.

They succeeded marvelously with it when they were forced to try it the first time on December 14 of that year. The temperature had dropped to –9 by eight in the evening. A thermometer in the barn showed 35 degrees at six o'clock. They heated some of the oil for the four pots which they had set up at suitable places and put enough oil in each to last for three or four hours. Meanwhile they intended to keep a close watch on what developed. They saw the temperature rise to 37 degrees around the pots, but noticed that it leveled off at 35 degrees elsewhere. They were overjoyed by the results. The element of frost was conquered, and all they needed to do was to keep a constant watch.

Mr Schafer, who had wondered how Wollsten's apples had held up through the cold wave, strolled over to see for himself. The smoke clouds in the barn could not be blown out and the door could not be kept open either, so the three used lanterns to walk around. They could scarcely see three feet ahead of them.

Seeing things in perfect shape, Mr Schafer's confidence in the ability of the two young men rose again. He himself had sold his entire crop long before because he had no way to hold it back. Grete served Mr Schafer a sandwich and some coffee. George was afire with the desire to show Mr Schafer some of the graphs he had drawn up on wheat and rye movements taken from statistics provided by the Board of Trade Year Books he had ordered from Chicago. These had arrived in the meantime.

George showed Mr Schafer that in some years wheat rose to two dollars and higher, and at other times fell sharply to sixty or seventy cents. He said that he could not yet account for such enormous fluctuations.

Russo-Jap. War 1904 & Grain Prices

George had found some old World Almanacs of 1904 through 1906 which gave the dates of events in that period. He checked the years 1904 and 1905, when the Russo-Japanese war had been fought. The pattern of wheat prices, he noticed, did not conform in any way with the events of the war. After a lag of four months after the war had begun, prices rose, stayed up for eight months, and then dropped precipitously in April of 1905, several months before the war ended. He found that no events in the United States had occurred during the month of April, 1905, either. And yet wheat dropped forty cents in less than one month. He felt, therefore, that while wars might influence grain prices, tending to increase values, yet the rise does not necessarily concur directly with the actual beginning of hostilities. Neither does its end produce an immediate drop in prices.

Dow Jones Averages

While Mr Schafer was there, George showed him the charts of several stocks, including U.S. Steel, Westinghouse, and Western Union. The charts showed how they had performed from day to day since he had been getting the "Evening Mail." Mr Schafer was much interested in this work. George had occasionally received some graphs from the brokers since he had first written to them in New York. Glowing letters about the next advance in share prices had also arrived, all urging that he hurry up and get in on the next rise.

Glowing letters about the next advance in share prices arrived, all urging that he get in on the next rise.

As George interpreted his charts, however, he was not so sure. Stock prices had been rising ever since November of 1907, when the mean price of 30 stocks, which was called the Dow Jones Averages, was computed at 55.00. Right now the computation was 98.47. It had been, in mid-November, 1909, as high as 100.57, but had hovered just below that level ever since.

At the time Grete and Jim had been married the price had touched 100.50, or .07 less than the record of mid-November. It looked to George like one of those broad tops, such as egg prices sometimes make.

George's Second Analysis on Markets

"I don't think this bull stuff will go much higher for a while," he said to Mr Schafer. "Not in stocks, anyway. Commodities, however, may go higher irrespective of what stocks do, since each works out its own pattern. I've found out that much."

Commodities may go higher irrespective of stocks since each works out its own pattern.

"What do you think of farm lands?" asked Mr Schafer.

"That's something I haven't checked into," George replied. "Off hand I'd say prices in properties are bound to rise, whether they be located in the city or the country, because of the tremendous influx of immigrants from all over the world. Just look at the three here. We need a farm – at least Jim and Grete need one. So do thousands each year. They will, too, until we've reached saturation point. Immigration may be restricted after a while, and then the situation will be different."

"That's what I think, too," agreed Schafer.

Jim Goes Hunting a Christmas Tree and Decorations

Jim was just ready to go out to look for a spruce or fir tree. He intended to surprise Grete with a tree so that they could have an old-fashioned Christmas. Snow had not yet come. He made excuses and left them to discuss the Russo-Japanese war and how it might affect the purchase of the farm on which he held an option. During the life of the option he would have to earn enough money to pay a sizable amount and get a loan from the bank or pay interest to Mr Schafer on the balance. George had discussed that with Mr Schafer already, and he felt that they had nothing to fear.

In his buggy, Jim started eastward toward the Southern Connecticut line. He knew there were some evergreen trees there. He found a group of cedars and some hemlocks, but he could not discover spruce or fir.

"I don't want to go too far," he thought as he cut down a hemlock. The tree was slightly taller than Jim himself.

As he drove home he purposely detoured to get through Upper Red Hook, since he thought again of Dingle's, which would probably have some of the old-fashioned Christmas decorations. They are manufactured mainly in Thuringia near the town of Sonneberg and are imported into the United States. Since there had not been much of a Christmas for Jim the year before, he felt that he must have the decorations now. He thought, too, that by the time Christmas came again, there might be another, a real American, in the family. Who could tell? He knew he was doing his part.

By that time he had reached Dingle's, had tied "Grimm," the mare, to a post, and entered the store.

"Yes," the salesgirl said, "we have plenty of those ornaments in the basement."

There he found all kinds of Christmas decorations packed in boxes, a dozen to the box. The colors were wonderful, and many were hand painted. Icicles he found, too, and glittering strings and candle holders which could be clamped to the tree. At one counter he found a small hill of walnuts, hazelnuts, and pecans. He bought half a pound of each. He didn't intend to spend a fortune just for Christmas.

"I'll have to get some gold and silver paper to put around the nuts and a colored wire to tie them to the tree," he reminded himself.

The salesgirl put all the breakable things into a special box. He had spent four dollars. Happy and contented, he drove home. Grete had not expected a Christmas tree nor decorations for it.

George was so taken up with his graphs that he didn't even notice the tree or the box. He did not even notice Jim.

"I'll make a tree stand this afternoon," Jim told Grete. "Let's eat something now, I'm hungry."

George had started to work another approach. He had seen an advertisement in the "Evening Mail" for the "Wall Street Journal," a paper devoted exclusively to finance. He had ordered a sample copy. In that copy there had happened to be an article on the "Dow Jones Averages," in which the writer explained the method of computing these averages. It told why certain stocks were selected, how the division and multiplication were made, and how the final figures were arrived at. The article mentioned, also, that a small booklet could be had showing the daily high and low levels of these averages back to the year 1897 for just fifty cents.

"That's grand!" thought George. "That's what I need to see what's happened throughout the years. It will show me what is likely to happen again."

George sent away for the book and soon it arrived. He spent a whole night studying it. In it he discovered one part showing the volume of trading from day to day from 1897 to the present. The variations in these figures astonished George. Some days, especially recently, a million and a half shares had been traded. Back in February there had been days when only 250,000 shares had changed hands. The market had been rising all year, and so had the volume of shares traded.

Price Movements After 1907

Back in 1907, when prices had declined steadily, he found that the volume was tremendous at the top area, dropping off gradually until very near to the bottom. There were often only 150,000 shares sold in a day, though there were exceptional days at low levels when more than a million shares were sold.

"Ah," he'd say to himself, "that's where they dumped stocks for fear that they would go much lower. They probably waited and didn't sell out until things looked hopeless."

"This is a top. Too many people want things at higher prices."

From charts of that time, which he plotted out in a hurry to get a better perspective of the situation, he could see this. Holding his pencil to his mouth, and chewing unconsciously at it, he did a lot of thinking.

There is something in the action of man which makes him see things rosier at noon than at daybreak, thought George. At dawn, when people are roused from sleep, they appear lively, eat something, and then busy themselves with their daily tasks. But in the markets those same people do not act like normal people. They act contrary to natural laws.

"Look," he said to himself, "instead of buying down at or near that low, they must have sold or dumped good stocks instead of buying them. And up here we again have heavy volume and high prices, pointing to the present. As sure as Christmas is coming, this is a top here. Too many people want things at high prices!"

His deductions were correct, as developments showed the following spring.

In order to plot the volume of the Stock Transactions for the years he had found in that new book, he entered dots on his chart paper representing the volume each day. He connected these dots with a ruler and then began his analysis. He did the same thing with the High and Low Values of the Stock Averages.

Caterpillar Movements

Suddenly, while looking at them (he had cut off the paper margin on the December side in order to be able to connect one year with the next) he noticed that *the entire movement resembled a Caterpillar crawling up a Branch*, parts of his belly bulging. After the formation had reached a peak the whole thing turned around. The Caterpillar Design was made in descending instead of ascending fashion.

In some years, George noticed that the caterpillar design idled along on level ground. It apparently had its fill of food and was resting. But this never lasted long. Sometimes a plateau occurred for as long as six months, but suddenly the change would come. There would be a march upwards followed by a recession and then the leveling off period again. However, when a rise started a second time the movement would keep on going and nothing would stop it until it had gone a long way. Prices would rise and Volume would do the same.

When a rise started a second time the movement would keep on going.

Now, George reasoned the caterpillar was trying to find the branch. George began to draw a line from the low point to a high point, but the results were unsatisfactory.

"Why, how dumb!" exclaimed George. "The young shoots, especially those of a birch or beech, are not just straight lines. They shoot up for two inches or so one way then turn the other way for about the same distance. This continues, and only later on, as they become larger, do the branches appear like a straight line."

So he made straight lines out of smaller periods, fitting them as close as possible to the patterns. In that way he could visualize how a caterpillar took its grip upon the individual segments of the young shoots.

Gaps Made in Price Structure

Once in a while George noticed that the *market would form holes in its movements* from the trading of one day. The market would suddenly jump much higher during the trading of the next day, leaving a space, or a price hole, at which no trading had occurred. For example, the averages might have been, for one day, between 87.50 and 88.02. The next day the averages might show 88.15 and 88.41, with a hole of .13 between the averages of the two days.

Whenever he saw that such a condition occurred he also noticed that a big move immediately developed in the same direction. He saw that if this phenomenon appeared on the way down, a big drop should be anticipated.

"These are the rattlers of the rattlesnake," it occurred to him.

"That's the beginning of a cycle," he declared. In wheat he noticed this more often than in stocks, probably, he concluded, because wheat is just wheat, and in the stock averages 20 or 30 stocks have been put together and averaged. All stocks do not move alike in the same trend, since some are laggards at a time when others are pushing hard. But, when plotting single stocks, George had noticed this.

He had saved all his copies of the "Evening Mail," stacking them in a suitcase and warning Grete not to use them to light the stove. He read back through some of these papers and paid particular attention to the comments by financial writers to discover, if he could, if something unusual had happened in the world on the days when such holes were made. Nothing unusual could be seen. True, they spoke about a strong market, about strong spots, about the rush of buying that came in the late afternoon just before the close, but what the cause of these "holes" in the averages was, they did not say.

"They ought to know," George thought. "They are right down in New York, where all the news arrives." George could only follow his charts.

George had learned quite a bit of economics during his school years. He knew how corporations were formed and understood the issuance of stocks and bonds to finance the enterprise. He knew about cartels to protect operations in foreign countries through the loan of patents and processes of a secret nature to foreign corporations which reciprocated in a similar way.

As a student he had been twice taken to the Munich Boerse to see how stocks and bonds traded, how the buyer bids, and how the seller offers at a slightly advanced price before giving in to close the trade. He knew something of financial statements, too. He knew how to read them, what to look for to see the position of a corporation in regard to its solvency and outlook in general. Always, however, he had a feeling that those operations, open to anyone with the desire to investigate and the common sense to judge, might not be so simple as they appeared. If they were, how was it that so many lose money? These people were intelligent and had money behind them. They had data and statements available, and yet they lost money. Why?

How was it that so many lose money?

Why did the big banking house of Maurer & Company at Munich, for instance, collapse in 1907? For years it apparently prospered. Everyone knew of the house. Many had their money invested with it. Agents of the concern visited smaller communities once a week, on market day, so that the farmers and business men might make deposits.

This firm had available every sort of information. Market reports came from London every day. George knew this because one of the bookkeepers would give George the postage stamps on the wrappers once a week. As a child, he had been interested in collecting stamps.

Grete Learns English

A few days after Grete arrived, Jim and George had agreed to try to speak only English so that Grete might learn the new language. This was hard on Grete at first. Once in a while the brothers would relent and speak in their native tongue for an evening. But George insisted that it was best that they speak English. Now, at Christmas, they heard for the first time a few words of English come from Grete's mouth. Both were amazed. Grete, who had never said an English word besides "Jim" or "George," now spoke a few words.

It was during this time that they all worked together to decorate the Christmas tree. The tree had been placed in the sitting room on a stool. The glittering balls, multi-colored and of every size, together with the nuts wrapped in silver and gold and the tree ornaments made Grete suddenly say: "Me like! Beautiful! Beautiful!"

"So!" interjected George. "There you are! Grete tries to tell us she can never learn English, and now she speaks it."

"You be quiet," she said to George, "or else I won't say another word in English."

"Keep trying, Grete," Jim encouraged her. "We want you to speak English, whether you make mistakes or not."

The first snow began to fall. In the morning a blanket six inches deep covered the landscape, the orchard, and the house. Jim had cleared away the leaves. Everything was spick and span and in readiness for the winter. A few repairs had been attended to around the chicken coops. One night a weasel had played havoc with a dozen chickens, all of which lay dead in the coop when Jim discovered them in the morning. Jim set a trap, and on the third day he caught the killer.

The eggs had increased in size by this time. Since chickens were not laying well prices had touched a new high.

It must be remembered that the boys and Grete had come from a place where religion was a large part in the lives of the people.

There the priest was often consulted on matters which did not concern religion. There the priest was honored and respected by all. He would scold the boys who would try to skip out before he had said: "Ite Missa Est."

Nothing was held more serious than to miss Mass on a Sunday. The priest himself would check carefully from his pulpit during the sermon to learn whose places were vacant. He knew them all. He was clever in learning from the others why those absent were not there. Only a few ever tried to outwit him.

Neither Jim nor Grete had ever sought to stay away from Mass and make excuses to the priest. George, however, had at times taken bicycle trips on Sundays. Fortunately for him, he could always say that his father or mother, living at Bruck, were ill and needed him. By the time he'd get there, Mass would be over there, also.

Interesting Stories from the Bible

When Jim had taken his job with Mr Schafer he soon became acquainted with the local Church and went there regularly on Sundays. So did George and Grete. They used the Bible Grete had brought with her, given to her, when she had left for America, by Jim's mother. Mother Wollsten wanted Grete to have it and use it. George also found time now and then to read it. He was especially interested in the story of Joseph and his brothers, in the story of Jacob while working for Laban where it reads that "Jacob put sticks in the troughs of the speckled, spotted and the ringstraked sheep" so that they would conceive in a certain manner. Those pages he had removed from the Bible and put with his charts to have them handy.

The story of the seven lean cows and the seven ugly ones gave him much to think about. He checked his charts for indications that the movement in the markets might last seven years. He had seen long ago that the regular seasons of the year do not show repeating movements. But he thought a certain number of caterpillars could possibly grow in seven years. Two and one-half caterpillars might grow one way and two and one-half the other during seven years. He recalled and read again the story in the Apocalypse that something happened to the woman in "Time and Times and Half a Time." However, he also was stuck with the third word of that sentence, "Times," because it was used in the plural form. Could it mean three and one-half times? Twice that much would give seven again.

"Time and Times and Half a Time."

In short, around that period, George had for the first time an inkling that certain types of these stories may pertain to matters that were far from religion proper. Especially, he noticed, these nomadic patriarchs were traveling "all the Time." They built cities, houses, and altars, and no sooner had they done building than they started to move on and kept going.

George did the same, true, while he worked on his charts. He went from stocks to grains, from December option into May option as he plotted prices. However, at least he stayed in one place, on Jim's farm at Upper Red Hook, while he did it. He had made many charts for which he found no use. They might as well never even have been made. Those he put away. But just to build something and then go immediately to some other part of a country sounded strange to him.

He was not unmindful of the statement that we have to believe all that is written of a country in the Bible. He believed every bit of it, with the reservation that he was to interpret some parts in his own way. There might be a second meaning to all these writings, he thought, just as there is in many men. They say one thing but mean something else. Some appear to be as meek as a lamb but prove to be treacherous and mean.

George thought again of stocks. How well they climb up; how people must have bought them in quantity as prices rose day after day. Then suddenly it would develop that they would show their true character. Look at the decline of 1903, for example. This chart he had before him. What a rude awakening those investors must have had when they bought stocks early in the year that fell away sharply by November.

He concluded by thinking that the movements of stocks he had checked so far carried a double face. One smiles and the other weeps. He must watch carefully for this change of face. Whoever is behind the stocks, be it the management of corporations or the output, the mining properties, oil wells, manufactures, merchandise, or services of some kind, none of these have much influence on the price of stocks. Stocks go up together in sympathy and they decline in sympathy, some more, some less. One may rise more than another, but when everybody wants to buy stocks, traders and investors themselves bid up the little stocks that have not risen.

Customers' Men

It was a good thing that George had so far not come into a broker's office down in the city. He might never have happened upon these essential truths. He discovered them while he was far away from the hustling and buzzing of ticker tape. Down there he would have heard smooth-shaven customers' men explain to him how much this company or that one earned, how much more they were to earn the next month, the next quarter, or the next year. He would have heard about frosts in Kansas that were premature, about the boll weevil that devoured cotton down in Texas. He would have found out that the grain prices at Winnipeg, Liverpool, and Buenos Aires differed considerably from the Chicago market. He would have heard that they often have movements which are completely contrary to the movement of grain prices at Chicago. Such knowledge would have bothered him. He was trying to find reasons for everything. He would not stop with shallow explanations.

One of the features of customers' men is that they have explanations for anything and everything a customer may inquire

One of the features of customers' men is that they have explanations for everything.

about. They have special folders containing current reports of any company whose stock is traded. These show how much the company earns, what it produces, where it is located, where the branch factories are, how many people it employs, etc. They carry little booklets wherein are shown the quotations of any stocks over a period of time so that this information can be provided at a moment's notice.

Like the masses of people in the world, customers' men constantly look at the brighter side of things. They are always worried that prices might decline and their income be curtailed, but seldom are they willing to admit it.

Unless a trader has gone through the wringer a few times and managed to survive a bear market, he never thinks of selling unless values have increased considerably. In the event that they do sell, they itch to buy again. The customers' man always knows from special services of some stock that it is in a seemingly favorable position to advance. Before the trader knows it, he has bought again at a higher level. This continues until he is trapped in a bear market.

Christmas Day

Christmas Day found the trio up bright and early. The best clothes had been made ready. Grete brushed them out the afternoon before. They were spotless. In the evening they celebrated their first Christmas Eve by the light of the decorated tree. They talked about their old home, about parents they had left behind, about the rest of the family. Grete did a little crying. Even Jim was temporarily depressed. But George reminded Grete to bring those "Lebkuchen" (honeycakes) she had baked two weeks before and to distribute some oranges. He turned the conversation into other channels to get them off the sentimental side which he considered unfit for a family which had the courage to start a new life in the United States.

"The early settlers," he would say, "had hardships far greater than these to go through. What have we had to bear so far? We have always had plenty. We seem to strike it right. We have started right at the bottom, at the time when everything was darkest. Remember the "Donner Party" Mr Schafer told us about? It trekked out from the Middle West sixty years ago, traveled for nearly two years by ox teams through mountains and deserts and perished when within a few miles of their destination, California. Our hard times do not compare with theirs."

Such language stopped Grete's crying. She brought the Lebkuchen and oranges to the table along with a bottle of California red wine. The rest of the evening passed quietly. Grete got a few small presents, as did Jim and George. Letters had arrived from the old country for Christmas which were scanned for the tenth or eleventh time. They wanted to be certain they had missed nothing.

George had a love for language, and his English had improved substantially during the six months he had been in America. From Jim he had learned many words used in conversation. From books he had learned technical terms and words used in market transactions. The Agricultural Year Books were also a great help in improving his vocabulary. Once a week, sometimes twice, George would spend a few hours with Mr Schafer. At Christmas time, however, there could be no visits because Mr Schafer had gone to Florida.

Mr Schafer was a bachelor whose home was run by an old housekeeper who had been in service with him for thirty or forty years. Schafer often spent the holidays in Florida, and in some years would go as far as California for a month.

The holidays passed quietly, but as soon as the new year came in George began to keep a chart of apple prices from day to day as they were reported in the Upper Red Hook Herald. Prices had jumped a little at the time of the first killing frost and had risen again before Christmas. In January the price rose nineteen cents within a few days, and toward the end of the month there was another seven-cent rise.

Periodically the brothers had inspected their apples to see how they were keeping. Most of them had been late varieties. It was but a matter of storing them. The apples were in fine condition. By mid-January they noticed an increase in egg production. Jim rushed eggs to the village egg broker on George's advice, since they felt that any day now egg prices would take a tumble as production increased.

Mr Schafer speaks of Astrology

Just about that time George began to delve into "Sepharial's Key to Successful Trading." He had read it through a few times, but most of the statements sounded too queer for him to believe. It contained many explanations of planetary movements and angular distances between the planets. It spoke of conjunctions, trines squares, oppositions, terms which he knew as words which belonged in the field of astronomy. What could these have to do with the markets?

Terms which he knew as words which belonged in the field of astronomy.

If he was to make a trial as to the truth of such statements he would have to produce for himself some ephemerides that showed the positions of the planets throughout the years and do some testing. The book had been published in London. It would take too long to write over to London.

George decided to consult with Mr Schafer, who had returned from his Florida trip as soon as he had a chance. He put the cards on the table, telling him straight out that he had bought a book which claimed that planets are involved in market movements and that he had decided to test these claims. He asked Mr Schafer where he could get ephemerides, tables which show from day to day where the planets are in the heaven at a certain time such as midnight and noon of each day. Schafer scratched his head. "Do you believe in such things? That's astrology, plain and simple.

Some of these fellows are plain goofy, if you want my opinion." George was depressed.

"We read about these fellows even in the Bible," admitted Schafer. "Egyptian pharaohs had astrologers with them. Ancient kings, they say, always had astrologers on hand. I think I read once that King Louis XIV of France insisted on the presence of an astrologer right at the time of delivery of the Dauphin, to make sure he could make note of his first cry. Of course, in those days even kings were more superstitious than the people are nowadays. I myself have never been interested. I don't depend on the stars, but I know where you can get those tables. Captains of boats use them. They are published by the government at Washington. Write to them."

"Thanks a lot," George said. "I'll do that as soon as I get home."

The subject of conversation changed. The trip to Florida was discussed. Mr Schafer described the beauty of that state so well that George warmed up to go there even tomorrow if he had the money. Schafer's description of the Everglades with their myriad strange beaked birds of all sizes that made raucus noises in the leafless trees fascinated George.

Only the fact that it was very late halted the conversation.

The American Ephemeris and Nautical Almanac

Soon George received an answer to his letter telling him that the 1910 edition of the American Ephemeris and Nautical Almanac would be forwarded upon receipt of $2.00. The issue of 1909 could be had for $1.50, and those of previous years for $1.00 a copy. He decided to send a five-dollar bill. That much he would risk on the Sepharial. He ordered four consecutive years, including the one for the year 1910.

The next morning Jim told him while they were going over the apples in the barn again that Grete was with child and that by late September a baby would arrive to increase the family.

"Grete must have eaten too many Lebkuchen on Christmas," George remarked dryly.

"No funny remarks," said Jim. "You know I am married and that Grete and myself want to have kids around us, not just a lot of books, charts, newspapers, and planets."

"Maybe I'll be able to figure out the child's future," smiled George as he left to congratulate Grete.

Grete was busy collecting eggs but had to listen to a sermon from George on how to rear children, what to feed them, how to bathe them, etc.

"Don't confound a mother's instinct," Grete interrupted at last. "We women know better than schools or books about how to bring up kids. You just leave the bathing and the feeding to me. Don't I feed well? Look at your belly. You're getting bigger and fatter every day. You may need an extra bath once in a while. The wash house over there is yours any time, and I shall heat the water without charge."

"Let's go down to the village," called Jim to both when he saw an opportunity to stop kidding. "Let's find out what they pay for apples today."

The Sale of the Stored Apple Crop

They hiked over to the village for the exercise, cold as the day was. The fruit broker informed them that the price for average run was $1.15 a bushel. He offered to come down to the farm to make an inspection and a final offer, since, depending upon quality and size, he might be able to pay more.

The time was approaching when Mr Schafer's rent had to be paid. They had nearly $850 in the bank by now; much of it was derived from the sale of the first lot of apples, as well as from the sale of their eggs. The lumber, straw and chicken feed had all been paid too; besides, there were no debts to worry about. They could have paid the rent without being obliged to sell the apples, but George advised that they should not try to hold off any longer.

Within an hour of their arrival home the broker drove out to the farm. He found the apples packed individually in soft paper, a thing he had not anticipated. Their condition was excellent, and his offer was $1.39 a bushel. Both George and Jim were astonished at such a differential, but G.J. Schaetzel & Co. was known to always offer the farmer a fair price. Schafer had told the boys of that long before.

The deal was made. More than 700 boxes went out before the barn was empty. They received a few dollars less than a thousand. The check went right to the bank for deposit. The president of the bank said that any time Jim wished to buy a farm to see him, since he would be willing to arrange a loan for him. No doubt the banker had inquired about this new account from Mr Schafer. Besides, he saw their balance increasing and learned that they met their bills promptly, things which please any banker.

"That's what bankers are in business for," commented George, "to lend money entrusted to them by their depositors. They seldom look at the clothes a man wears. They look instead at his business ability and acumen."

Grete was all excited when she heard that they had received almost $1000 for the apple crop.

"Forty-two hundred marks in a year, not figuring the eggs and milk. No farmer could do that in Germany," she exclaimed.

"You stop counting in German marks," Jim scolded. "I told you long ago to feel yourself to be a real American and to act as Americans do. We are here to stay. We must think in dollars, just as we must speak English. We'll make our living here and so will the kids."

George went to his chart in the living room where he had installed himself in a corner. From there he could glimpse what was going on in the kitchen, see what was happening at the barn, and view the weather. From there, too, he could see the county road winding toward Upper Red Hook.

The Nautical Almanacs Arrive

The Ephemerides from Washington arrived in good order. George was all excited. What size the books had, he thought. What a precious package for five dollars.

Pulling out one as fast as he could get the wrapping off, he sat over in his corner chair and pored over the pages.

"Let's see," he said aloud. "October, 1909. Well, that's all right. I can take that too. 'Apparent Right Ascension, Diff. for one hour, Apparent Declination, Diff. for one hour; mean Sun,'" he read. Turning to another page he continued, "'Orionis, Groombridge, Leporis, mean Solar Date.'" Turning yet again, he read, "'Satellites of Jupiter, 1909.'"

"I don't think I got the right books," he said to Grete who was busy cleaning the mirror. It's all astronomy, but not the one that shows about conjunctions and squares and such things." His pep was all gone. He was so happy a few minutes ago, but way down in the dumps now. A five spot, spent for nothing. He got a hold of that old Sepharial again, paged through it, began to read for a while; what he read, he couldn't say. He was reading and thinking all at the same time how to get ephemerides that would show trines and oppositions between two planets. "There was a mistake somewhere." He got up, unpacked the rest of the books; the years were there alright, but the contents were for astronomers, but not for astrologers. "Captains may have use for that book. Schafer couldn't know, of course." He had advised him as well as he knew. He was too hasty, he thought, such as he had been at other times too. He remembered the "Auer Dult" at Munich, where several years ago he would buy and buy again books, for which he thought he might have use, but in reality, he had no earthly use, ever. They just filled the room he had with his uncle and aunt. Some good ones came out of the lot, though, books on teaching, another on Sanscrit, which he studied for a while for no reason whatever, but he did. Stamps came to his mind too. Had he not spent a lot of money on foreign postage stamps too? For what? Looking at monkeys from Labuan, at ostriches from New South Wales, at some battle wagons of United States revenue stamps? The time he spent to paste them into the album, the money he spent to find out their value on catalogues and, when, before joining Jim he wanted to sell them to a stamp dealer at Munich, he offered him a few marks. That fellow would say: "You had the fun with it, I have to find others that like to have fun. It would be different if you had rare stamps!" He took them home again and they were still with his uncle. Thoroughly disgusted he was for a while about stamp collecting.

Jim and George Order Baby Chicks

The day was ruined. Into the suitcase with the newspapers went the four books. Out to the yard George went, trying to count the chickens. There was a lot of money walking around, he thought, also baby chicks could soon be had. "We better place an order early; the early bird catches the worm." He called Jim who had begun with his tree pruning job because it was bearably warm that day. "Let's order a flock of chicks now," he said. "We can put them in the apple barn! They are advertising them already for future delivery, as soon as it is warm enough to ship." "OK with me," said Jim. "How many shall we buy? We could build an addition over there for a run, all we do is make a runway fenced in from the barn door alongside the wall into a fenced-in place. Some of our chickens can take over the mothering of the babies." Jim figured out the amount of wire that would be required, together with the wooden posts, and went down to the mill to order wire and posts.

George Makes Charts of Planets' Paths from Ephemeris

The Ephemerides bothered George. In the evening he took them out again, looked them over. On page 299 he found something: Venus, Apparent Right Ascension, Apparent Declination; on page 224 he saw Saturn, Apparent Right Ascension for each day, March to August; the same pages carried also the Apparent Declination. But, here! Page 250 began with Mercury heliocentric Longitude, followed by a table for Venus in heliocentric given for Greenwich mean Noon in degrees, minutes and seconds. "I am coming to something that may be it!" He looked through page after page until he came to "Part II, 'Astronomical ephemerides for the Meridian of Washington.'" "I think," he said to himself, "I am going to plot those heliocentric coordinates of the various planets and see what comes out of them. I will use a different color for each planet." He took a chart sheet and figured out how to get 360° into the space available. He plotted Mercury as first, using the year 1909. The first entry for January 1st was 296°. The minutes and seconds he had to ignore, because he even had difficulty in weighing the 6 degrees of the 296° correctly, since the sheet was rather cramped when 360° had to go on it. He had used one square for each 10° of the chart paper.

Mercury Heliocentric Motion in Longitude

By January 17th the motion of that planet ran off his sheet. Mercury had reached 360°. "Whew! That runs fast!" he thought. "What now? Shall I put another sheet above and continue or shall I begin at the bottom again?" He started January 17th with 0° at the bottom and in this fashion he plotted Mercury through the whole year to its last day.

Mercury was plotted in black. Venus he plotted next in green. That planet did not run so fast. The subsequent were still less in their speed. It was way after midnight when he had the first chart, the one for 1909, completed. "Six hours' work, an hour per planet," he said. He tried to plot the Moon, but he could not find any heliocentric position for it, so he passed her up. But he plotted the Sun. He could hardly see the figures any more, which made him finally stop till the next day.

During the next few days Jim had to work alone. The fence could not be erected anyhow, since the ground was frozen deep. Jim kept on pruning his trees. It was a rather tiring job and took time and judgment. But experience is the best teacher. After a dozen of them were pruned, the work went considerably faster. Without straining himself unduly, he finished the job by the end of February. Fertilizer had been spread around already in December before the snow came.

George Makes Deductions After Plotting Planets' Paths

George kept up his regular run of charts diligently for stocks, for grains, for poultry and eggs, as well as for apples, even though they had been sold. The newly plotted planets' chart was now scrutinized. He saw quickly that when the planets crossed each other, that must be a conjunction. But, how could he see when they were forming squares, trines or oppositions? A new depression set in upon him. "It's wrong, it's dead wrong, all that stuff is no good!" he'd say to himself. "There are other books, I am sure, only I will have to go down to New York and find out about it. No other way, unless I go there! I'll see a broker at the same time. Maybe I can get some more books down there, too!" But he had not even checked the conjunctions to see whether or not they had any effect upon markets! "Yes, I've got to do that and do it now!" He spread his Dow Jones average chart before him, the wheat and rye charts, to check their tops and bottoms for the year 1909 and began.

He spread his Dow Jones average charts, to check their tops and bottoms.

A Major Discovery – the Crossing of Saturn and Jupiter by Mercury

In the book is given the wheat chart of 1909 as well as the planets' graph as George had produced it out of the Ephemerides (see Appendix). A few minutes later we hear him holler blue murder: "Jim, come in, Grete look! I got it!" "Don't get so unnecessarily excited," Grete answered, approaching with a laugh towards the table. "What have you found now? What?" "What makes the grains go up and down! That's what I've found," George answered, a little piqued. Jim thought something was amiss. He rushed off his pruning job, limping a little on one leg from standing lopsided on the ladder the last ten minutes, which made his one foot sort of fall asleep on him. Jim had not run that fast around the corner for a long time. Peter, the cat, was nearly knocked over as it sat in the door stoop, thinking about a chance to catch a mouse somewhere. "What happened?" he shot forth. "Just look, just look, here is the thing I have been looking for!" "All I can see is a lot of lines," said Jim, while Grete added, "I can't see any more either." But in order to gratify George they sat on the couch, looked and listened. George quickly let loose an oratory about the wheat chart of 1909, about the planets he had plotted for that year out of the book that came the day before, at whose plotting he pointed. "Now, here is the planet Mercury which runs off the sheet once in a while," he continued. "It does so each time whenever it reaches 360°, you know."

They knew nothing, in truth. They just looked and said "Aha." "Then here is Saturn, there is Jupiter and the others. Now watch!" he said, "watch close! Whenever that Mercury crosses this Saturn line there is a top! and we go down thereafter for a week or even two or three weeks. At least wheat makes a top. That's something worth knowing. Now look at Jupiter! Whenever Mercury crosses its line, we go up. It makes no difference to me whether the movement has started before they meet, as long as I know wheat goes up higher. I'll find out yet why they sometimes start before that time. I can't find out everything in one minute."

Whenever that Mercury crosses this Saturn line there is a top!

"That's good," said Jim, a little peeved to be called from his pruning job. "You know, George," he said, "with these lines I can't prune our apple trees! It takes elbow grease. You just keep on and when you have another one just like that," he added, "you can call me again."

So saying, Jim went back to the job; also Grete resumed her

work. It was time for her to set up dinner, to cook a few pots of potatoes for the chickens. Work never came to an end for her. She liked it, was happy at it. It was her life.

George didn't even half hear the sarcastic words of Jim; he was already figuring how to go on to find other points by means of these planets. "Where was I all these years?" he said a few times. To those professors of economics he could now tell something better than what they tried to preach and teach him about economic movements of commodity prices. This thing will work with stocks too, no doubt, he said. They never will believe it! They'd be out of a job, teaching, because it is so easy. Suddenly, some thought shot through his head. He went out to Jim. George found him in a tree, and called up to him: "Before we have dinner, I will tell you when we'll get our chicks!" "I thought we had decided about the chicks a week ago, that's why I went down to order the wire and posts," Jim called down from his tree, but kept on pruning. "There is some little change about that, since I found out how the planets run," said George. "We must follow them; otherwise we do just nicely the right things at the wrong time. We have to buy those chicks just before Jupiter is passed by Mercury so that they can go up like grain does whenever Jupiter is passed by Mercury. I showed it to you a little while ago. Supposing we got them when Mercury is crossed; they are all apt to die on us, or some disease may overtake them. You know," he said, "they always picture Saturn with a big scythe!" "Well," said Jim, "you keep on looking at your stars! I got to finish this tree before we eat, and it is getting late. It looks like snow, too, which may stop my work for a while. Tell Grete to bring me some coffee, I am thirsty." George returned to his important work. His thoughts were so taken up with the discovery that he forgot all about telling Grete of Jim and his thirst. He began to plot planets for the current year to see when he would himself go over to the hatcheries to pick up the chicks at the right time. All he needed for the time being was the day when Mercury would run over Jupiter. He would use that special day, rain or shine. "But," he said: "Wait a minute, I better let them be born on that day! . . . because," he continued, "if we take chicks that have been born while the trend was still down, we may have dead chicks when they come here." He looked at the wheat chart of August 12th 1909, the day Mercury crossed Jupiter. The market had declined in wheat just to this day and then turned around. Only from that day on it started an upmove.

Jim Pays His Rent to Mr Schafer

Suddenly he remembered that they had decided to go over to Mr Schafer in the evening to pay the balance for the rent. It was not due yet, but "just as well get rid of that debt," he thought. Yes, we can be back in an hour or so. I can tell Mr Schafer at the same time of the great find. It was January 31st 1910. He immediately prepared a check for the amount, so that Jim only had to sign it, when he came in.

Part of the planets for 1910 had been plotted. He looked for the next crossing of Jupiter. It was due on February 8th, in a little more than a week, tomorrow, Tuesday in a week. That was rather early for chicks. They might not even be ready . . . For a while he quietly looked at how the wheat picture had developed since the beginning of the year. Grains had been sagging since New Year with a small come-back that started on the nineteenth. Last Saturday the market had again begun to sag slightly. That was the day the last box of apples was moved out of the barn. Thus, he figured, prices could react until this eighth Tuesday a week and get going up again for a while. "But," he added, "that caterpillar has been winding itself upwards for a heck of a long time, for more than a year already!" That has to come to an end.

The next Saturn crossing was due to come only by April 5th or 6th. George figured that probably nothing serious in the way of a decline would arrive before that time, anyhow. He then wrote a letter to the hatchery immediately to find out when they could buy the first chicks, even were it in small lots of a few hundred at a time. The barn would simply have to have several windows in a hurry so that some light would penetrate; these windows would have to be made in a way that enabled them to shut tightly during the winter in order to store the next apple crop. The best way, he thought, would be to get a carpenter to do the job. The mill had several carpenters working, so he decided to hire one or two first thing next morning.

Dinner was ready. The last chicken killed by the weasel was served. The steam of the potatoes in their jackets cast irregular clouds over it. Kale, covered with a white sauce, was near Grete's place. Big slices of bread were seen next to each plate. An old-fashioned pudding boiled to a finish in a tin container, which again sat on the stove in a pan filled with boiling water. They had a plain but healthy meal. Neither Jim nor Grete lacked an appetite, and even George could dig in heartily. Grete began to hint about a trip to the village to buy material for baby's clothes because, she said, "I need a lot of time to make them, and I had better be prepared early."

George is Supposed to Move to the Barn

"We'll have to see a doctor too," said Jim, "who can tell us when to expect it." "You'll buy a muzzle too, while you are at it," cut in George, "so that when I work I can't hear any crying until I am into the work, and then you may take it off." "All you will have to do is move into the barn if he annoys you," Grete retorted laughingly. She had said "he" without thinking, but underneath her mind spoke the truth. She wished to have a boy, at least to make a start. George, trying to smooth out matters again, said he would take her to town tomorrow. "I am going to hire carpenters to put windows in the barn," he said, "and while I go to the mill, you can do some shopping. Just point to the things, stretch your arms this far or that far to show the sales girl how long a piece you want to have." "Leave that to me," said Grete, "I know how to get things now. I practised all afternoon, while I cleaned and cooked, what I will say. There are ladies at the store who will understand me." George explained to Jim about the windows, as well as about the letter that would go off tomorrow to the hatchery. He also told him about that important eighth of February, on which day things ought to pop up. "When we go over to Mr Schafer's in a little while, I shall take my grain chart along and show him some things that he does not know."

Another Meeting at Schafer's

Schafer welcomed the boys as usual. He inquired of the price which they had received for their apples and was much surprised when he heard that Schaetzel & Company paid a dollar and thirty-nine cents a bushel for the apples. "I received eighty-four cents for mine," he said. "You are doing much better than an old timer," he added. "I'll have to learn a few things from you, I can see that." "Oh," interrupted George, "that apple deal which brought us 40% more than yours is nothing compared to what I have found!

I can tell when wheat has to move up and when it has to come down.

I can tell you now when wheat has to move up and when it has to come down, rain or no rain, frost or no frost in Nebraska, out west. Mr Schafer was sort of already geared to be fed with surprises by the, young men. Some of their ideas he had already incorporated into his own methods of handling the farms, and others were in a fair way to be tested this year. George talked about the Ephemerides he had told him to get from Washington, then showed him the sheet where the grain movements for 1909 had been plotted. Above it was the pattern of the planets' motions taken out of that Nautical Almanac. "I just can't understand," he said, "what people have so much against astrology, when you hear them talk about it. Newspapers, too, poke fun at it. If they only knew how I laugh at their comments about what they think grains will do. Each time they think wheat goes down, you can very near make a bet that it runs up fast and yet they think they can judge about astrology, of which they know as little as, well – let them sing. Mr Schafer, you'll have to sing with us, because I'll show you." After all this introductory speech, he spread the chart, pointed to the crossings of Saturn and Jupiter over Mercury during the year 1909, and during the first part of 1910. "See here," he said, "on the eighth, Tuesday in a week we will have a low just because Jupiter is passed by Mercury. On the fifth of January last, we had a high just because Mr Saturn, the scytheman, said hello to Mercury. There it is and I dare you to say no." He went carefully over the entire year of 1909 to verify his statements. "Of course, I shall make charts now for the two other years. I have the books for them and then I will be doubly sure. However, if eight times in succession something works, I don't believe it will stop doing so. And should it miss once in a while, then something still more important than those two big planets, is there. The whole world knows Jupiter and Saturn are good luck and bad luck. Only they do not know the combination of their ways of operation. They do not know it is Mercury, in combination with them, that makes them click. They do not operate in geocentric motions, the motions which astrologers use exclusively, but they operate in, let us call it 'celestial motion' i.e. in the heliocentric way. I am certain a lot of people have tried the Sun, but, as I can show you, it's a dud, if one uses the Sun." He showed him by examples that it was so.

Schafer took it all in. He had never paid any attention to stars. The suggestion to get those books from Washington was a mere guess. He had figured that since Agricultural Year Books were produced each year as well as Commercial Year Books, Year Books on Mining, etc., they would also produce Star Year Books. Because he remembered that ships are run by the star positions to find ports, he added "ships' captains" to his words.

"Of course," Schafer said, "we grow apples and not wheat. We ourselves do not care to know when wheat prices go up and down." "What do you mean?" said George. "Don't you think we can make money with such knowledge even though we grow apples? Can't we trade wheat in Chicago and yet attend to our own crops? You have explained about those things yourself a few months ago about the technical parts, I mean about the mechanics of trading grain futures. In a couple of months I will have checked many more years whether or not this Saturn and this Jupiter ever change their minds and the next thing I will do is to order twenty more years of those Ephemerides from Washington as soon as I get home now." Schafer made no further answer, except to add, "It looks as if you have something there alright."

From the way the boys had been acting he could readily see that foreign blood was well worth introduction. It brings ideas to say the least. Those people bring courage, they are enterprising; some chaff comes along with the good grain, which is unavoidable. There is occasionally a wormy apple among the good ones.

More Back Years of Nautical Almanacs Ordered by George

Two letters went off the next morning from the Upper Red Hook Post Office, one to Pine Plains, where a large hatchery had supplied for Jim the baby chicks last Spring, another to Washington for twenty additional volumes of Nautical Almanacs of past years. George never was stingy when it came to buying books. "The further back I can test Jupiter, the better I can see what he does," he thought. "And Saturn, that devil, will show his face too, as well as Mercury. Business, the double crosser, should indicate the changes," he concluded. Grete had come along with him to buy some materials. George walked over to the mill to get carpenters' items. There was little building at this time of the year. Men and material could be had immediately. The mill also supplied the necessary glass for the windows. The job cost them about eighty dollars. After he had made them a small pencil drawing to show the number of windows, their size and place, the foreman told them that two men would be there on the job by seven next morning.

Grete and George Buy at Dingle's

George had retraced his way to the village, met Grete at Dingle's busy buying little socks, a cap, a woolen blanket with blue borders – in fact, everything she bought was in blue. It was to be a boy, and if – well – that's out. "Got a muzzle?" George asked with a smile. "You just keep quiet and don't you bother me. I am busy now," said Grete. "You can look at those books over there until I call you," she added, pointing towards the book department in the far corner where farmers' calendars and almanacs were on display, aside of books on agriculture and poultry raising, together with an assortment of fiction. He paged through one of those poultry books trying to find out when chicks are hatched the earliest but could find nothing on the specific subject. Then he took hold of one of the almanacs. "Let's see," he said. "February. Moon in Scorpio on the first, in Sagittarius on the fourth, in Capricorn on the sixth. Sun in Aquarius. Sun conjunct Moon on the ninth. Sunrise February first at 7:01; Sun set at 5:15," he read.

"That is not for grains, but for farmers to know when to get up and when to stop work. What they are to use the Moon for, don't know, but it is printed. It may be for those who once in a while get 'Moon struck' to know when they are due to walk around so that they can clear their bedroom of unnecessary things."

Grete had come to him by now, handed him a large package and said, "Get thee going towards home, George." From reading the Bible in English of late she had learned that the German personal pronoun "du—you, familiar" is rendered in English as "thee." Grete had found that funny and began to use it once in a while with George, especially when she wanted to incorporate in the meaning the idea of "George, your Grace, please . . ." His lips contracted on hearing it, his eyes seemed to take on a different color and expression, as if he wanted to say, "You little rascal, don't try to make a handy-man out of me."

Jim Gets Fooled With a Bag of Cement

A short while afterwards we see both treading down the road towards home. George carried the package on his shoulder, one finger had turned whitish yellow from holding on to the string while Grete began counting telephone poles and street trees at the same time in their own sequences. George started to count his steps aloud to confuse her and succeeded marvelously. By that time they had reached close to home and their thoughts began to turn quickly towards tasks that awaited them there.

Jim saw them coming down the road from his perch in one of the fruit trees. It had appeared to him as if George carried a bag of cement on his shoulders. He made his guess about its possible use. "What's got into him now?" he mused. "That brother of mine has a new idea every hour. This one must have grown on his way to town." He saw him shift the bag of cement over to the other shoulder with comparative ease, which told him he was wrong this time to accuse his brother. He was equally certain that the package could not contain material for the baby, since a small baby would not require material in such quantities. His baby was to start like all the others as a tiny tot of about eight pounds, while the package must weigh some twenty-five or thirty pounds. He judged its weight from the manner George had shifted it. He had given Grete a blank check with his signature so that she could buy the necessary things. She could not have bought the whole baby department at Dingle's, that was out of the question. Curiosity and the idea that she might really have bought enough goods to see junior through high school made him come down the ladder. Carefully approaching the subject as to the contents of the package, he said, "All fixed up with the carpenters for the windows, George? Hallo Grete! Did you get what you wanted?" "Oh, Jim," said Grete, "George just would not let me count either telephone posts or the street trees; he always butted in. George was reading up on the calendars at the store while I bought a nice warm blanket for baby, little shoes, a bassinet, cute, you'll see, and some socks and material to make clothes." So saying, they reached the living room. Jim felt relieved when he considered that the bulk of the package was caused by the bassinet. "I thought you had bought out Dingle's," he said. He just could not keep back his thoughts, that had proved wrong. Every piece was looked over, judged and appraised as to its usefulness. Even George could see that Grete had good taste. Blue was the color, anyhow, which he liked.

The unexpected find of the special planets' action made George delay his intended trip to New York to look for other kinds of ephemerides. However, the time between now and the arrival of the new books was used to plot the planets' paths in heliocentric longitude for the years 1907 and 1908 so that he could verify the effects of all the conjunctions. He had not touched any of the angles as yet such as the squares, trines, oppositions, which Sepharial's book had spoken so much about. This he intended to do later on.

On Geocentric Positions of Planets

Incidently, it must be stated that in Sepharial's book nothing whatever was mentioned about heliocentric places or positions of the planets. Everything treated was intended for geocentric positions. There are special small books published in London that contain the places of planets geocentrically which are used by astrologers to make horoscopes. Had George possessed one of those it would have been easy for him to see when the planets come to a conjunction, to a square or trine or to an opposition, which they call "aspects," since these booklets contain a special column for them. Those aspects mean absolutely nothing for trading grains, nor for anything else and are merely illusions. True, they hit once in a while a top or a bottom, but he who puts any reliance in them will soon find himself in hot water. Besides, their arrival is so frequent that every day or two one such aspect might be due. The direction of the movement cannot be judged either, since a square may bring an upmove or a downmove and so with all the rest of the aspects. One's own personal judgment as to the possible direction of a move when those aspects show a turn is usually just contrary to what actually happens. Therefore they should be shunned. George, by luck, worked according to the instruction of the Sepharial book, but used something else, the heliocentric positions, without being conscious of the difference. He had hit on the right way, whereas others chew up something that could be stretched like a rubber band. One always finds excuses as well as angles to meet the situation after things have happened. He who starts the way astrological books teach will find himself quickly in a forest, like Little Red Riding Hood, from which there is no safe return. Grimm's as well as Andersen's Fairy Tales are merely books that attempt to teach the right ways, but those are considered as children's books, unworthy for a grown-up who "knows it all" to delve into. At any rate, the average astrologer or he who tries to use astrology as a means to discover movements in markets, be they of grains, of cotton or of stocks, wades through angles and aspects for years. After about eight or ten years he will have all the experience to measure angles and aspects in a hurry but all that is useless to find tops or bottoms. Whatever he tries to forecast with their aid will fly around like a feather in the wind; it may fly a mile, but a rain drop may down it in one minute.

Was it intuition or just merely dumb luck that made George unconsciously commit the apparent big error of using heliocentric positions of planets and not the geocentric ones as taught in astrology books?

After plotting the heliocentric positions of the planets Jupiter, Saturn and Mercury for the years 1907 and 1908, he proceeded to compare the ups and downs in wheat with the crossings. The results turned out somewhat different than he had expected with his enthusiasm that knew no end. It proved to him that Jupiter was not at all times favorable inclined. Jupiter did shine on May 23, 1908 for three days to the tune of a four cents advance. However, then it faltered, losing the four cents advance and an additional three cents besides. On the other hand, Saturn turned out to be at times favorably inclined and not always a mere scytheman. Saturn was crossed on April 29th by Mercury which was the beginning of an advance as far as to the place when Jupiter was crossed by Mercury towards the end, and so it happened at other places.

"I will have to see what the other years show," he said, "then I will have to find out how to locate the unregistered tops and bottoms (those that are not shown by the crossings of Saturn or of Jupiter), as well as the reason why they change their minds once in a while." His personal trend had apparently begun to turn down. He was rather quiet and spiritless that evening, because "after every action must follow a reaction."

From Plutarch's Lives

Plutarch said, "Greedily let us never gain, lest vengeance follow in their train." We do not want to say that George was a greedy sort of man because that word applies to material accumulations more than to study and learning. However, we may use this idea in connection with all things where an extreme attempt is made to gain a certain end fast, faster and fastest. By beginning something fast we are already moving in the higher brackets. But when we compare the natural formation of the stalagmites and stalactites such as can be seen in caves which were built by drops of water leaving their mineral contents as deposits to form them, we have Nature as the patient mother who had already worked a few million years to produce them. Of course, our lives do not run in such cycles. Ours are rather short and yet, out of little acorns big oaks grow. Anything that starts with a bang such as a four platform circus performance, such a one moves to another place over night. Neither Jim nor George has become rich since their arrival in the New World but so far as we can see each one has laid a solid foundation of a kind that is peculiar to each one's personal endeavor and aspiration. After a year and a half Jim had Grete come to be married. He had rented the farm after he had worked for Mr Schafer for a whole year. Then he took an option to buy the rented farm. Most likely there won't be quintuplets in the family to make a good start. Grete is satisfied to begin with one, even though she is a little picky, wanting a boy instead of what the Lord will provide. On the other hand, George seems to be progressing on quite different paths, slow but sure in an attempt to solve certain puzzles of Nature, on a path that is trodden by few men. Why so few people get on this path is due primarily to the education, both at home and in schools, due to beliefs and superstitions disseminated by certain elements that have one believe rather than know. In due time we shall see that he pulls out all the weeds that grow in the field called "Grain Market."

Some may object, saying, "That loafer isn't making any money by just playing around the way he does." He is not exactly a charitable case in the home of Grete and Jim, but he is not very far away from being such. However, we can see that certain ideas of his had been used to advantage by Jim which never would have grown in his own head. We remember he had brought a little money of his own along from Europe but turned it right over to Jim to help along. He had no receipt; he had no bank account. What's the idea? Does he intend to keep on living off the air surrounding Upper Red Hook? All we can see is that he feels fine, even though temporarily on a down grade because matters do not develop just at this moment the way he had them figured out. In short, he manages to keep alive on the surface; inside, however, he is very much alive as to things to come.

The Barn is Changed to Accommodate the Baby Chicks

The carpenters were on time the next morning. Jim was up as usual; even George was out early. He directed the work, marked the places where the windows had to be placed. It took some time to make the openings. The lumber wagon brought complete frames of the given size and description. George, in his simplicity, had thought they would make them there. It took the two men just a day and a half to finish the job. The glazier took another day to insert the glass. By that time an answer had come back from the hatchery stating that two hundred and fifty chicks would be ready for delivery on the tenth of the month. "That's fine," said George after reading the letter. "Jim, you and Grete can drive over while I shall tend to the place. Grete has never been over to Pine Plains yet anyhow. It'll do her good."

February can be very cold in that part of the county and plenty of snow may be expected in some years. Other years there are when the weather is more reasonable. Then temperatures may linger around freezing, especially after a week or ten days of the month have passed. This happened also in the year 1910. There had been plenty of snow but the roads had been cleared with an old-fashioned triangular wooden plough. It was a pleasure to take a trip to Pine Plains. Finely ground grits had been ordered. Both had worked hard to prepare feeding troughs, to repair the ones of last year. They had made several attempts to get the barn dry with small fires and succeeded in raising the temperature several degrees above freezing, and Jim considered it warm enough for the chicks.

Jim and Grete Drive to Pine Plains

The old mare was glad to have something to do outside for a change. She took great strides forward at the slightest movement of the reins. Grete and Jim were tucked under warm blankets. A ten-mile drive by buggy was quite a ride. They passed through rolling country, the orchards gradually disappeared the further they moved from the village. Pastures with batches of cedars were passed, everything was well fenced but a thin snow blanket still covered the landscape. Cattle could only roam there during the summer months. A few crows could be heard here and there. Most of the fences were of field stone, some three feet high gathered years ago out of the fields so as to make the land clear. Some of these stones were real boulders, weighing easily four to five hundred pounds. Leafless poison ivy cluttered the stone fences all over.

Grete admired the scenery. Gradually the conversation went over to discussing their future. Certain matters they did not want to discuss right in front of the brother who, like a pest, was constantly around. They discussed seeing the doctor real soon so that they would do the right things for the welfare of the child. They spoke of George and his queer ideas which were quite foreign to both, who knew farming and the three R's. They needed not much more. George began to get on their nerves. He himself had noticed it and yet, he was not quite ready to leave them. They talked of the old country, and the time went so fast that while Pine Plains seemed to them to be still quite a way off, a church steeple told them otherwise. At the hatchery of Clark Edson & Sons they found everything quiet and calm so as to give the hens a chance to attend to their work of breeding. They were told that within an hour their baby chicks would be ready packed to withstand the cold. Jim had taken tarpaulins along to protect the brood on their journey. In the meantime they had a bite to eat in the village. When they returned they found the chicks all loaded and wrapped, chattering with each other contendedly. Six hundred they could get. By four o'clock in the afternoon they arrived back home and before night had arrived, the little flock was installed in the barn to grow up and become chickens.

George Decides to Go to New York

The next morning George told Jim and Grete that he was going to New York, that he wanted Jim to give him a check for two hundred and fifty dollars, representing the funds he had brought along from Europe. "I am going to New York; you don't need the money for the farm right now, but I can use it to try to trade some wheat down there, as soon as I arrive," he told him. "Listen," said Jim,

"I will give you seven hundred and fifty dollars to lose. George," he continued, "you are going to walk on ice down there. I spoke to Mr Schafer myself the other day while you were over at the mill and he told me 'Watch George, it won't be long. He will soon go to New York to lose the little money he has on the 'Change. I tried it years ago and know what can happen. Of course, I never approached the market the way he does. He may have luck, but in Wall Street, it's always the unexpected that happens there. It's a hard game, nerve-racking, it brings sleepless nights and it takes cold blooded people who have plenty of funds besides.' He was right. Now you are ready to leave. I hope Mr Schafer's statements do not turn into truth. However, in case things go sour on you, you know we are here; even though you don't mind me saying that you are a nuisance, once in a while, with your books and your ideas," he added jokingly.

In Wall Street, it's always the unexpected that happens there.

"I told you I wanted to get only two hundred and fifty dollars and not more, but since you have the feeling you can spare an extra five hundred and pull through the summer until the apple crop is ready again, I will take it. With careful trading and just a little luck I believe I can make it with that what I have learned, irrespective of the experience of our good neighbor. Keep the books that come from Washington for me until I ask for them or until I shall be back again."

George packed his belongings. Jim made out the check and handed him an extra twenty to get him to New York without having to cash it. Grete said she just knew that something would happen while he was away. It gave George a chance to size up the situation and condition to make a solid and fast decision.

"Now, Grete, don't cry," he said. "I will be back for visits once in a while, but I have to use an entirely different road than Jim to make a living. I have tried my best to show Jim that I also know a little about farming, even though I have never before worked at it. I will keep Jim posted when to buy and sell his products."

So saying, he took up his suitcase, gave a big kiss to Grete, and a solid handshake to Jim and went off. On the way to the station he dropped in to Mr Schafer, told him briefly of his intentions and after a few minutes talk he left, bound for New York.

CHAPTER VI

GEORGE WOLLSTEN GOES TO NEW YORK TO TRADE STOCKS AND GRAINS

It was the day before Lincoln's birthday, 1910 when George Wollsten came into New York from Upper Red Hook. At four o'clock in the afternoon we see him sitting in the cafeteria of the Grand Central Station, at the same table where they had been four months ago when Grete became married to Jim.

Sepp Muller

New York had much more snow than Upper Red Hook, piled in big heaps even though the streets generally had been cleared for traffic. He was reading the "Telegram" to look for a suitable room to live. There did not seem to be a shortage of rooms. The prices ranged from $1.50 to $5.00 per week. He had been in New York only twice, the day he had landed and the day Jim and Grete had been married, the famous 5th of October last year, when they had walked from the book store as far as Columbus Circle. This drift of thoughts brought him to the idea to take quarters with Mr Holten's place instead of hunting around for a room. Pretty soon we find George sitting in an easy chair of the lobby of the YMCA, where Mr Holten had secured for him a nice room at a reasonable rate. His specific worry had been to obtain a large-size table on which he could spread his charts of wheat, as well as a bookcase to store his special books. Both had been promised to him by the clerk. Holten and George were just now discussing Jim and Grete, farm life, chickens and eggs, apples, but Holten showed himself such a novice on these subjects that George was forced to change the subject. He even welcomed the weakness of Mr Holten, who knew a chicken only in a roasted condition and the egg only when fried or boiled. "City fellow," he thought. He shifted the conversation over to stock and grain trading on the Exchange. "That's another thing," said Holten, "with which I have never bothered. But a friend of mine knows all about it. He got what they call down there such 'a trimming' that his hairs fall out ever since. He is well-nigh bald now. He told me that he had some mighty fine stocks on what they call 'margin,' but that thing gave out; he supplied more of it for a while, but the 'Change ate that one up too. The more he put up, the faster the stocks dropped, until he was as flat as that carpet here. He had in mind to see his folks in Europe with the profits that he intended to make. At first his stocks went up, in fact, he could have gone five times across the big pond with his 'paper profits,' but then, he wanted some extra money for gifts (and in German this same word means poison) to take along with an extra hundred he wanted to see Paris. He had it all figured out down to the cent. But some fellows down in Wall Street must have been aware of his plans and they somehow stopped the advance in stocks. So he is still here. We will go to see him some day over in Yorkville." "Where is Yorkville?" asked George, imagining that it would be somewhere in the country outside of New York. "That's on the East side of New York City, around 86th Street," said Holten. "He has a hardware store. His name is Sepp Muller. Let's see, he may still be at the store. I will call him up. Tomorrow is Lincoln's Day, so he will be closed. I will ask him to come over and explain to you all about stocks. He knows more about them than I do." Holten went to the phone near the desk. After a while he came back all smiles, saying that some Club had an outing with dance and dinner over at the Hofbrau in Long Island City, just across the Bridge, and they had agreed to take him tomorrow. Sepp Muller would come here by three in the afternoon.

On holidays Ellis Island was a rather deserted place. Only a skeleton crew was maintained to watch the "left-overs" of ships that came in the day before which for some reason or other had been kept there. Holten's duty was to assist immigrants to get located. It was charitable work, supported by a philanthropic fund over which the YMCA had supervision. Several men speaking all kinds of languages were associated with Holten in the work. He had absolutely nothing to do with the hotel part, but being a bachelor, he spent much of his free time around the place, especially when he was able to find a few immigrants who needed his help. Holten had told him about several unusual cases that came to his attention, when the clock of the lobby struck eight. George had to pick up his luggage from the depot; besides, he had become hungry. In order to satisfy this want he had to tell Holten about it, which cut short the conversation, else they might have been sitting there until midnight. It was agreed that George was to meet him the next day by three o'clock.

By ten o'clock that evening we find George unpacking his belongings in his new room. A big table had been moved in, also a small table with a suitable bookcase he had found. "I will have to enter my charts now," he said, pulling out of his coat the "Telegram" of the afternoon. "I hope they have the prices," he added. Due to his concentration on getting located he forgot all about the market, such a one-track mind he seemed to have developed. "Gee," he said, "this is Friday, then a holiday and a Sunday. This gives me a good chance to get ready for Monday to make a good start. Ah! they all went up, while I came down," he said, looking at the grain quotations. The Dow Jones averages had closed at 89.07, up 1.22. The volume of transactions was much less than during the previous day, when a lot of traders and investors must have sold out their holdings because ever since the New Year started, the industrials had declined from 98.34 to 85.03 by February 8th. This was a 13 points drop. Investors can only stand that much in the way of a decline before they decide to get out to allow stocks to decline without the investors. "Let others have the fun now," they probably think.

Over a million shares had been dumped on Wednesday, February 9th. They must have all thought the market would go lower now; why would they otherwise have sold all their stocks? "But, here," said George, "prices have come up four dollars already. Wheat also had run up one cent and a half on Friday, four cents since Tuesday's low." He made the entries in his chart, looked over the pattern, looked at his planets that were plotted on the sheet above by pasting two sheets together. He had noticed a registry number on the margin of the paper – No. 358-143L, Keuffel & Esser, Fulton Street, NYC. "When I need some more I shall just ask for the number," he said to himself.

"That Jupiter surely exerts some pull, a sort of a suction, since Mercury has crossed over it. I will buy some wheat on Monday first thing. It is bound to go higher for a week or ten days anyhow; that is what has happened before, whenever Jupiter did some pushing. This man Muller must tell me where I can find a good broker; no use asking Mr Holten about it." He perused the odd sequences of the ups and downs on the grain pattern of the chart. At times prices would move up for a week, at other times it took weeks of slow upmove before a reaction would set in. Sometimes the reaction would be four or five cents, at other times they might amount to ten and twelve cents and more. "How can I get an idea to know ahead of time when it is a nickel or when it is a dime?" he asked himself. "What is it that I am plotting here anyhow?" pointing to the planets' lines. "These lines represent the path of the heliocentric coordinates of Jupiter, Saturn and of Mercury. This is what it says in the Nautical Almanac. Helios means in Greek 'light' and centric is something that moves around a centre. It is the path of a planet as made around the Sun, whereas the geocentric path would be the path as described around Geo – the earth."

Pretty soon we find George engulfed in the study of the "Use of Tables" found in the back of the Nautical Almanacs for 1909 on pages 561–591. It was three in the morning when he turned out the light.

He felt as if he knew just as much now as he did before he ever began to read these explanations. "It takes time to learn about those things, I can see that now. In fact, I know very, very little in spite of all my years of study. I wonder how those grain and stock traders acquire their wisdom to trade. Are they born with a silver spoon in their mouth or do they try to work with some laws and rules that are easier than the way I try to approach the subject?"

Mr Sepp Muller arrived a few minutes before three. Holten and George had been talking in the lobby for a while about the weather, about President Lincoln – that he came from a small place in the Middle West, that he freed the slaves. A colored porter sweeping the lobby evidently gave the impetus. George had watched the boy very closely, analyzed his features, his curly hair. He was a tall, slender and snappily dressed boy, wearing a nifty brown sweater which made his appearance still darker, even though the high white collar and the snow-white shirt formed a pleasant contrast. "That's the first black man I ever saw close by," he said in German to Holten so that the man could not understand him. "But," continuing in English he added, "how can they be distinguished from one another? I will never be able to do so, unless it be by height or waist line." "You will learn of that after you have talked to a few and looked at them closely. They are a happy, contented tribe; they do good work and are usually willing. After you get used to seeing them, you don't even think of their black color."

George was introduced to Mr Muller as "my friend from upstate," to which Mr Holten added that "this gentleman intends to take over where you had left off in Wall Street." "I hope," said Mr Muller, as if he had been an old acquaintance, "that you will make enough profit down there to take a trip to Europe just for once. I tried it, but I am still here and those fellows got my money. It was a good thing that I stopped before I lost my business and my head." George came right back at him to show his interest in the ways and methods he had used and asked him which broker he had done business with and added, "I came down from up-state to trade grains and stocks as a business and not just merely to make enough profits to take a trip to Europe." "Trade grains," said Muller, as soon as he had the chance to talk. "Do you want to get burst in a week?" Mr Holten cut short the conversation to get them on the way to Long Island. They boarded a trolley at Columbus Circle which brought them to the bridge. In less than half an hour they had reached their destination. While crossing the East River, George admired the size of the bridge, the traffic that went over it, as well as the navigation that went on below on the water. Everything that could float was there: tug boats, barges, steamers, pleasure craft. The panorama of Brooklyn and lower New York came to view, as did large advertising signs, big factories and piers. Since the two companions had lived for many years in New York such a view was natural to them. Neither of them had been more than 30 miles beyond the city limits. In spite of that they could talk about other cities and towns as if they had been there quite frequently.

The food was excellent, even though the atmosphere had not been quite to his liking. Discussions ranged on subjects in which he had not the slightest interest. He tried to be as sociable as possible. He tried soon to wean Holten and Muller away from the party as softly as circumstances would allow so that he could have the chance to discuss markets with a man that had gone through the mill. By about seven o'clock they were finally convinced to leave.

It was pretty late that night when Mr Muller left George's room, after having given away practically all that he thought worth telling to that newcomer in Wall Street, George Wollsten. George had used an old rule: listen and say nothing until the other side has talked itself dry. Muller began by explaining how in early January of 1916 a bull movement in stocks had inveigled him to go every day to the stock market, leaving his wife to attend to the business in the store. To begin trading he first bought a few odd lots of 50 shares of various stocks. The market went down a little which suited him well because it gave him the opportunity to buy some more stocks a little cheaper so that when the market really began to rise again, he would have a lower average price. Markets did rise once more, so he said, around mid-July just when he had made new purchases at the suggestion of the customer's man. He had accumulated nice profits by October, when the Dow Jones averages had reached above 96, in that his stocks had been well selected. However, he did not want to go to Europe in the winter and decided to postpone the trip for the following June. This gave him a chance to hold his positions and that way make a real haul out of Wall Street. He had seen other men trade back and forth. Some made nice profits in one transaction, but lost them again on others. He himself liked to stay with stocks for big swings. This he made his main rule. However, when Spring came he found many of his chickens missing that he had counted in the previous October. In fact, he had big losses by that time. The Averages had dropped to 76 or thereabouts. They had even called him for margin, which he supplied, because they just could not do that to him . . . prices would not decline to nothing when business and general conditions were just wonderful. Prices did rise again – he knew it all the time – they came nearly back to the levels where he had acquired the second lot of stocks and his stocks had been performing even better than the Averages. He could have sold with very small losses, had he wanted to.

The trip to Europe was not going to be passed up. He had his heart set on it. He carried a time table in his pocket that contained all the sailing dates of steamers. His passport for Europe had long been ordered from Washington, since someone had mentioned he might need it. By Decoration Day of 1907 he definitely postponed his trip for that year, since prices had declined again and had declined to a still more dangerous place, very nearly to the level where they had been the previous March. He was not a man who would give up the ship in a hurry. "And even should they go lower, it will be still alright with Sepp Muller," he said. "I can put up more margin if necessary. My business can stand it. And, if I make the trip next year, what of it! I have been so many years away from the place where I was born that a year up or down will not make an iota of difference."

By mid-October prices had dropped sufficiently to exhaust his second margin, but like a good soldier Muller brought along some additional ammunition to fight the battle; he was to be the winner; he was going to make that trip to Europe. "No back talk," he said to his wife. "I know better than you what I am doing. True, stocks go down, but they also go up. Our business is good even though it also has declined a little bit, but it will be better before we know it."

Things and events turned much different than he ever had thought. Losses had accrued on paper that were well nigh staggering for his means. For two weeks he had not been down at all to watch the market. As soon as the papers came out in the afternoon that carried the closing prices, it was he who got the first copy from the adjoining stationery store. He'd close his eyes while opening the financial page that would tell him how he stood at the moment. "Shall I look at the prices, or shall I wait a while?" he asked himself. While fumbling with the pages, a cold chill ran down his back; goose pimples crawled up the other way. "Down again, darn it, and a whole point. Is that ever going to stop? Well, it will go up tomorrow, it usually does so on a Tuesday," he mused. This policy of cheating himself he kept up for a while, hoping against hope. What made him rather disconcerted was the fact that just his stocks would lead the parade downwards. When things had been bullish his stocks had been the strongest by far and many of his trader friends envied him for that. On November 12th he received another call for more margin. What now? Business had suffered much because he did not attend to it properly. He could not do a hardware business on the ticker tape, that thin strip of yellowish "serpentine" that tells of actualities instead of dreams which is found in every broker's office in a place therein called the Board Room. He was a well known figure of that place. He knew everyone by their first name and with newcomers it would be but a few days since they undoubtedly would come to "milk" him for some good information. He was Sepp to all. He would tell tales about this stock having been at 100 and the other one at 105 whereas now they are 32 and 28⅛ respectively. But, he would say, "they will come back and have right now the earmarks to do so."

Sepp Muller ignored the broker, that is, his margin call. He just could not go down. He did not even dare to call Mr Mayer, his customer's man on the phone, since he had made himself "out of town on business" to any phone callers for more than a week. He waited anxiously for the next paper at 11 a.m. which brought the first 15 minutes of transactions. Down again. He was frantic with fear. However, at about 3 p.m. he suddenly calmed down as if by magic. His fear was gone. He felt like a new man. That afternoon he did not even buy a paper but went home to take a much needed rest. He said to himself, "No use fighting the battle any longer. Those darn stocks are going down, they are bound to go lower now. There is just no bottom in sight, it's impossible. Business becomes poorer, everything goes haywire, I will have to save at least the few dollars that are left."

The morning's mail brought one more letter from the broker for additional funds by 11 a.m. in the morning or else. "They won't have a chance on the 'else,' I will be there in person just before the market opens and sell those stocks 'at the market.' I'll show them who is the smartest."

Quiet reigned in the offices at those times. What was turmoil a few months ago was like a funeral parlor then. Is it because Sepp Muller has stopped being an active trader that all the other friends had also stopped coming there? These were ideas that passed through the mind of Sepp when he entered the broker's office a few minutes before ten. He used to come down with high spirits to meet his associates that now, too, were strangely missing. Only Mr Mayer, the customer's man, was busy checking some reports of those customers whose accounts were to be "dumped" at eleven. He happened to look up just as Sepp turned the corner. His Christian name was Joseph so the name has no reference to a good English word that is used in botany. Mr Mayer brought forth a forced smile, went towards him, shook hands and said, "Lovely morning, Mr Muller. Haven't seen you for ages. How was your business trip? Tried to get you on the phone several times." He acted wonderfully in spite of the death warrant right on top of his desk. "No," said Sepp, "I have changed my mind about this market. I am going to sell out before they will catch me." "Where shall I put them in?" said Mayer. "At what price?" "Oh, make it 'at market,'" said Sepp haughtily, "no use dickering about an eighth."

Shaking all over, his last little bit of energy dissipated so as to be able to put it over on the customer's man, to show that he also could face the firing squad if need be, he walked to his usual seat around the Ticker Table. Two or three faces unknown to him sat around also. Another read aloud some statements that came over the ticker tape about the suspension of a Member of the Stock Exchange on account of some Rule and Paragraph of the Constitution of the Association. Two minutes of ten. "I hope they will open up until I am out," he said to himself dryly, "then they can go wherever they want to go," he added.

The ticker began to print a bunch of letters that gave no sense whatever, even dollar signs and Pound Sterling signs became mixed with them. They were testing the machine on the other side. "Let's have it," he suddenly burst forth so that the other three men looked at him and wondered who he might be. On the quiet he added, "Let's have it over with, then I can go. I'll get even with them some time."

Mr Mayer nonchalantly separated Sepp's margin call from the

many others which he had received from the margin clerk at 9 a.m. "Roberts, McTarvich, Knob, Dagnin . . ." he read down the list, some twenty-five of them. "All fine boys. Who ever thought the market would catch them?" He was himself anxiously awaiting the opening to see where stocks would open so as to call the boys if they might not be persuaded to dig up a little more of that mazuma* required to hold on to them. That merciless fellow of a Daugherty would not close an eye this time and let one of them slip by his margin sheet. It did happen in grains once in a while that he could slip one or the other through below the deadline since Daugherty did not pay too much attention to the grain accounts.

Suddenly the ticker began to move. It said: "November 20, 1907." Then it stopped dead. Cold sweat ran down on Sepp and goose pimples began to crawl up once more, but his chills were gone. It was a hot place. Off they go! 1000 U.S. Steel at 8, off half a point, and so on the line. Some stocks were down a whole point on big volume. Five minutes after ten stocks began to rally. Sepp's stocks had not appeared as yet. "Mine are not out yet, they are not sold at the low; they may catch that rally now and open much higher," Sepp thought. However, he did not say a word. Breathlessly he watched each letter appear, each number and eighth come out from under the wheel. For ten minutes the battle had been going on. Prices had risen a point already. Steel was up to 9 again. He felt relaxed in all his misery. "I'll cancel the order," he said. "I will put up some more money right now. It looks better all around to me. Maybe they won't go any lower now. It may be the bottom." So saying he rushed over to Mr Mayer and told him, "Cancel the order. Rush! Send it through. They haven't sold them yet. Nobody even seems to want my stocks not even 'at the market!' Quick, before they will take them on the rally!"

Mayer rushed to the window of the Order Clerk, writing on a

*An American slang word for US dollars.

slip as he ran to cancel the whole order. A voice could be heard from the inside, "We will try our best." Sepp kept watching the ticker. None of his stocks appeared as yet. A minute later, the voice came through the order window. "Too late, sold." "I haven't seen them on the tape," retorted Sepp, swallowing a few times. He had not quite finished the sentence when one after the other came running across the tape. Every one opened half a point lower compared to yesterday's close. "They just had to wait until I would cancel the order, then they grabbed them," he said. Sepp kept sitting motionless for a while at the ticker tape. Mr Mayer handed him a slip that showed his stocks had been sold, together with the price realized for them, and printed on the tape for his benefit. He knew of those slips but had never had one himself. He had bought in early January 1906 and again in March 1907 when as he thought he had bought the big bargains.

He figured out the differential of purchase and sale in his mind and found he still had nearly $400 left of the $8500 he had put into the venture.

Without so much as looking at Mr Mayer he walked out, never to return to the broker to this day.

"True," he said, "Mr Mayer gives me once in a while a ring when he sees something is moving but I will wait a while to get back into the market. I have watched them move and the market looks good to me right now. There are hundreds of stocks that are just now beginning to move. You come at a real opportune time to buy, Mr Wollsten. When you go down to X and Co., see my friend Mayer. He is a fine fellow. He'll pick runners for you right on Monday morning, I bet. But, leave grains alone! They are dynamite. I've seen more people burst in them than in stocks."

So saying, he got up and took his leave. "Come and see me one of these days, any time you need information on how to trade or some of the tricks of the game. You can have them all for the asking."

For half an hour George sat motionless in the chair digesting what he had heard from an experienced trader who unfortunately lost a lot of money on Wall Street. He placed the charts of 1906 and 1907 in front of him on the big table, joining them. Then he looked. "So," he said, "Muller bought in January of 1906 and some more in March. He let them go down for more than 40 points measured by the averages and sold right smack at the low. If he thinks I can use this method to learn, he don't know George.

"I learned from him 'what not to do."

But, in spite of all the mistakes he has made, I have learned a lot from him, that is I learned from him 'what not to do.' One can learn a lot from the mistakes of others. I will see him occasionally. Maybe I can give him a hand to regain some of his losses. He is a fine fellow but not a market trader."

It reminded him of his old music teacher who after eight years of instruction had told him that he was a good pupil but never would be a musician.

Muller was of a type that would never admit mistakes unless warmed up. True, he was a great talker who every day saw roses blooming yet had never noticed the thorns. During the conversation with such types one has to keep perfectly quiet, say "Yes" once in a while, add to it "Is that so?" in order not to make listening too monotonous. They do not like to be interrupted with questions, else their phantasy stops working. One must never laugh at them as they come forth revealing serious errors, but keep a quiet listening attitude. When they are all done with their story they suddenly come back "to earth." They look at one as if their own story was full of doubts. If anything was not as clear as desired, one merely has to say "That I just can't believe." "Oh, you don't believe that?" such a type will say. "It was this way . . . etc." Then they repeat that specific part very carefully to be certain that nothing was omitted. Sepp had told the truth and nothing but the truth.

George Makes His First Trade in Wheat

Monday morning early we see George Wollsten ride down town to see Mr Mayer of X & Co. Stock and Grain Brokers. It was nine-thirty when he arrived at the office. Sepp had furnished full information how to reach the place. It took but thirty minutes. Mr Mayer was a slender man of about thirty-five, with shrewd eyes, who sized up Mr Wollsten hurriedly, including the size of his pocket book.

"I am Mr George Wollsten," George began, introducing himself. "I want to open an account with you. Here is a check for $750.00 to start." He endorsed the check and continued, "Buy at the opening one contract of May wheat." Mr Mayer was somewhat surprised since he had underestimated the newcomer, the friend of Sepp. He had heard about this before George ever reached his desk to talk to him. Upon entering the long Customer's Room he saw an elevated place, some six inches higher than the regular floor with a dozen or more desks in a long row. Behind each of these sat dignified men. The whole affair had an appearance of a dozen judges sitting at court all at once. He had addressed the first one, asking for Mr Mayer, and had stated at the same time that a Mr Sepp Muller had sent him. "How is Sepp?" asked that man, but continuing in the same breath, "Mr Mayer is down there, five desks further."

Customer's men have eagle eyes; also extremely sensitive ears that are apt to catch even what is whispered by someone among the crowd anywhere about the room. Once in a while valuable information has been obtained with the aid of good ears and relayed to customers directly or by phone.

Tickers mounted on round tables were placed on the lower level of the room. One or two people were found sitting around some of the tickers. It was early yet. On the wall side of the room was the big Board with letters of stock abbreviations. The Board had long grooves so that green cards with numbers could be inserted. To each stock had been assigned three cards, one to show the opening price, another the high and a third the low price as they were made during the trading. A boy was just busy removing those which had been left from the previous day's operations. Others just removed small square tablets showing ⅛, ¼, ⅜ up to ⅞ which had been placed next to the full number of the green cards whenever such fractions had been reached by the price of a stock. They tucked them into small boxes on a leathern belt attached around their waist. On the far side George saw small cages, the order clerk's window and that of the nemesis of traders, the margin clerk. Behind the desks were windows that opened out above the neighboring roofs. A beautiful sight could be had over the city.

Yes, Mr Mayer was somewhat befuddled. Usually his customers would first discuss with him the situation about buying or selling stocks before ever thinking of making a commitment. He then would assist them to consult some bulky books that gave details about the corporations' assets, operation and outlook, together with many other matters of importance to traders. It was rather against "Wall Street" etiquette just to come into the broker's office and buy something. One needed more or less the sanction of the little emperor. In case a customer wanted to trade wheat, Mr Mayer would consult with him the various government releases about crops, aside from studying weather reports from the grain belt. Liverpool's, Buenos Aires' and Winnipeg's markets had to be looked over until finally some action could be taken. If a customer grew somewhat impatient, Mayer usually would say, "You must be very careful, else you might get stuck; no use plunging; the market is here every day."

"But this stranger comes here, tells me to place an order and sits down near the grain ticker in the far corner. He is not related to Sepp, I am sure," he said to himself.

Just a handful of people traded grains at this office. They kept more to themselves, more apart from stock traders. When one scrutinized closely, one would even discover a marked difference of manner, face and action compared to stock traders. These people look for entirely different indications to find out the probable trend of grains than stock traders use to discover trend of stocks. A corporation with a dozen factories all over the East can work and operate even when it rains cats and dogs, but not the farmer nor the grain seeds. Grain traders do not care whether U.S. Steel operates with a 50% capacity or with 75%, just as little as stock traders bother whether or not it rains in Saskatchewan.

Mr Mayer had taken the order together with the check to the order clerk's cage. From there the order was channeled over to the Chicago Pit.

The Board Room began to fill rapidly. Mostly men of mature age seemed to assemble and trade. George was by far the youngest among the crowd. He stayed by the grain ticker. The Big Board was to open at 10 a.m. sharp, whereas grains would start at 10:30 a.m. From this time differential he could quickly recognize who was trading stocks and who was on the grains.

Stocks opened. George walked over to watch the stock ticker. He saw some traders give orders to buy or sell to various customers' men. He approached Mayer to ask if he had any booklet that would give the abbreviations of stocks or something that would make matters clear. "Of course, Mr Wollsten, we have," said Mayer. He pulled a copy out of his drawer and handed it to him. "You come from up-state? I presume," said Mayer to begin a conversation. "Grow much wheat up there? Oats, probably," he added. "We grow apples up our way and some mighty good ones," said George. Mayer thought to himself, "That's where my next Fall's apples will hail from," but aloud he said, "The market is very strong today. We are in a real bull market from the looks of it. Steel is up a point, Dupont up two, even the little fellows pop up. Look! that three dollar stock XX is up a whole dollar, what a market!"

It was just half-past-ten when the grain ticker began to tick. It had a somewhat different buzz and tick than the others. George walked over to it to watch where May wheat would open. Several elderly gentlemen had taken seats around it. George had to lean over to get a peep at it, to see what comes out from under the wheel. "Why, they also use abbreviations for grains!" he said, something he had not known of. RK 66¼, WN 111⅜, ON 38, WK 112½, he read from the tape. It was necessary to go back to Mayer to ask for a booklet of grain abbreviations. With a smile, Mr Mayer gave him a piece of paper which he had prepared himself:

W wheat; R rye; O oats; C corn; B barley
K May; N July; U September; Z December.

"Thanks, Mr Mayer," said George, "that's a help." He walked back to the ticker. By that time the serpentine tape had reached the floor, which gave George an opportunity to start from the beginning to see what had happened in the Chicago Pit so far. He found his May wheat had opened at 1.12⅛. He saw July oats had opened at 38, May rye at 66¼. Several times again WK appeared with advancing prices to 1.12⅝. "It's going my way, that is the way Jupiter said it would go," he thought. Mayer handed him a slip which stated that they had bought for his account and risk 5000 bushels of May wheat at 1.12⅛. "That's fine," he said to Mr Mayer. "Thanks!"

The room filled up more and more with traders. The conversations going on around the room caused quite a bit of noise; the tickers ticked each their peculiar ticks, sometimes they kept quiet, sometimes they ticked just a little and again they rushed out prices rapidly, only to be completely quiet once more. Periodically everything seemed to be quiet around the room. Then the noise was again resumed. He thought of the frogs croaking in the old pond at home which also stopped their concerts as soon as they heard somebody approaching. One would begin, then another. Gradually the whole orchestra would be in full swing, only to stop at noises again. He thought of Ovid's Metamorphosis and of the Frogs of Aristophanes.

He watched the grain ticker again and saw his wheat had reacted back to 1.12⅛, the place where he had bought it. A portion of the Board was reserved to register grain prices the same way as they registered stocks. He noticed the marking for May wheat as follows: WK opens 1.12⅛; high 1.12⅝; low 1.12; last 1.12⅛. The other grains, as well as cotton, had been assigned their places on the Board.

Afterwards he scrutinized the Stock Board. Two boys were kept busy changing the fluctuations of prices. Each one with a piece of run tape in hand was posting the last sales prices to keep customers abreast of the market. "It will take me quite some time to get wise to all those abbreviations and symbols. To remember the names of the various corporations is still another matter and then I don't know yet what they do or can do, what they manufacture or sell," he thought. "But everything takes time; I can't do everything at once. As long as Jupiter does not fail me, I will catch on to that soon," he said. A look at the grain ticker showed him his wheat had advanced again to 1.12⅜.

"I wonder what Grete and Jim are doing now," George suddenly thought of them. "Grete should be gathering eggs and Jim will be worrying how to make the holes for the fence posts," he mused.

Around noon he went out for a bite to eat. What a crowd of people he found in the streets! There were plenty of eating places but a great rush prevailed everywhere. He looked for a place less crowded. "I am now one of those ants that creep around lower New York to make a living," he said to himself. "Everything seems to be mixed here too just like on the Stock Board: bosses, clerks, stenos, assistants, all with one common thought to satisfy the belly. Up there the stocks try to outdo each other by blowing themselves up into dollar values to satisfy traders and investors." He passed a place where it said on a wooden blackboard, "Free Lunch; Mug of Beer Five Cents: Pig's Knuckles, Liver & Onions." The place was not crowded. He found the place to be a bar. A long counter was full of assorted meats, salads; hot dishes also could be had as had been marked on the blackboard. He watched a moment to see how the affair had to be tackled. He noticed that everybody just helped himself. Sliced bread was found in masses in a basket. Customers made their own sandwiches and each had a mug of beer. To be sure he would not do anything wrong he asked the man behind the counter how much a meal would cost him. "Did you buy your beer?" asked the man. "When you have the beer, then help yourself to anything you want." "Then all eats are free around here?" asked George. "It says so on the board outside," retorted the man. George was dumbfounded. "That's America for you," he thought, "generous in giving away food. How much profits must there be in this mug of beer for a nickel?" he wondered.

In less than half an hour George was back at the ticker. His wheat had been up to 1.12¾. He saw it on the Board, but the last sale was 1.12½. "I must not expect too much the first day," he said to himself. "All good things take time. In fact, I shall go home and do some work now. That wheat will move all by itself. I have seen and learned enough to-day that was new to me and I need some time to digest this," he added. "I think I'll go home," he said to Mr Mayer. "Shall I call you at the close? Glad to do it," said Mayer. "Thanks, don't bother. I'll see it in the paper," said George. "By the way," said Mr Mayer, "will you fill out this card so that we may know where to address your mail. Our statistician often has stocks that show a good advance and then he sends out letters to customers about them; besides, confirmations will be sent to you on all trades which you make, that's why," he concluded.

Half an hour later George was home. Overcoat and hat had disappeared in the closet. He lay down on the bed for a while, thinking about the future. "The future seems to generate out of the past like a plant comes out of a seed. The seed disappears: after a while nobody thinks what has happened to it. They see only the plant or the tree that has grown out of it. Take those ancient

Greek and Latin books, written nearly two or three thousand years ago. There could have been but one original written by one or several people. This was the seed. Two thousand years later copies of what had been written are still spread all over the world. Schools and scientists seriously study their contents to-day. The seed has either disappeared or is kept in a safe place in some Museum. It has grown a mental tree of enormous size. They must have known the time to put out seed," he thought. "Did they use a Jupiter crossing to start? Or did they just sit down and write because they just wanted to write something?" George was very much interested in the past of things, especially in the past of grain prices. He could not work up too much enthusiasm for stocks. "I will work in them some other time," he would say, "because no man can serve two Lords. One thing after another. Two is company, but three is a crowd. Myself and wheat are two; the third has to wait. Multitude, of which much is spoken in books, is apt to get me all mixed up," he concluded.

He had fallen asleep and all was dark when he awoke. His watch showed 5:15. It was not his habit to sleep during afternoons, but the excitement of this important day had been too much. Like the seed that is consigned to the ground before it can sprout, so he needed a little darkness and calm.

He washed up, went down to get the paper and had an early dinner at the same time. His wheat had gone up to 1.13¼ and closed at 1.12⅞. He felt good when he returned to his room. On the way he met Mr Holten in the lobby and had a few words with him, thanking him at the same time for introducing him to Mr Muller, but made it rather short so as to get to work.

He wrote a long letter to Grete and Jim giving them details of those events that would be of interest to them. About the market he told them very little. "They don't understand it anyhow, so why waste time and paper?" he thought. He wrote Jim to send down the books as soon as they arrived.

For two days George checked the average length of one of the swings in wheat, that is of a complete upmove or of one downwards. He found that small swings in one direction last about 9 days. Just by that, many days later his wheat had climbed to 1.14½. There he sold out. The transaction gave him a hundred dollars' profit after deducting the commission of the broker. This profit put him on easy street for a while. He wanted some more time to work out certain ideas that were more or less dark to him before he would make another trade. For a whole week he bothered little about the market except to plot the daily performance in his chart. He kept charts of several stocks, of the Dow Jones averages, also of cotton and of the other grains. His room was a bed room, office and sitting room all at one time. It had a hot and cold shower attached which made it quite comfortable. George was all set for the time being. Grete or Jim would not disturb him any further. The farm, as nice as it was to live with them, was not close enough to the market. He knew he had to be closer. On the other hand, he thought that Mr Mayer as well as the traders that stayed at the Board day in and day out from the time the market opened until its close, who watched every sale that passed underneath the wheel, were entirely too close for their own welfare.

One day he remembered about the astronomy book he had wanted to buy. He also recalled that on the ride over to Long Island City with Muller and Holten they had passed several book shops. He took a stroll through 59th Street. In one of the stores he acquired a copy of Herschel's Astronomy and one of Norton. As soon as he came back he began to study them. He soon discovered that there are two ways to measure planets' positions, one as seen from the earth, the other if we imagined ourselves to be on the Sun and were to look from it out into space to view the planets from there. The way planets are viewed from the Sun was contained in the Tables furnished by the Nautical Almanac, but the other way, "That's a horse of a different color," he said. "I shall have to try to obtain some of those ephemerides and see how they look and what I can do with them." The clerk at the desk soon directed him to a place where he could find astrological books and ephemerides. While on his way down to 32nd Street he felt as if in the one week he had become somewhat acquainted with the town. It was not as hard as he had first thought it would be. There was an East Side and a West Side. Streets had numbers from 1 to 180 or 242. Avenues ran through the length of the Island which were also numbered. Was that hard? Only the downtown part of the City had street names.

We soon see George in the store asking for ephemerides for astrologers. "What year?" asked a little old lady that waited on him. "Give me four or five years backward including the current year," he said. She soon brought some small blue paper-covered booklets from the rear, saying, "Fifty cents a piece." He paid her, comparing at the same time the size with the ones from Washington. The name on each of the booklets said "Raphael's Ephemerides of Planets' Places." A few people were sitting in the small reading room that was connected with the store. He unpacked his own again there, paged through it to verify that they really were planetary tables. They contained a maze of figures, but instead of positions being in straight degrees and minutes from 0° to 360°, they were shown with the signs attached, such as Aries, Taurus, etc. He wrapped them up again and went home.

The market had played around without doing much for the whole week. Wheat had receded to 1.13. The next morning, it was the 25th of February, George went down early to buy himself another contract of wheat because after idling for a week he figured it ought to get a push and Jupiter, after it is crossed, keeps up the good work for a while anyhow. "I may make another two points to keep me going," he said.

He paid 1.13⅛ for it. The opening was the low for the day. He talked a very little while with the broker and went home early to work again.

Somehow or other the little blue books which contained the geocentric positions of the planets did not appeal to him. He saw quickly that the positions given therein were entirely different than those in the Nautical Almanacs; he saw that Mercury and the others were moving backwards too when viewed from the earth, whereas by heliocentric view they always moved forward. "Of course, we have two lives," he mused, "one represents our main work and endeavor which always moves forward, the other is pleasure. I will quite often go back to visit Grete and Jim; I will also some time go back to visit my folks in Europe, but that will not take me away from my general forward movement. If I do go back it's just for fun and play but I can't do anything constructive with such movements. So I consider the geocentric movements of planets to represent their fun and pleasure, while their movement in heliocentric view is the real thing, the real forward movement. One is for astrologers, the other is for scientific work." He put them in his suitcase where the back pages of his newspapers lay at rest.

Certain people have a talent to choose things that are good for them while they leave others alone. Adam was one of those lucky ones, had not Eve later on given him that apple, a fruit that is round and looks like one of those gaps which the market likes to make at times. The serpent was the anterior cause. George suddenly thought of Sepp Muller and how he got bitten by the stock market serpent. He looked over the stock pattern. There he saw that serpent winding itself up and down, and up and down, striking once in a while. He also imagined he could see the apple into which Eve bit. He imagined his old violin which he was obliged to scrape for many years and recalled those two f's, one on each side, that allow the sound to come out of the box. What about the word "If"? Does the "I" of this word not sound like "up, joohoo" and does its "f" not sound like the smell of a foul egg, with the egg between the I and the F? Is Mrs Adam merely the counter part, the F of the I? The German word for breath is "Atem." "There you are," he said, "breathe up and breathe down. I have to consult the Bible sometime," he continued, "if it does not give me some cues about market movements!"

By putting the small ephemerides to the side George saved himself many years of drudgery to wade through something that would have taught him astrology. There is something to astrology, no doubt; several major changes would have to be made before it becomes useful. A certain fellow by the name of Bayer had worked out a method of astrology which took him fully twelve years to complete. He had made it out of one single horoscope, the way astrologers use five others, all arrived from that one. By this means all events that could happen would come forth. However, it takes about two days just to erect the framework, with complicated calculations.

The methods which George produced, as we soon shall see, are so much simpler and easier and to the point for trading, that results are almost immediate without much effort. The average astrologer who puts his work to the test in markets will be a failure, a positive failure. That is why they cling to forecasting people's future. It matters little whether aunt Fiffy comes for her visit on the 18th or the 27th, when the horoscope says: "Relatives come to your house," but with markets one can be a wreck in less than a week.

George looked again at his stock chart for the time Mr Muller was run through the wringer. "If Jupiter does not cause an upmove when it is crossed by Mercury, something is fishy and it is a top," he said. "This applies to grains, possibly also to people."

Especially one thought made him keep away from the geocentric positions: "If there are influences from the cosmos working on the mind of the people that live on earth, it cannot very well be an influence that connects with the earth proper such as a geocentric conjunction between Jupiter and Mercury, for example." He thought of a thunderstorm as a cosmic phenomenon caused by air overloaded and overheated with electricity. "True, the air is part of the earth: so is the tree into which the lightning passes to enter the earth. However, that which develops the excess of electricity is neither the air nor the earth. It's beyond it. This may be against all laws of physics as taught in schools, but I now make my own laws."

The Ellipses

George could see perfectly that Jupiter, Saturn and Mercury could affect heliocentrically the little bits of brains of the ants that crawl around the earth and verified the facts from his charts. "Of course," he continued, while looking now at a picture in Herschel's Astronomy, "all planets run around the Sun in ellipses, yes, in ellipses. . . . Ell . . . ip . . . s . . . IS." He dropped the book, looked at the 1904–1905 wheat charts and cried out, "El . . . ipse . . . IS. Like hell it is!" His Latin came to help him: ipse can mean "itself" or "of one's own accord" or "alone." He saw now ellipses in his wheat chart, even though there were none visible to anybody. Such a condition we call vision. "There they are," he said. "Parts of them are clearly visible, others are seemingly invisible, like the Moon with its phases. At the time of the last sickle one can often discern the entire contour of the Moon and yet but one quarter of it shines brightly. I can complete an ellipse around these movements," he said, "which will look like a bath tub to fit them into, nay, they fitted themselves that way," he added. He had looked at the wheat prices on his chart from June 5 to August 22, 1904; also at the part from March 9th to April 26th of the same year. They had taught him drawing in school, so it was not difficult to draw an ellipse fairly accurately around the periods. One was a long and narrow ellipse, the other was rather short and fat.

All planets run around the Sun in ellipses.

"I can complete an ellipse around these movements."

He went down to the desk. On the way he met Holten. "Where can I buy some celluloid sheets?" he accosted him. "Celluloid? What do you want to do with celluloid, Mr Wollsten? Artists use that. You can get some over at 45th Street on Sixth Ave., just above the Hippodrome, there are the Artists' Supply Stores."

"Thanks a million," said George, and rushed out of the door as it was getting late. He bought an entire sheet to make sure he would not run short. George had figured that it would take a good many ellipses of all sorts and he'd try out which ones would fit best. How he would arrive at selecting the right ones was part of his study and work. On the way home he paged through in his mind old mathematics books to recall the correct construction of an ellipse. "Two circles, major and minor axis, no, I better get me a book," he mused. On 59th Street he picked up an old geometry book that gave the details. "Those things are cheap, twenty-five cents," he said, as he continued home, "but who can put those things to use?" Triumphantly he walked through the lobby; Mr Holten could not make out what had struck George. As much as he had a desire to invite Holten up to his room, he decided against it. He would be distracted by his presence and he had a lot of melted gold on the fire that required immediate attention before it would cool off. "And time is money," he thought. The "Evening Mail" he picked up before he came home. Wheat had advanced to 1.14¾ and it closed at 1.14½. It was a Friday again, one of his lucky days.

That evening he made five ellipses of various sizes, a fat one, a lean one, a long one, a thin one and one of baby size. The lengths and widths had been selected on account of various patterns formed by the movement of wheat.

Saturday was but a short day. Wheat closed at 1 o'clock. He did not go down. Shortly before the close he called Mr Mayer on the phone to get an idea what wheat was doing. He heard: 1.14⅞ high, 1.14⅜ low and last. "I will be down Monday early to watch it," he told Mayer. From the quotation he figured that wheat must keep going now. "If it does not make a push upward Monday, I will sell out and may even take a short position," he said.

About that time Jim at Upper Red Hook had driven over to Pine Plains to bring the rest of the chicks home. The first batch did well. His fruit trees were all pruned; the snow began to disappear.

During some years even in March heavy snow falls could be expected. At spots facing the south the earth began to get soft and chickens walked all the way from the coops to try for real early worms. Grete was busy making her baby's clothes. They had seen a doctor who informed them that they could expect their baby by early September. "Your wife is a strong and healthy woman, so don't worry about anything," he told Jim.

The chickens had increased laying ever since George left, though prices dropped in proportion. All told, Jim had bought 1500 chicks. The barn housed them comfortably. Of course the feed cost had increased with such a quantity, but the revenues would in due order do the same. He planned to sell off the old hens with the exception of a few for home use so as to make place for the little brood as soon as they had outgrown the barn. He even planned to construct a second chicken coop.

Things had turned rather quiet about the house. Life even seemed to have become a little monotonous. Jim could not work much outside. He looked after the chickens and cut wood for the stove. Much of his time was used to read the "Upper Red Hook Herald" as soon as the delivery boy had brought his copy.

He had decided to order lumber for the new coop and started to build. The job kept him busy into early April. He wanted to make a good job of it so that should George come once for a visit he could show his ability as a carpenter.

George worked with the ellipses. He soon saw that there were endless possibilities:

George had worked over Sunday with the ellipses. He tried them in all sorts of ways. He soon saw that there were endless possibilities to lay from bottoms, from tops, from gaps; there were possibilities to set them straight up, to lay them sidewise across from a top or from a bottom, to lay them at an angle, to fit them through consecutive higher bottoms upwards or through consecutive lower tops when the trend led down. He had produced them on celluloid. On the first one he pricked holes with a pin, patiently, all around the periphery, until it gave him the contour. The actual drawing had been made on paper and, by laying the celluloid over it, he reproduced it on to the celluloid that was transparent. It was a tedious job. Afterwards he trimmed it all around with scissors. Mr Holten was the man who dug up a pair somewhere. George's face would shine during those tests periodically like the full Moon; at times his face would be like that of the New Moon, disappointment being clearly drawn on to it. The ups and downs of markets mirrored themselves remarkably in his physiognomy.

Monday, the last day of February, George arrived on time at Mr Mayer's office. Wheat had opened unchanged. During the next 15 minutes it became strong and the price ran up 1 ½ points in a rush of buying. Because he saw that new advance, his thoughts wandered off to Sepp Muller when he had told him of his trading experience. It was Sepp Muller that made him get up, walk over to Mayer and say, "Sell two May contracts at the market." Meekly Mr Mayer took the order. A few minutes later he received a slip that showed 10M WK sold at 1.15¾. George put the slip into his pocket without saying a word. Mayer had expected to hear at least a few words about why he shorted wheat when it looked so good, when everybody talked about the big advance that was just now beginning. Disappointed, he retired to the "judge's dais." After a while George asked Mr Mayer for a check of $100 from his account and soon left to do some more work at home.

He was trying out other ways and means to discover when wheat would turn up from a low or down from a high. All sorts of ideas had developed while riding subways. He had seen a stock trader who used a "system" by keeping tabs on 15 different stocks of which he took prices every quarter hour, added those prices carefully and made a chart with the aid of this special average. Another trader, Mr Peeper, had talked to him during the morning. He asked him whether he kept charts. "I see you come only once in a while to the office, stay for a while and beat it out again." George answered him that he traded solely on intuition. "If they look good I buy, if they look better I sell them," he said. "Why, you take terrible chances that way," replied Mr Peeper. "You should use charts. I'll show you," he said opening a binder that was carefully tied with several ribbons. He had about a hundred charts of all sorts of stocks neatly plotted. George saw trend lines drawn on those charts that connected a low with the next following low, also high points connected with the next high points, so that a sort of a channel was indicated. Through this channel the trend was supposed to run. When the channel was violated, that is, should prices push through it either above or below, he expected the trend to change. George sized up the idea quickly, especially the virtue of those lines. But he noticed that just at critical places this channel would many times be exceeded by a point or even two and instead of continuing in that direction, prices would go completely the opposite way. "Those charts are very beautiful," he said to Peeper, but thought, "I'll check on this as soon as I get home." Suddenly Peeper said, "Have you heard about the new charts which they use?" "Not me," said George, "which ones?" "They now make weight charts by combining the number of advances and declines of the stocks that are traded every day in a certain proportion. I think they take the advances three consecutive days and deduct two consecutive declines. Finally they obtain a difference which they plot on a chart. After they have plotted it for several days a line is produced which waves up and down in irregular fashion, but turns around just about when a top or bottom is made." "That sounds very interesting, Mr Peeper," said George. "Tell me that once more, I want to mark it down; I have a poor memory for such complicated things." He picked a pad off Mayer's desk whose eyes threw lances because he had not asked permission to use it, but George

They take the advances three consecutive days and deduct two consecutive declines.

was the customer and the customer is always in the right, so Mayer had to take out another pad from his third drawer and put it in the very same place. It simply meant "Keep it."

Mr Peeper repeated. "Take 15 stocks, I believe; then separate those which advanced to-day from those that declined to-day. Do so for three consecutive days. On the third day you add up the total value that shows on the advancing side. Of those that declined you make your total already on the second day, because only two days are used to make that total, so that on the third you make your total for this column out of the declines of the second and third day.

"Whatever value appears from the advancing column, from that is deducted the declining column. The result is then plotted each day."

"I got that now," said George. "Do you happen to have such a chart?" he asked. Peeper fumbled through his carton of charts and found one that showed these wavy lines. George noticed a sort of zero line drawn in it around which the serpent wound itself. The values seemed to him to run at times into plus and at other times into minus. The pattern looked to him more like the picture of Mercury with Aesculapius, only it was lying sidewise instead of standing. He saw Adam again, he saw Eventide, he saw Day and Night. "Why," he thought, "that man has the first chapter of Genesis solved and don't know it. However, they took six days that time," he added. He was all afire on the inside. He spoke for half an hour with Mr Peeper, thanked him for what he had shown him and went home to put all this to the test. There he had his charts as well as the time to do so.

For several days thereafter George went down town each day to sort of snoop around whether or not any other ideas were floating around the "Street." The wavy line was as big a monster to him as was the actual grain chart with the only difference that it wound itself around a centre axis, whereas the grain chart had the form of a roof, running upward in the bull cycle and downward in the bear cycle. He had not done anything with it as yet since the ellipses kept him occupied sufficiently for the time being. He thought of Ecclesiastes where it says, "There is a time for everything; a time to sow, and a time to reap, a time to give and a time to take," while he drew the two axes through the ellipses, the major and the minor.

His search for additional ideas down town convinced him that every trader in the Board Room had some sort of a "system" which he followed, that was supposed to reveal the trend of markets. How could they otherwise get up the nerve to trade so often? Some indication must cause them to act. The great majority used daily high and low charts with trend lines drawn in underneath two consecutive low levels while the trend rose or above two consecutive high levels when the trend declined. Supposing the market's trend reached that line a third time, that is where they would buy or respectively sell, expecting that the price would be chased back again from such a channel line. It might take a week or two weeks until the price would reach that "wall," it may never be reached or it may pass the wall with a bang.

Every trader in the Board Room had some sort of a "system" which he followed.

One morning Mr Mayer introduced George to a kindly looking old gentleman, Mr Rotolo. It was he who always received the piece of yellow tape from the boys after they had posted the prices from it on the Board. They were as used to doing it as an old lady passes the rosary beads.

Mr Rotolo kept a "Sale to Sale chart." He used a regular chart sheet, ignored the dates shown on top and bottom margins and plotted on each small line one sale after the other as shown by the tape of one option, May wheat, at the present time. Each day the chart's January 1st was his opening price line. Rotolo, dark haired, with a moustache like bicycle handles of a high wheeler, was about 50 years old. His accent told of his Italian origin. He was a native of Riva on Lake Garda. During all the thirty years in the country he was not able to shake off the accent. He was happy when somebody looked at his work. He made his trades rather on the quiet whenever his trend line indicated a change. Other traders did not pay much attention to him since they considered his "system" too involved; besides it required nearly five hours' constant watch and marking. It was more "business like" to listen to some wild cat story or to read the newspapers. He was the "Queer Duck" for the other grain traders, although when grains were boiling they never failed to try to take advantage of his patient detailed work. Like a painter paints his landscape with cattle, trees and clouds, so he plotted sale after sale every day. Once in a while, for want of better ways to kill time, one or the other would come over to inquire of him, "Rotolo, what's new? Let's see the chart! Is that dip going to become an abyss? What do you think of it?" the visitor would say, worried, but hiding his emotions as much as possible. From his charts Rotolo would measure very closely the times when Reynolds or Lopez would call for a visit.

Around the ticker tape more stories were told in one day than were printed in the newspaper. The subjects touched most anything. The other day they chewed over Stanley's travels through Africa while grains moved quiet. When the story reached the situation where the natives were about ready to roast him, one of the more tender-hearted trader-listeners gave an order to sell out his grain. It looked so dead, ready to "fall out of bed." That way the time passed every day; always something else came up for discussion. If they had no news the ticker would supply fluctuations.

George spent much time with Mr Rotolo, who had given him a lot of back charts of the "Sale to Sale" type. "But watch out," said Rotolo, "I keep equal spaces for the hours! In case there is too much trading in one hour, my points are set very close together; in quiet hours the points are farther apart, but note, each day ends with April 25th of the chart! If I did not do that my pattern would not talk to me. I have tried it in many different ways already and this way I found best." "I see," said George, "you keep rhythm like the organist who plays 8th and 16th notes and yet stays in his regular time." "That is what the fellows don't understand; when they see a fast run away they think it keeps on running, but it is often times only some little news from Washington or that Iowa may have a shower. After that we are back in time," he said. George thought Rotolo's arguments rather clever. He had not thought to compare the movement of grains with church music so far. "There are many slants to this market timing," he said. "It will be years before I really shall finish learning."

He had not thought to compare the movement with church music. There are many slants to this market timing.

He made another comparison. "When they serve a dinner, we first get some ripe olives, a sardine, some slices of salami. Then they bring on the soup, followed by a nice fish. After the fish comes the roast meat, possibly a roasted duck or turkey. As the final dish we will get sweets. On holidays there might even be champagne. Nuts are supposed to end the meal. After such lavish dinners there is bound to follow a show of the best vaudeville in town. The market seems to provide us with similar courses in the form of a banquet." George remembered having had a few of such dinners. However, invariably he felt quite uncomfortable after it was all over. The stomach was overloaded. "Isn't it the very same way with the meal dished up for traders in the market?" he asked himself.

In the meantime the additional volumes of Ephemerides had been sent down by Jim. Immediately he began to plot all the years back to see whether or not Jupiter, Saturn and Mercury kept faith with him. For ten days he compared, sized up and set ellipses into his charts. The results appeared good to him even though much had to be cleared up. He found many cases where Jupiter had made a top from which a big decline would start. Saturn did similar tricks. Even the prices, however carefully he set ellipses,

Ellipses once in a while run just enough to make one think the trend does continue.

would once in a while run outside of the periphery, just enough to make one think the trend does continue, and yet the trend turns around to form an ellipse the opposite way.

"Of course," he mused, "were it that easy, many a clever trader would just grab each move without ever taking a loss." But the world was not built of one mountain; that would be monotonous! We need hills and dales in grains movements as well as with ourselves; we are bound to make errors. "I wonder," he continued, "if ellipses do not make a blunder once in a while themselves! Supposing I consider the ellipse as a bath tub or, better yet, as a barrel which I fill with water. Now, that barrel may spring a leak," George pointed on his chart where the movement of wheat had trespassed by a point beyond the ellipse circumference for a few days. "Someone higher up who watches over those movements must have noticed it and quickly plugged up the leak, which made the movement of wheat get back inside of the ellipse."

Whenever George looked at the market's action he always tried to associate actions of nature, whether they were related with weeds, grasses, trees, animals, parts of man's body, mountains or valleys.

One day he decided that one length of an ellipse was to be considered as one cycle. Such cycles had various lengths because the angles to set the ellipse varied. The ellipses varied in themselves. But they had nothing in common with our year's length nor with the four seasons, that is with the Sun. However, he thought that since it was only a matter of two planets, Jupiter and Saturn, crossed by Mercury, the number of ellipses should be reduced to merely two to keep up the harmony. Like an inventor who had to make many models for his invention, so George, on May 9th of that year, completed two ellipses.

One ellipse measured 6.25 inches; the other measured 9.25 inches. They had the same width of 1.95 inches.

For some reason he combined them into one, by using the same minor axes. (See Figure VI.1).

FIGURE VI.1
The Six-Inch Ellipse With Half of Nine-Inch Ellipse Inserted

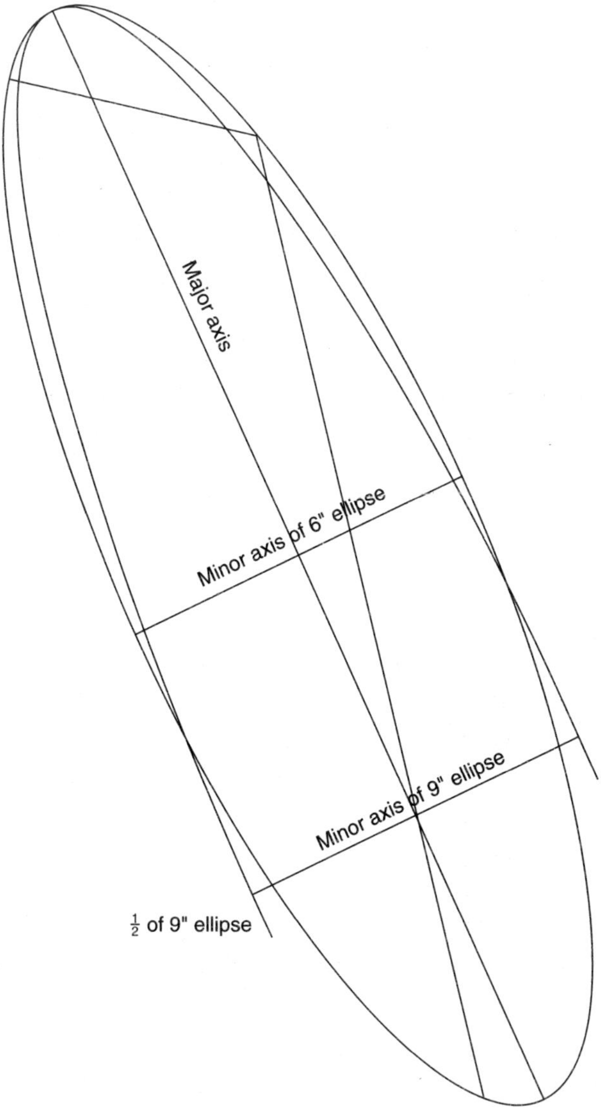

This was not the only innovation George made on this 9th day of May. He made one more important discovery.

He made one more important discovery.

The 71° and 78° Angles

He used a transparent semi-circular protractor and drew into it the 71° as well as the 78° angle from the centre outward to the periphery of it. He had noticed that if he set this protractor to a low place, the trend would first run up the 78° line then fall back to the 71° angle, run up on it for a while and only when the trend broke the 71° angle was it all over with the upmove. From a top he would do the same thing by laying the protractor the opposite way. He scratched lines into the protractor with a pin point again and ran some ink through the grooves to make them visible. At times when very big moves occurred, such as happened in 1904, he would simply add a ruler to extend the lines beyond the protractor.

George carried a long positions ever since the first of the month. Six points' profit had accrued so far. Jupiter told him that on this day will be a top of importance and not a "jump-up" place. Therefore he sold two contracts on May 9th. Besides, he sold two more, which made him short. He had increased his trading from one contract to two contracts. His judgment was right. He had also noticed that stocks did not recover very well from the sharp drop they had suffered during April. Matters discussed by traders around the tickers sounded too hopeful for him. He never could forget Muller's story.

The discovery about the 71° and 78° angles helped George in many ways. His analysis was correct. Wheat had been walking up on a 78° angle since May 2nd. On Monday it had advanced two points, but in spite of all that advance, it walked across the 78° line of his protractor to be ready to go down to the 71° line. Besides, when he had set his six-inch ellipse upright into the low place of

April 20th he could see a regular pocket had been formed, whose left side was the high of March 31st, whose right side was this very day, Jupiter's day and the "valley" low place was shown for April 20th. To-day's high was just one point higher compared to the high of March 31st. "That's just fine," he said. "That extra point must have caused everybody to buy and the shorts that were put out around the low levels are running to cover here for fear the market will run through on the upside."

The information obtained from Mr Peeper and Mr Rotolo had not been used as yet. "On their ideas I will start work pretty soon," he said.

A few days later wheat started a sharp comeback after it had receded 5 cents. "That's alright," he said. "I will keep my short position just the same." He had found out that after a valley is made, be it a big one or a small one, the market often times holds until Mercury reaches 0°. It does not need the crossing of a planet, just as long as the heliocentric coordinate of Mercury shows 0°. He had seen it happen quite often. However, the change may occur just a few days before or after that 0° is reached.

He did not like the idea too much that Mercury at its zero point would not register on the exact day at 0° and was trying to find out the cause of this failure. He considered it was not an actual conjunction of planets, but merely an action of Mercury proper at the time it passed 0° heliocentrically.

After the middle of May wheat turned down again. It had missed the top of May 9th by just one point, that is one cent. New York became quite warm already. He thought again of Jim and Grete and decided to take a run up to see them. He had ordered the "Evening Mail" to be sent to Upper Red Hook for a month, packed his charts and the other tools to do some work in the country. The commitments he left intact. For safety's sake he placed what is called a "stop loss order." He said to Mr Mayer, "Stop my September wheat ¼ point above the high of May 9th" (at 1.16½). The last commitment he had made in September wheat instead of May wheat, which option ran out during the month.

Thursday, May 19th, during the afternoon, George came walking into Jim's farm. He had forgotten to notify them. Nobody was at the house. Grete was in the new chicken coop feeding the chicks. Jim was in town on an errand. He had sold the entire lot of last year's chickens. While George began unpacking his belongings, Grete came back to the kitchen to prepare supper. "Why, George!" she exclaimed. "When did you get here? Hungry, I presume, from the long ride?" "You look good, all browned already," said George. "Where is Jim? Haven't seen him nowhere around." "He is in town. We sold the old chickens to make room for the young brood. That was alright to do, wasn't it?" she asked. "How do you like the run we made for the chickens?" she said, looking out from the window. "Looks alright to me," said George. "There is Jim coming now!" he added as he glanced through the apple trees to the road. "He will be as much surprised as I was," said Grete.

The kitchen door opened. "Grete, that . . ." He was just going to say something when he saw George at the sofa. "When did you get here, George? I thought so; one nice day you'd be just fed up with the city and with those stars of yours, with your charts and all the other crazy things. Only the other day I had said to Grete: watch, one nice day George will be back and we will have to look for a larger farm." He shook his hand heartily while George bit on his teeth to withstand the pain of the hand shake. "I just come for a visit," he said, "and to bring you back the $500 which you let me have to get started." "No sir, they are yours," said Jim. "You also worked here. In case I do need them some time I shall ask you for them but I just received that amount for the rest of the old chickens." They sat on the sofa. Grete began to prepare the evening meal. "We will finish the stew of yesterday," she said, "but I will make some pancakes for you, special. See if there are any eggs in the coop!" Dutifully George went to the coop and came back with six of them. Two he had in the left pocket, two in the right, two in one hand which gave him a chance to close the coop without breaking any. "Is that all?" said Grete when she saw him marching across the yard with but two eggs. "Your chickens are not that lazy," he said jokingly, pulling the others from his pockets.

That evening George did not get to work. He had to tell of his doings in New York, also about Mr Holten. He himself was anxious to hear how things had gone and how Mr Schafer was doing. In a short while more information was gleaned on both sides than a dozen letters could have conveyed. Grete had changed her girlish figure quite a bit during the last three months. George told them that he had made nearly $1500.00 trading wheat down at New York. "And all this money was made with those crazy stars which I found in the books from Washington," he added. "Of course," said Jim, "you have learned in school many things which I never have heard nor will hear, but everyone has his own way to make a living, just like each bee knows where to go to get its honey. Have you seen my bee hives already?" "You got bees now?" said George, somewhat surprised. "Yes, I started with three hives about a month ago when a lost swarm landed in that apple tree next to the chicken fence. I put them in a hive and to make it worth while I bought two more swarms over near Pine Plains. They cost me $25.00. One has a Western Queen." "Why just a Western Queen? Aren't the Eastern ones good enough for you?" said George. "They claim that the Western Queens make the workers bring in from 10 to 12 pounds more honey each year than the Eastern Queens do, but I will tell you next fall. I will keep track of each hive and I know where the Western Queen is," he said.

George told them that he intended to stay about three weeks or four at the most, unless "you want to get rid of me sooner," he added. "You are at home here as we are, even though you were a nuisance the last few weeks with your old planets and stars but you can be much alone now – we are busy outside with so many things that do not interest you whatever, that the whole house is just yours." "Only let me in once in a while to see that you are not starving while we are out," added Grete.

The next day George paid a visit to Mr Schafer, who was delighted to see him. He inquired of him how he was getting along down in the big city. George told him briefly that his progress was slow but steady, that his idea about captains of boats and the celestial Time Tables had been wonderful. "I have a lot to learn, though, but Rome wasn't built in one day." While they chatted Mr Schafer brought him through his extensive orchards. He had to admire the Newton Pippins which he had set out last Spring and informed him that it was Geneva Stock on French seedlings. "They should bear in four or five years. The only trouble with us now is the Western competition that may keep prices down, but our exports increase according to the Commerce Year Book," he added.

After a while George made a tour through Upper Red Hook. The place had grown close to him during the half year he had lived there. It seemed to be home to him. The constant rush to get places down at New York formed a big contrast to the quiet, easy-going life around here. Yet the happy villagers also reach their goal. He walked through Dingle's, then went to the bank to open an account of his own with the check Jim refused to accept. The president recognized him and asked a few questions about where he had kept himself for the last several months. Then he walked down to the mill, even though he had nothing in particular to do there. But old thoughts come back. What change had come to him within the short space of time! He was now a full-fledged grain trader. Before he felt himself a nuisance. He now had a foot-hold on something worthwhile. Part of the way he whistled old Vienna tunes and came back hungry like a tiger. The fresh air had done him good. Not for once did he think of his grain commitments or whether prices had gone up or down. What did he care just then? He carried a stop, just in case. If the prices did decline as he expected, so much the better.

Jim was again in his trees. This time he looked over the branches to see if one or the other was interfering with more important branches. In that case he would do some "thinning." However, it was more the joy of looking at the swelling fruit, as small as they were. "Too bad," he mused, "that George could not see the trees in bloom, the solid mass of flowers all over." Any heart could feel the trend of Nature, how it produced beauty and food. His bees lived then in Paradise. The pastures had now become their gathering grounds. All sorts of flowers produced multicolored carpets there.

A good meal awaited the brothers who both came in at the same time. Smoked ham with potato salad and pickles supplied the table. Bread Pudding was the dessert.

Grete had fixed the table for George again the way he used to have it during the winter. Even the suitcase was in its proper place where he used to keep his paper file and the books. She laid out the charts for him, together with pencil and ruler, everything so that "His Grace" merely had to sit down and get going.

"Don't you make such a fuss of me, I just won't have that," said George when he saw the nice arrangement. "You have your own business to attend to and I have plenty of time for a few weeks," he added. Just the same he felt flattered.

George began to work now with those advances and declines of which he had taken notes from Mr Peeper. Of course, Mr Peeper used the combinations for all the stocks that were traded, the total of which ran to some 350 varieties. This gave him a big stumbling block when he tried it for wheat. One always had enough stocks that would show plus signs, also a certain number that would show minus signs after trading was over. With wheat, however, there was but one wheat, and three active options thereof. He had considered to use all the grains, oats, corn, rye together with wheat, possibly barley too, each in the three options. This would give him 15 changeable units. The test was to be made for about six months back to see what sort of a wavy line would result. The old newspaper file came in handy now. Of each day he had kept but the market page.

His first step was to copy the closing prices of each grain and of each option patiently on sheets, but after two hours' work he changed his mind about the procedure. "To arrive at any pattern would take weeks that way," he decided. "I will take wheat alone and one option only. When the option is about to expire I shall switch over into the next option. I shall only use the price differential from one day to the next and give each day its plus or minus sign, depending upon whether we advanced or declined." Part of the work he could use – the daily high price of one wheat option. After complete tabulation of the rest he produced a double column, from day to day, that showed how much was the advance and how much the decline. In order to make adding easier he used decimals instead of fractions, so that ⅛ would be marked as 12 or 13, ⅜ would be marked as 37 or 38, etc. Out of this he made two more columns, the one containing the total of three days taken from the "advances" column and the other containing the total from the "declines" column. Of this he used but two consecutive days.

George had patience. In less than one week a pattern appeared that looked similar to the picture seen from Peeper.

He began to check the days when the line had turned down to see whether grain would decline in harmony. He discovered soon that the line contained a lot of unnecessary kinks that would fool a trader into thinking the trend had changed. Yet the line would straighten out again and prices would continue mounting. The line would do the same while it moved down into the minus side.

"Man-made stuff," he said. "This product is in crude state and needs refining. Nature is hidden in it, I can see from the winding line. The kinks must be straightened out as much as possible before I can use this line. It needs different combinations. Whoever thought of such combinations first was a clever man who tried for rhythm. But I have to make out of a buggy one of those automobiles that come more and more in use."

While George worked on his problems on the farm, September wheat had taken a tumble to 1.02. Yesterday's reports showed it had broken the low level of April 20th. "Is this the beginning of the bear market?" said George. "Was the movement from April 20th to May 9th the last kick-up before a big slide is due? Mr Jupiter, please tell me of that!" He looked for the time when Saturn would be crossed again by Mercury. The chart showed July 5th. Mercury would hit 0° on June 30th. "Those days will become the critical days. But that's a long way off; for two weeks we decline already and after all, wheat is worth something," he mused. He looked at the chart into which he had drawn from the top of May 9th his 78° and 71° angle. The 71° angle was now definitely broken. It appeared to him as if prices tried now for the 78° angle. He decided to cover his shorts as soon as the 71° angle was crossed upwards again.

"Even though I may be late by one day in covering, I shall see in the morning paper and there is time enough to get in touch with Mr Mayer before the market opens. I will even 'double up,' which will make me long again." He was somewhat nervous all day but tried to hide it from Grete and Jim. A few times he was on the verge of going back to New York in case a sharp turn-about-face would occur. Yet his Jupiter told him there was no rush. He himself (Jupiter) had turned down prices, so why hurry and expect them to go the other way without the planets' assistance? Sepp came to his mind again. He also saw Mr Mayer, whose opinion he had never asked. Mayer had asked him twice to join his Golf Club where he used to enjoy a game twice a week. He had asked him to see a boxing fight. Once he even had tickets for Madison Square Garden. But George had to refuse that day because he had a test to make that evening which he considered of more importance. With Muller and Holten he went to see one a week later. It was plain that Mayer was fishing to find out where George obtained his dope when the others had been buying right and left right in front of him. Mayer had even repeated orders, reading slips aloud saying, "Is this correct, Mr Wind, buy 5 contracts WZ market?" and, in spite of these warnings, George would walk away from the grains to chat with Peeper of the stock crowd without giving wheat even a tumble as soon as he had sold out and shorted it. Mayer could make neither head nor tail of him. "What nerve of that up-stater" as he called him, when he spoke to some of his intimates while George was away. "What nerve that man Wollsten has is unbelievable. Things look attractive and he goes short! He'll burst one nice day, we'll live to see it. He is just the counter part of Sepp Muller, you may remember him." But George did not want to burst; he had come to New York to do business. He had come to stay.

During Saturday, May 28th wheat dropped 6¼ cents in spite of the short day. His option had declined to 96.

George Collides With Jim and Grete

On Sunday he went to the village Drugstore three blocks out of his way to buy a New York paper. When he looked at the quotations he hardly could believe it.

"That's 20 points profit I am in. What a drop in 3 weeks," he said as he walked back to the church where Grete and Jim waited for him. "Such speed cannot keep up for a long time. I believe I shall go back Decoration Day to be at the Office bright and early. No, I shall stay and phone Mayer to cover the shorts, at least I have clinched that profit and then . . ." he nearly knocked down Jim and Grete who were waiting at the corner. He had walked with eyes wide open but did not see them until he had the collision. "Where do you keep your eyes, in your pocket?" asked Jim. "You nearly knocked us over in broad daylight." "Excuse me both. I just did not see you," said George. "I was thinking of going back to New York because that wheat market dropped too much yesterday to be very healthy for the shorts and I am short too." "Whatever that means is no reason to walk all over us," said Jim.

All three were a little put out on account of that accident. George was sorry; Grete didn't mind it at all, but she had to take her husband's part. She also became somewhat quiet. In order to smooth out the situation, George invited them for a short trip to New York. He arranged it that Mr Schafer's man was going to take care of feeding the flock, the horse and Peter as well for a few days. One can invite brother and sister-in-law when six hundred dollars come flown in over night! "You both have been working hard and need a holiday," he told them. "Instead of cooking a meal we shall eat in the Dining Car," he continued. "Now you can laugh, because you have succeeded to smooth out matters and even take us along with you," said Jim. "I was just figuring what kind of a meal we shall have on the train," retorted George. "What's so funny about that? You are not going to feed us peanuts and cough drops on the way down? Otherwise you shall have here fried eggs morning. noon and night until you stop laughing. Don't forget, he who laughs last, laughs best." Jim was in a regular fighting mood.

George Takes Jim and Grete to New York

Grete had put the finishing touches to her household. A suitcase that contained everything for a two-day trip was ready. George had enough clothes and linen at home. His own toilet articles he had sneaked into Grete's suitcase while she turned her back. They caught the 11:17 just in time, changing at Poughkeepsie to the Montreal Limited going south. They had just made themselves comfortable when a boy passed through, calling "Last call for Lunch." A few minutes later they were seated at a table in the Diner. Jim and Grete gazed at the novelty of the thing. "I like that," said Grete, "don't you?" Grete was looking at her husband who glanced at George, expecting from him a come-back about what he had said of peanuts and cough drops. George, who quickly noticed it, said, "You'll see, the food is delicious." It was good. "It's seldom that two holidays come in succession, so we might just as well take advantage of them and I don't make six hundred dollars every day either. These are exceptions and we might just as well take them," said George.

He lodged them at the St. Andrews. That hotel was close by. He selected a nice room with all conveniences and a fine view over to the Jersey side. Grete was all eyes. What a difference between this place and their farm home! She admired the bell boys with their uniforms and shiny buttons; she was a little scared of the big lobby that appeared to her as if it were the entrance to a big castle of some duke or prince. Jim was similarly surprised. He recalled his Albergo Chiave d'Oro. That one had no carpets that made one feel as if walking on dough. They felt as if they were out of place, especially when they noticed people that sat around had been waiting and watching for them, at least it appeared to them that way. First Grete turned red, then white. Jim was glad when an elevator swallowed them, to be carried to some other unknown place. George, of course, enjoyed the scene. He had to get even with Jim.

Gradually their pulse became normal again. "I shall leave you both alone for about two hours. I will go to my hotel. In the meantime you can take a rest, and a nice hot bath. I'll show you the hot water. At seven I will be back and take you out for peanuts and cough drops," he added.

At his hotel he found Mr Holten sitting in an easy chair blowing rings with a Sunday Havana. "Will you join me for a small party in about two hours?" he asked him, patting him on the shoulder. "Since when are you throwing parties? What got into you, Mr Wollsten?" Holten asked as he blew a nice oblong one due to the patting that had coincided with his expulsive movement. "Jim and his wife are at the St. Andrews for a visit. I will take them back home on Monday noon." "Is that so?" said Holten. "Of course I will join you." "Meet me at 6:50. I will be seeing you then," said George and went up to his room.

George was all in. He had to lie down for a while to size up the situation about his wheat and its drop yesterday. "I just can't believe it." He got up, went down to the lobby and bought two other Sunday papers to see what quotations they contained. "Same thing," he said.

About an hour later George began to wash up, but had to stop suddenly. He began to search the telephone book for the number of Jim's hotel. "Give me 57212 please. Room 418 and keep on ringing it," he told the operator after he had the hotel connection. After a while he heard, "Jim Wollsten, yes." "Jim, this is George. Get me that toilet bag with the razor which I put into Grete's suitcase. I can't go out without combing my hair. I forgot to take it along. Take a cab, it is not far." "Grete thought there was a fire or something," said Jim on the phone. "I am soaking wet, had to jump out of the water for you. I will be down soon if I can find the bag."

Half an hour later Jim entered, all polished up. "You scared us for a while with your phone call. Here is your comb. I had to leave Grete all alone to worry that I find the way back and she's having the baby," he said. "I'd better go right back." "No, wait; we will call her on the telephone right now and tell her of your safe arrival." He called the number again. After a while a faint voice came saying, "Mrs Wollsten, who are you?" "Grete, hallo Grete, this is George. Jim has arrived and we will be back soon, don't you worry," he said.

Pretty soon we see the trio walk up Broadway to meet Grete. Holten remembered her, of course, from the day she had arrived, and was pleasantly surprised to hear her speak quite a bit of English. Occasionally a German word would be mixed in. "Glad to see you," he said, when they met in the lobby. "You have quickly become used to our country. Jim and George have told me all about your nice farm and about the apples and the chickens. We have decided to go to the Hippodrome after dinner," he added. "What home you say?" asked Grete. The little party had reached the dining room of the hotel where a good meal was waiting for them. Later on they took in a show at the Hippodrome, which ended the day perfectly.

After Grete and Jim had retired she said to him, "How true is the proverb 'the unexpected happens often'? Who would have thought this morning that we would be in New York at night and see a beautiful show besides? What will the morrow bring?"

On the way home George was thinking hard how to entertain them the next day. "I have it," he exclaimed, half asleep already. He got out of bed again, called 57212 again, Room 418. "As sure as we are in New York that's George," said Grete as she answered the ring. "That night owl don't know when it's time to sleep." "I'll meet you both at 7:30 all ready to go, that's all, good night," he said and hung up.

Jim and Grete happily awaited George at the appointed time. "We will have breakfast right here," said George. They coaxed a few waiters out of their folded arms – waiters who stood in corners awaiting their entrance to assign them a good table. One pulled out the chairs, another began to pour ice water, a third tendered the menus, a fourth with pencil and pad in hand seemed to wait impatiently for the order, sizing up the situation and combination of the early guests. He quickly noticed that one of the party was a man who knew his way around. The others seemed to be visitors from a small place – the hands told him that farming was their line. After the orders had been given, George asked them how they liked New York so far. He talked of everything except of the plans for to-day.

The Trip to Washington

Pretty soon we find them in a busy subway train whose cars carried signs "Brooklyn." They left the train at Pennsylvania Station. After walking through a maze of underground passages they reached the main station which had opened but a few years ago. "What do you want with us at this station?" said Jim. "We take a run down to Washington," said George. "We have to look over that city so that we know where those ephemerides have come from. Besides, you have seen enough of New York and we never have been there." For a long time he had in mind to see Washington for once but something always came up to prevent the trip. Besides, Grete and Jim would have something to remember for a long time. The idea had come to him just as he tried to fall asleep last night.

George bought three return tickets for Washington. The Southern Limited was just about ready to leave. In four hours the Capitol was reached. It gave them about six hours to enjoy the sights. George, the snooper, was able to find the Capitol Building without asking directions. They went to see many other interesting places in the city. Someone pointed out the Government Printing Offices, a huge building in which the "Books of Gold" had been printed. They even discovered the White House.

"Mr Schafer will be surprised when he gets from us a card mailed from Washington," said Grete as they were on the way back to New York.

As the train approached the city the conversation turned to things of to-morrow. The holidays had come to an end.

George had figured he would take Jim down with him to the Broker's Office to show him the inside of the place where he traded. He intended to watch wheat and make a decision during the first 15 minutes of trading. Grete was to take things easy. Jim liked the plan. They had talked about the apple crop, about bees, and chickens, also about the wheat, oat and rye crops of the mid-West. George had not bothered much with any grain except wheat. He had kept charts of each.

However, he had seen that they had somewhat different movements than wheat which showed in the charts. "Oats might take a sharp drop while wheat keeps up its strength or declines but a cent," he remarked. "I can't have too many irons in the fire, one is enough," he said.

The train pulled back into Penn Station. Soon we see them in the subway. Compared to the morning the cars were loaded now to capacity. "Theatergoers," said George at Times Square, when the train had to accept another load of mankind. They had to stand in the car, changing weight from one leg to the other, holding on to straps from a bar above them, surrounded by odors of human flesh. Big fans on the ceiling tried to blow them out through small openings near the ceiling. George estimated that a car carried about 200 people on the inside, with some 25 standing on each outside platform. He had counted ten cars as the train had pulled into the station. As they left the subway George said to Jim, "Your whole population of Upper Red Hook would disappear in one of those trains just like Jonah in the whale."

George and Jim Visit the Broker's Office

Shortly before ten o'clock Jim and George entered the Broker's Office. Mayer had missed George. He had called the hotel twice to report of the big break in wheat on Saturday, but "Mr Wollsten is not in" was the answer. He just could not understand how anyone can stay away from the tape when profits accrue at such terrific speeds. He had even inquired of the order clerk whether or not Mr Wollsten had placed some kind of an order directly. This was a few minutes ago. "Did that fellow have an accident somewhere?" he asked the clerk. Mayer was all upset about George and his twenty points' profit. Two thousand dollars ahead and the fellow don't even bother about it was beyond his capacity.

Mayer's sharp eyes had espied George as he entered when only the nose was showing as yet. "He brings another fellow now, I wonder who he could be," he thought. By that time both had walked down, passing the high tribunals at their right, Jim was somewhat confused like any stranger that comes for the first time to such a place. He walked close behind George. "This is my brother, Mr Jim Wollsten," said George to Mr Mayer to introduce him. I am going to show him 'your' place." Mayer was quite flattered. Interiorly he thought, "Not a bad fellow, he has much respect for me; I like him." "Mr Wollsten," he began, "wheat has dropped to 94 and I did not know where to lay my hands on you. Don't you remember that early this month they talked of an unusually dry summer and now they talk of a bumper crop. That's just what caused the drop." "That's interesting," answered George. "How fast things can change, don't they?" Suspicious about that answer, Mayer could not make out whether George was kidding or whether he meant just what he said. However, he took advantage of the time, saying, 'Stocks are down again, Steel was off half a point at the opening. This won't help wheat very much." As he thought fast like all customers' men do, he remembered that George was short and not long like the others. He added, "Cut your losses short, but let your profits run, that's the way we say in Wall Street." All the while he watched Jim, who wheeled his hat between the fingers.

"Are you trading up in Albany, Mr Wollsten?" he suddenly came out, figuring there might be a chance to get another account. "No, I grow apples: I won't have anything to do with them stars no . . ." George turned red, saying immediately to Jim, "Look, these things here bring out the sales of all stocks as soon as they are consummated," pointing at the tickers but thinking at the same time, "Darn fool, what a mistake did I make to take you along."

However, the damage was done. He knew so now. Mr Mayer, who always took George as an enigma, unsolvable, had now heard something that gave him a clue as to the source of George's wisdom. He came right out saying, "I always had a hunch that you are a clever astrologer, Mr Wollsten." "Oh yeah?" said George. In order to change the subject he said, "I am going to watch this market for a few minutes, then we shall go again." They sat down, chatting about unimportant things; George tasted gall in his throat, so mad he was. But it lasted only a few minutes. He himself thought fast. Jim had noticed nothing out of the ordinary.

George knew what to do. As fast as his spirit had dropped as fast did it come back. In fact he laughed a few times when his brother asked some questions.

WU opened off a cent. A few sales came at this price, then it dropped another half a cent. Suddenly George called: "Mr Mayer, buy me 10M September wheat at the market." Mayer had been awaiting this order for quite a while and placed it immediately through the order window. George waited quietly to find out the price at which he covered it. It was unfortunate that Jim had popped out about the stars. He was a farmer but not a trader. This man Mayer does not like it too well because I do not ask him any questions. I have to work alone and not do a lot of chatting about the stars. Therefore I better quit this place and change brokers. It is not Mayer's fault, but my own to have taken Jim along, but sometimes innocent people have to suffer for others' mistakes."

"92¼, Mr Wollsten," said Mayer, handing him a slip. "Fine," said George. "By the way, will you tell them to close my account and let me have a check for to-morrow or the next day? I am going upstate," he continued. Mr Mayer grew pale. He had done very little business of late since markets had been sagging, and grains had dropped too. He could ill afford to lose a customer. Rapidly the events of the last half hour passed through Mayer's mind. He knew it. It was on account of those evil stars. He should have shut up and acted as if he had not heard the words about the stars. "But, Mr Wollsten you do very well in your trading, what makes you stop so suddenly?" was all he could bring forth. He worked on a "long shot," saying, "Mr Wollsten, let's go out for a moment, I want to tell you something." He took George by the arm. George told Jim to wait a while. Mayer brought George out to a corner of the big vestibule. Nobody was around. "I know why you go to some other broker and not upstate. Your brother has said something or was going to which you wanted to keep a secret. I will never tell anybody nor make any remark whatever. I will try to get your orders filled as fast as possible. I believe you have noticed it. Please stay.

You know that time when Sepp Muller sold out I was just about laid off through no fault of my own. I have a feeling that we go into a bear market." He thought very fast to make sure he would not spoil the "build-up" he had made by talking himself out of it again, so he added: "I really don't know. The market can go either way." "Alright," said George. "You have heard nothing, seen nothing and you let it be that way. I will stay with you. Cancel the order." Satisfied both ways, they marched back into the trading room and Mayer took to his dais from which he could overlook his realm. He had acted just on time, fast, furious, and had won. George took his seat on the "witness chair" next to the judge.

He was telling Mr Mayer that he intended to go up-state in a few minutes to take a rest for a week or ten days. "Take this order down: Buy open stop 15M September wheat at 94." He intended to buy wheat only when and if the price had reached 94. On the tape it was still selling at 92½ or well below the price at which he had entered the order. He had good reasons for such decision. "I may phone or wire you in case I decide to have this changed," he added. Mr Mayer made out the order and brought it to the window. His pep was well exhausted from the last hour's events. He did not even want to know when George would come back, what he would do up there – nothing. All he could bring out was that he hoped he would have a nice time and would enjoy himself while away.

As soon as George and Jim had vanished into the outer rooms Mayer felt relieved. The customer's man at the adjoining desk had noticed something had gone amiss with Mayer's customer whom he had known but slightly. It happened occasionally that arguments would arise because some customer's man would make "cuckoo eyes" at another's customer, that they talked to him without being asked first by him. It was petty jealousy. They were somewhat afraid of each other. One might take a position with some other broker and it was possible that he might drag the other's customer along with him.

"What happened to your man?" he would say to find out if Mayer had lost a customer. "Wasn't he satisfied with the price?" Mayer, happy, answered him, "He will be my star customer after a while, you shall see. But, you leave your paws off him if you know what's good for you," he added. "Don't you snoop around and watch my business! Attend to your own!" There were no partitions between one desk and the next, but he who knows the "inside" also knows that an invisible Chinese Wall runs through. Borrowing a witness chair from the neighbor to seat a customer might cause trouble for a week, although he had no earthly use for it at the time. One was supposed to bring one up from the lower level.

Mayer began to call various customers by telephone now to tell them about the market's doings. He took a cue from George's action that a low level was imminent, otherwise that fox who used stars would not have covered his shorts. He himself had tried a little about astrology a few years ago when he had some customers that always spoke to him about the stars. However, he had also found out that when big moves came the star operators did not fare any better than the regular run and disappeared with them in good time. For a long time he had discounted those things, but here comes that fox and seemingly makes them work. He remembered very well that only a few months ago he had started with 5,000 bushels and here he gives me an order for 15,000 already. His account could stand eight or even nine contracts, that is 40,000 bushels or so, if he felt like buying that many. "Wollsten might be an exception," he thought.

"That's a mad house," said Jim as they emerged from the place. "How can you stand it in there, that ticking, talking and everything? I am glad I don't have to make my living that way. You can have all of it. A day or two in the city is enough for me for a long time. The thought bothers me that something may go haywire at home, which is a thing you seemingly can't understand. I shall be happy to get home again. We will leave this afternoon, at least

Grete and myself will, in case you have some more places to go to," he added. "No, that's all. I will come along with you for a few weeks. I have been working quite a bit," said George. Jim looked at him as if he wanted to say "you and your work." But he kept quiet not to offend his brother who after all had shown them a good time.

When they reached the hotel Grete was ready to join them. After a final meal they selected the 4:20 to bring them home.

In a month or so it would have been too late for Grete to undertake such a strenuous trip. For weeks the conversation centered on the trip to New York and Washington.

Improvements Made on "Jiggle Line"

George's vacation was actually the beginning of serious work and study. The jiggly line bothered him. "How can I straighten that line so that it does not have so many kinks? I shall try some other combinations such as four units on one side and two units on the other, or I can try five units on one side and three on the other. It may give better results." He worked the period from January to May again.

He began to use the following combination: On the advance side he first used four units, carried them out into the next column and out of this second column he again made a new unit. using three units to obtain a third total which he placed into the third column. On the declining side he used three units to obtain a total for a second column and repeated it into a third column.

On the advance side he first used four units. On the declining side he used three units.

A little sketch will illustrate this better than words can convey.

Date		Advances	Wheat 1910
April	20	0	no advance between dates
	21	187	advanced 1⅞ points
	22	112	advanced 1⅛ points
	23	75	advanced ¾ points
	25	75	advanced ¾ points
	26	0	no advance
	27	0	no advance
	28	37	advanced ⅜ points
	29	12	advanced ⅛ points
	30	50	advanced ½ points

The actual Table for the advancing side looked as follows for the period of April 20th to April 30th:

Date		Advances	4 Units	3 Units
April	20	0		
	21	187		
	22	112		
	23	75	375	
	25	75	450	
	26	0	262	1087
	27	0	150	862
	28	37	187	600
	29	12	50	387
	30	50	100	337

First he added the total of advances from April 20th, 21st, 22nd and 23rd, that is four consecutive values which had given him a value of 375. This value placed over into the column marked "4 Units." We note that for April 20th he had placed a 0, because there had been no advance from the preceding day; in fact, the market had declined on April 20th. However, on April 21st, 22nd and 23rd the highs of each of these days had improved, which made him enter the values 187, 112 and 75 for those days. He used points instead of eighths to make figuring easier.

The next addition computation included April 21st, 22nd, 23rd and 25th. He had dropped the value that was produced on April 20th. For the 24th he had no value. It was a Sunday. The new value was 450, composed of 187, 112, 75 and once more 75. This 450 he placed on the line of April 25th. To obtain the next value he used April 22nd, 23rd, 25th and 26th, which showed 112, 75, 75 and 0 because on April 26th there was no advance. He had to omit the number 187 of April 21st, else he would have used 5 units instead of 4. The new value was 262, which he placed on the line of April 26th next column to the 0. This way he carried out the series carefully.

For the second row, marked "3 Units," he now began to make the totals that originated out of the column marked "4 Units," the same way as he had done before, but used 3 units only and not 4 units. Thus, for April 26th he had an entry in the "3" Column amounting to 1087 which was produced as follows: It contained first all the values that were produced since April 20th and that had been carried in units of fours into the first column as 375, 450 and 262. The three had then been added also and carried as a unit into the second column as 1087. On April 27th he had to enter number 862 into the 2nd column, being the addition of 450, 262 and 150 of column marked "4 Units."

This was done for all the months. The same way he proceeded with the declines of the advancing side. At present he produced a snake line that had to do only with the highs of each trading day. The lows of each day had been ignored just then, but later he used the same rules to make one for the lows.

In case wheat had made higher one day compared to the previous day, he had to mark 0 in the column because in such case there had been no decline. The pattern for the decline column looked as follows:

Date		Declines	
April	20	137	declined 1⅜ points
	21	0	no decline
	22	0	no decline
	23	0	no decline
	25	0	no decline
	26	63	declined ⅝ points
	27	225	declined 2¼ points

For the operation of the declining side he used combinations of 3 units for the first column and 2 units for the second column. The pattern looked then as follows:

Date		Declines	3 Units	2 Units
April	20	137		
	21	0		
	22	0	137	
	23	0	0	137
	25	0	0	0
	26	63	63	63
	27	225	225	288

The advancing side was then combined with the declining side and the daily difference calculated by taking for each day the final value. For example on April 26th his number for plotting was 1025 which represented the difference of:

3 units value of advances	1087
less 2 units value of declined	63
	1024

Since quarters do not end in 24 nor halves in 49 or 51, he had to call the value 1025.

It was tedious, painstaking work to compute 5 months of figures that had to be exact and not approximate.

The line improved with the new method. It had not quite as

many kinks as were found in the original line, yet it was fooling in places.

In that week he tried some other combinations that promised still better results.

In the meantime grains had drifted still somewhat lower and stopped. Prices idled around until the middle of June.

George had laid his 6-inch ellipse in such a way that its axis ran over the 71° angle downwards. The upper end of the ellipse had been placed into the top of May 9th. He had noticed the lower end of the ellipse fell on June 30th. This was the day when Mercury would reach 0°.

He saw much more.

He noticed that the 78° angle in connection with the ellipse thus laid touched the periphery of the ellipse on June 7th, 1910 and to his astonishment it was there when the "rally top" was made which had begun on June 4th. Not only was this very important to him, but, "Grete! Look!" – she happened to be in the house sewing. She had to look at the high of June 7th; she had to imagine that on June 4th was the hinge of the open door of her chicken coop that was closed every night.

"Now watch," said George. "This uptrend from June 4th to June 7th is your chicken coop door. There is the hinge," he said, pointing to June 4th. "Do you see the way the ellipse lies? This chicken coop door was supposed to be closed so that weasels cannot enter, but someone opened it. Had it been closed, it would have just touched the intersection of the 78° angle as well as the periphery of the ellipse.*

"The rally was 3¼ points and the intersection of the ellipse with the 78° angle is exactly 3¼ points below the hinge's place of June

*There is an unusual technique and methodology in this illustration of the weasels and the chicken coop. In the typical great master's style, the author gives a starting point, then leaves it up to the market student to puzzle over it and evolve it from there.

4th. Some weasel will get away with the chickens, because it is open! Understand that, Grete?" he asked her. "Perfectly, perfectly, don't I open and close that chicken coop every day? You are not trying to teach me anything about opening and closing my chicken coop?" George had not even heard what she had said, else he might have come back with some of his nasty retributions. "The real low was on June 7th in spite of the fact that the chart shows a low on the 4th and another low on the 13th. That is what fools traders. What time is it, Grete?" "We will eat in ten minutes, call Jim. He is in the barn," she answered. "Must be near seven," he muttered as he walked over to call Jim. "Wow, that's a find. I will call Mayer tomorrow to buy at the market instead of waiting for the 71° angle to be crossed. That angle will be crossed when the weasels come," he said.

George worked once more on his 43-32 combination. He had noticed that the line had worked itself deeply down into the minus side, way below the zero centre line, but on June 10th it had turned around for the first time. "That's another confirmation that the trend is due to change. It just tells you to buy. I will call at ten. No, I better go down myself and take the first train in the morning. I have several other things to attend to besides," he said.

That's another confirmation that the trend is due to change. It just tells you to buy.

Plans to Build and Hire Help on Farm

At the dinner table he informed Jim and Grete of his intentions to go back to New York, saying that he was not good for anything on the farm as it was. He told them he would send a man to help around, for Grete's sake. Jim really needed help. Grete had to reduce her activities. The chicks were growing into chickens by the hour. It took time to feed the flock, to keep everything in clean condition. Jim could see the point and was just about ready to debate on this subject with George. George suggested yet that he remove a few apple trees near Schafer's line that had not done so well last year and again this year they were full of leaves but lacked fruit. They had noticed rosin came out of these trees just above the ground. "Build a little house in their place so that the helper will have sleeping quarters. Order lumber tomorrow and get carpenters from the mill. Let them build. I will send you $1000 as soon as I am back in town to start it. Many people want work. I may be able to find a suitable man for you. I will send up a new dress or two for you, Grete, that will again make you a perfect 36." "You seem to know too much about married life; where did you grow all that knowledge?" retorted Grete. "In those Washington books, I presume. You haven't reduced yourself while up here! Look at the front window," she added.

George had noticed himself that the fresh country air, the substantial food, the twelve hours daily at his work table had increased his waistline considerably during the four weeks he had now been on the farm. He thought he would work it off in town in a short time. "I will leave on the first train tomorrow; don't forget to call me," he told them before they retired for the night.

George Back in New York Buys Wheat at 90¼

"Back again, Mr Wollsten," said Mr Mayer when George had come to the broker at 10:15. "Glad to see you back in the saddle. Your September wheat has not gone up to 94 as yet, so you still are on the side lines," he said. "Cancel that order and make it read 'at market'," he said. Peeper had come down from the stocks to greet him, asking where he had kept himself during this hot spell. "I was up state but it was pretty hot there too. Where could a fellow go during the summer to be cooler?" he asked him. "90¼ bought," called Mayer to interrupt the conversation. Such "cutting-in" was natural at the broker, since everyone who had orders to be filled was anxious to learn the price obtained. George was satisfied with the price and felt that the week had started nicely. The interruption suited Mr Peeper well. It gave him a chance to think about a cooler place to answer George's question. "Have you ever been at Atlantic City? They have cool breezes there and a broker's office, too, else, without a broker go up in the Maine woods, around Bangor. There are places out West, but, that's too far away. It would take a week to get there." "Where would that be?" asked George. "Somewhere near San Francisco, in California, I heard it was nice and cool during the summer all along the Coast, a little windy, also foggy at times, they say. I have never been there. Eardley told me only a few days ago. He lived there for many years," he replied. "You mean where they had the big fire a few years ago?" said George. "Yes, Eardley was right in that city then; that's why he left. He is from California, but I have forgotten the place. You know him, don't you? the fellow that plays those Puts and Calls," said Peeper. "What do you mean by 'Puts and Calls'?" George asked. "Stop kidding," said Peeper, "you as market operator would not know what they are!" "You have shown me a few things on the market already; why do you doubt me when I say I don't know? Is it to my advantage to pretend to know when in fact I know very little and admit it? We can't all be born professors, else there would be no pupils to be fed knowledge to," he added. Peeper did not know exactly himself what they were, but he knew that much: they were dangerous. They gave the buyer certain rights to buy or sell stocks within a certain time limit. Points were involved too. An authority on technical parts of markets, Mr Mayer had to be consulted by both. "Wollsten would like to know what 'Puts and Calls' are," said Peeper. To keep both in the dark and in suspense he told them, "That's the very same thing as 'bids and offers' in grains." "Thanks, professor," said George jokingly. "Now explain them to us at the same time, since we are ignorant of them too." "You will pardon me for a while," said Mayer, a little nervous, "I will be back as soon as I can, but right now I have to watch several margin calls that expire by eleven . . ." (he whispered in George's ear) and aloud, "if you really are in earnest." George really had never heard of any of these four things, whatever they might be or mean. Peeper became engulfed again in the tapes action while George thought, "There is plenty to learn about trading yet, about simple matters that need no Almanacs or charts . . ."

Puts and Calls; Bids and Offers

Mayer was now ready to come back to explain, but George came to him saying, "You had booklets of Stock abbreviations, don't you have any about those new things?" Mayer said he had one somewhere. He began to remove from his lower left drawer papers, charts, newspaper clippings, a tooth brush, two pipes and many other things. It gave him a chance to dispose of these things in the waste basket. "Put and Call Brokers publish those booklets which explain all about trading in them," be muttered a few times, "but I can't find the one I have." Suddenly he had a bright idea. He called a Put and Call Broker saying, "Send a boy with two booklets, I have a customer for Puts and Calls." Inside of ten minutes he had not only the booklet for Puts and Calls, but also one about Bids and Offers, since George told Mayer right there and then to call a Bid and Offer Broker to send booklets also. Each of the booklets was accompanied by extra sheets, which contained quotations for the week. The Put and Call sheet listed about 20 stocks. The first stock on the list was Baltimore and Ohio. It said: 10 points up for Calls, 8 points down for Puts, 30 days.

This meant, "During a period of 30 days beginning with today the buyer obtains the right to call 100 shares provided the stock advanced during the 30 days 10 points or more." It had to advance nearly 12 points, however, to come out even because there was a cost of $137.50 per 100 shares, besides the broker's commission for buying them in the open market.

For the declining side the matter was just in reverse. The market for B & O would have to decline at least 10 points before any profit would come forth for the taker of a Put. In normal markets they are difficult to profit by. If one knew, however, when a big rise was due or a big drop, then a 30 days' Call or Put, as the case might be, could produce very big profits. They also had "straddles" quoted, which operated on both sides. They did cost a little more but gave the buyer a chance for up or down in one paper.

Bids and Offers operated similarly, but they were used for grains only. They had 1 day bids or offers, 1 week's or 1 month's. In Puts and Calls they had 7 days', 30 days', 60 days' and even 90 days' time limits with different charges and different point quotations for each unit.

Mayer explained to George that in case he wanted any momentary quotes on a certain stock for a Put or a Call he would call his friend, W. P. Price, who specializes in Puts and Calls. "He might even shave off a point," he said, "because what he wants and what we bid is different. One has to bargain things with them the same way as in regular trading. And, we might have him use the next sale to write his paper, the one that comes after the deal is agreed." "No, thanks, I want to go to a cool place and ask Peeper about one. What brought us to speak about Puts and Calls I don't remember anymore."

A look on the Board showed that WU had advanced half a point by that time. George thought it a good omen. During April he had been nipped a few times for a point or two, but had noticed that as soon as he had made a commitment and the market went immediately against him – that was bad. On the other hand, he had noticed that as soon as the first few sales went with his commitment, he was able to close the deal with a profit.

The booklets on Puts and Calls, and on Bids and Offers he took home for his file, marked "Future Reference."

George Buys a Stamp Collection

On the way home George walked for once through Nassau Street to explore lower Manhattan. On the way he gradually became "stamp-conscious" again. It happened that in this old narrow street were dozens of postage stamp stores which sold stamps to collectors. Force of habit to investigate made him look in the windows at displays; gradually a spirit got hold of him that made him go into a store. He merely wanted to "look," possibly buy a few to just play around with his old hobby for recreation's sake. As it happened, he walked out with a collection containing some 6000 various stamps and a catalogue that showed the prices. Besides he had bought hinges, tweezers and a magnifying glass to scrutinize those little labels. A watermark detector and perforation gauge he did not forget. He had also bought a shoe box full of mixed stamps, which some office boy had brought in. For the box he paid but three dollars. With its contents he expected to have more fun than even with the collection. He used to collect stamps as a youngster. With them he traveled all over the globe. He had the Liberian Elephant, the Australian Ostrich, the Venezuelan Columbus stamp among his treasures.

Four days he was lost to the world. Only hunger made him leave the stamps for a while. Even wheat was neglected; He did not care whether it went down or up. But, to find in the shoe box a penny stamp that was not as yet in his collection, that was important! Mayer had to call him twice a day to give him at least some prices.

A few minutes ago he had called him excitedly stating that wheat was up to 97 already for September option, and adding that July option was even stronger. "OK with me, keep pushing, thanks just the same," said George. He stopped for a while to get back his senses, because, he said, "Am I a stamp fiend or a grain trader?"

Like one who comes out of a daze, he remembered that he had to watch Mercury when it was due to cross the 0° point. He was even behind with his chart entries. He had to catch up figuring his 43–32 line whose entries had stopped the day he had left Upper Red Hook. He had not written to the folks either. "They know weeds keep growing," he said, "but I better write." This is what he wrote: "Dear Grete & Jim: Am collecting stamps now; will write later: also will look for the boy soon. Sincerely, George."

"There he goes," said Grete, "he starts with some other foolish thing now, collecting postage stamps. Who ever heard of that? And here he adds 'Save all the stamps of the envelopes that come but leave the teeth on them.'" Many people collect stamps, others collect coins, minerals, match boxes, the same way as we collect eggs and apples pretty soon," said Jim.

The letter made George think about the farm hand. During the evening he spoke to Mr Holten about finding a suitable man. A few days later Holten introduced a couple to him, Robert and Paula, whom he thought would be able to fill the place. George explained them their duties, told them they would receive $40.00 a month and found. Robert was to help the brother, Paula was to assist in the kitchen and tend to the flock of chickens. "If after a while you can find something better, go to it," said George. Overjoyed at finding a job, the newly landed couple agreed to accept, Robert told George that they had brought along their own bedding. also a commode that had been in the family for nearly two hundred years and came filled with useful things.

"We can go up right now together," said George. "To-morrow is Sunday. We can catch the 4:20 if we hurry." Holten was happy that he had given someone a start again.

No doubt other representatives of that philanthropic society acted in a similar way with Dutchmen, Poles, Russians or Greeks, working up connections with business men, farmers, etc., who were willing to take a chance with immigrants to give them a start. They had to become absorbed somehow and somewhere, which the general public never knew anything of.

In the hurry to catch the train George even forgot to lock the door, but told Holten in the lobby to take care of that. They took a cab and caught their train just on time. About 9 o'clock in the evening they reached their destination. Grete and Jim were just about ready to turn in. It was getting dark when the trio walked up to the house. "Do you see what I see?" asked Grete as she looked out of the window to have a last look if everything was in order outside. "One of those squirrels again knocking off our apples?" he said. "No, guess again!" By this time he saw George. "That's him all over," he said to Grete as he walked to the door. "It's a couple for us," said Grete.

Somehow it was arranged that all could find sleeping accommodation as the lights went out near midnight.

The next day, after church, George went thoroughly into details about the way Jim should proceed with his farm. He felt that his own work was getting crowded. He told him to train the couple carefully so that they would have assistants for a long time. He spoke about the new house – that he should make it larger and more comfortable and use it for themselves, and leave the new couple in the old house. "About farming, that's your business. I tried to steer you in the right commercial way of conducting it. From now on I won't butt into your affairs anymore. Only if you should need money for expansion, tell me. If I have it, it's yours," he added.

After a pleasant afternoon he left again for New York, wishing the new people a good beginning.

Back in New York that night, he again went at his stamps, pasted and transferred until daylight. He had not thought of sleep. Those labels had such magnetic forces in them that he just could not keep away. Each stamp that was pasted was checked off in the catalogue so that he would know just what he had. Some stamps were printed on watermarked paper; the same kind might be without a watermark. There were stamps on woven paper, ribbed, thin, granite, laid paper, etc. Some stamps with certain perforations commanded much higher prices than with other perforations. Color differentials were important. "There is a lot to learn about stamps," he said, "but I have to stop for a day." It was five o'clock.

About eleven Mr Mayer called, "Mr Wollsten, wheat just crossed the buck, now an eighth, a quarter." George rubbed his eyes as he listened. "Say that again, I didn't hear right," he said.

"Your September wheat is right now at 1.00¼," came Mayer. "Sell all of mine at the market," said George. "Okey-doke," retorted Mayer and hung up.

After George got dressed to resume his stamp session Mr Mayer was back on the phone. "Sold 15M at 1.00⅛, Mr Wollsten," he said. "Alright, I shall see you to-morrow," was George's answer.

"That's about $1,500 – in two weeks," George figured in his mind. "Those Swedes used to have nice stamps when they first issued them," he continued, admiring them in his album. He jumped from Sweden to Zanzibar, but had no stamps thereof, so retraced and landed in India, of which he had a large assortment, mostly with the head of Queen Victoria.

We must note that George was of a type that could jump from one subject to another without much difficulty. While he pasted stamps or tested watermarks and perforations he thought up ideas how to straighten the line into better shape so that it would kick over a day before the change of trend would come, both at a low as well as at a high. He knew the combination which he used was not quite right. He had not counted how many hours were spent to straighten the line so far, but it had become straighter. The original crude line of Mr Peeper was not even recognizable anymore. He did not even remember how his first notes read. George had another ability. He could forget quickly anything that was unimportant or burdensome. Rotolo's ideas he had never put to test as yet, because it would require his presence at the Board to keep a tab on each fluctuation. He felt he could make money faster especially if he would apply ellipses with such plottings, but he said, "No use getting rich too fast. If I use the 71° angle and the 78° angle also with such a sale to sale chart, I may get things down too fine and might mistake a few grass blades for a church steeple. I would be jumping around like a chicken without a head. I'd better leave well enough alone, for right now," he added.

Survey of Situation

The 30th of June had been uppermost in his mind. It was the main reason why he sold out. He had made $3,000 in such a short time that he felt it was time to survey the situation to see what he had achieved before looking for additional profits.

His first major discovery was Jupiter, Saturn and Mercury. Of next importance he considered the ellipses in combination with the planets' crossing by fitting their setting into such crossings. He could not do without the 71° and 78° angle. The next important help was in the jiggle line of advances and declines in combination.

His first major discovery was Jupiter, Saturn and Mercury. Of next importance he considered the ellipses.

"All these things can be used also for stocks," he said, "in case I wanted to trade stocks for a change, or cotton or some other commodity."

Rotolo's idea did not leave him. He thought it needed some sort of a change, the same as was the case with Peeper's.

The 10 Kopec Stamp – Discovery of "Polish Ellipse"

George was just about ready to paste the 10 kopec stamp of Poland into his collection. It was the only stamp that country ever had issued. "A page with just one stamp! Probably they did not write very much," he said and kept thinking of Rotolo.

"I think I will go the other way. Instead of plotting sale by sale, I will plot the bigger swings, four points or more in extent, but plot them in time proportions on a very small scale. I shall use one point for each little line on my chart and as to time I shall call one square across one month." This he did.

The pattern produced is shown as an insert at the end of the book, giving the wheat chart of 1910–1911.

In 10 minutes he had the picture in miniature properly proportioned and usable. The ellipse could not be used. However, he soon invented something new that would be useful. He put on his thinking cap, and just for fun began to measure with his 6" ellipse the size of the 10 kopec stamp for height and width. He did so with the center of the ellipse. He found that the height of the Polish 10 kopec stamp was as wide as ½ of the ½ of his axis, while the width measured exactly ¾ of that ½. Why did they decide to make that lonely stamp just ½ as tall as ½ of my minor axis and why ¾ as wide as this half of the ½ of the minor axis?

This is what he did then: He divided the half minor axis of the 6″ ellipse into four parts and drew lines through the points. He drew them parallel to the major axis, but omitted the first quarter line next to the centre axis for certain reasons. He merely made a small mark where its beginning should be.

The exact size and construction of this small gadget is shown (the Polish Ellipse).

The exact size and construction of this small gadget is shown in Figure VI.2. (the Polish Ellipse).

This was the rule he formulated for himself: At a major low set low point (marked A) of this "Quarter Ellipse" at the low point straight up, curve to the right. As we move up, watch for reactions amounting to 4 points or more. If and when one such reaction occurs, then move the gadget away from the low and set it into the reaction low place with the middle line, marked B straight up. On the following reaction of 4 points or over shift the gadget again and set the ¾ line to the new location low. This point is marked C. Set it always straight up, never sidewise or at an angle. Now: whenever the ellipse is broken by the performance of wheat, then the trend changes completely.

Application of "Polish Ellipse"

As soon as the trend did change, Aladdin changed his lamp. In A Thousand and One Nights the story says that Aladdin's palace had been moved from China to Africa. In this case the Polish Ellipse is now set on top, pointing downwards and the performance repeated the down way, shifting it whenever a 4-point move or

FIGURE VI.2
The "Polish Ellipse"

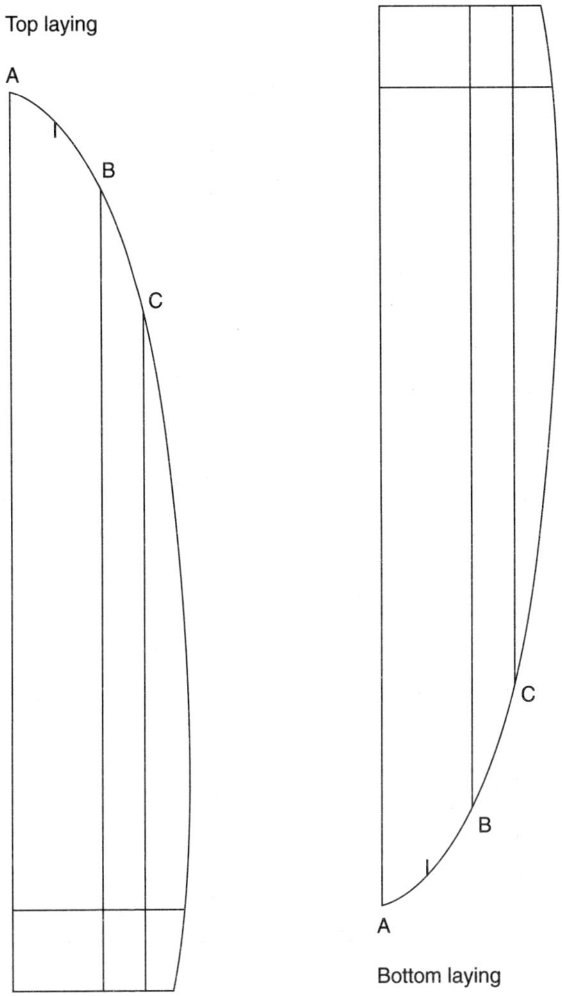

more happens in form of a rally, until the width of the ellipse is completely passed through.

In this case the Polish Ellipse is now set on top, pointing downwards.

Checking past performances, he noticed that extreme moves within one such "Quarter Ellipse" could amount to as much as the length of it. He had noticed this situation particularly during the Philippines War of 1899.

He demonstrated for himself the action and setting of this new invention for the period of April to the present time.

George set the low point of the "Polish Ellipse" into his miniature chart on April 20th when it had made 1.03, after the reaction from April 25th to 29th he had to shift it so that point B was the guide. The next shift had to happen when a 5-point reaction set in on May 9th. This time the "Polish Ellipse" was set to the new place of May 11th with point marked C at this low.

He had noticed how the price had crept up inside of the ellipse curve to near the old top of May 9th, but then it fell out of the narrow space. "So that," he said, "I should have sold more as we declined and nothing would have had to be feared, since a brand new move had begun that belonged to a new 'Polish Ellipse.' Here I have to set the ellipse downward and consider the May 9th top as the first place, the May 13th top as the second place to shift to point B whose line goes to that top. Point C will have to be set into the May 25th top, even though wheat rallied but 3¾ points, but I have to use my judgment too and not just cold inflexible rules . . . This procedure would have made me cover and buy wheat around 93 in June, as soon as the line of the 'Polish Ellipse' was broken upwards."

(The same way he would have proceeded with his operations in the subsequent upswing which, if he had followed that rule to the dot, would have taken him out of long positions and caused him to go short around 1.07 by July 21st or 22nd, 1910.)

"Now, into the album with you, you good for nothing," he said, "you are damaged, two perforations are missing on you, and besides, at the catalogue cost price of $5.00 you should look better.

"When Mercury comes to 0° I shall leave for San Francisco to see something of the West. I don't even know where they grow wheat – before they take the harvest home," he continued, switching into an entirely different line of thought all of a sudden. After I once see the Pit at Chicago, I shall continue until the train stops on the Pacific Coast."

George withdrew some money from the broker's account. Mr Mayer had told him he should use either direct or give-up orders through another broker. "Any broker will execute your order if you state that your account is with us," said Mayer.

A day or two went by to purchase the necessary equipment for the trip. One of the new-fangled wardrobe trunks had long been on his "want list." It was the first article be bought. Two summer suits, linen, fancy shoes, hiking boots and even a swimming suit together with other articles, he purchased. He had to call Sepp Muller to cancel the fishing trip that had been arranged for the 4th of July. His stamp collection including the shoe box with stamps, the catalogue and other paraphernalia went into the wardrobe trunk, which he had shipped on the ticket. All that he carried was a suitcase and an overnight bag. He said good-bye to Mr Holten who was greatly surprised to see him leave so suddenly for the other side of the country.

Off to the Pit at Chicago

The 4:20 carried him off towards Chicago. The train did not stop at Upper Red Hook, since it was but a small place. He used a sleeper this time, a novelty which he enjoyed greatly. The seats were more comfortable; small tables had been supplied which allowed him to enter his charts. Quotations he had from the "Evening Mail" of which he was able to obtain a copy before his departure. He began to read the newspaper to pass the time, looking once in a while at the scenery that passed. He had dinner. When he came back he found his bed all made ready by a porter. George retired early; he needed some extra sleep. The stamps and the "Polish Ellipse" had upset him a little, not to speak of the trip into the unknown.

At dawn he raised the shades to peep and survey the whereabouts of his train. Pastures, fences, a few trees here and there, also several farm houses passed in quick succession. A large station, marked "South Bend," was reached. It was a quiet city with some factories that were waking from the last night in June. He had an early breakfast on the train and by eight o'clock sharp La Salle Street Station was reached. He had no idea of Chicago. All he knew was that it had the "Wheat Pit."

George soon found a suitable hotel. A clerk gave him directions how to find the Grain Pit, how he had to go about to be allowed to see it in person.

At 9:30 he witnessed the opening of grains from an open balcony high above the actual trading floor. He saw three rings, some six feet in diameter, of shiny iron structure. Brokers were standing around them, awaiting patiently the signal to begin trading. The customers for whom they bought or sold grains were located all over the world. They, too, were waiting at brokers' offices with their eyes glued to a small wheel to see what would happen.

Bang, bang! sounded a bell. In a split second loud voices, hand waving, fingers flew into the air that belonged to the floor traders assembled around the rings.

The first day of July was really a wild day, as wild as they can make them in the Pit. George could not make out prices whatsoever. Once in a while he thought he heard someone cry "a quarter," then "three eighths." To the left he noticed a giant Board on which boys began to mark prices. They had some contraptions hanging around their heads. Giant letters showed sections for wheat, corn, oats, rye and barley. Smaller letters indicated by K, N,

U, Z, marked the months of the options. Underneath he could now see the quotations marked with chalk, that is, the actual sales that had just occurred.

He saw his September wheat had opened at $97\frac{3}{8}$ to $97\frac{1}{4}$ on what is termed a "split-opening." Such situations occur when too much is offered (in a declining market just then). First all that is taken at $97\frac{3}{8}$ would be absorbed; however, some of the opening orders might not have been filled. They will be taken up one eighth lower and yet are considered as part of the opening.

The price reacted quickly to $97\frac{1}{8}$, but right now the price was $97\frac{3}{8}$. Some visitor of the gallery had pointed to the rye pit. Less people were assembled around its ring. A little further beyond was the oats pit. "There does not seem to be much trading in them just at this time" said the stranger. "They don't plant much of it anyhow, of late," he continued. "Wheat is our main crop, isn't it?" he asked George, to keep up the conversation.

But George was watching wheat. "Yesterday it had touched $97\frac{1}{4}$ and to-day with all the transactions it would not go lower, besides, there are several holidays coming and, what about Mercury at 0°? . . ." George walked off. He was looking for a broker. He had seen the Pit. He decided to buy wheat right now, because, he said, "The trend has changed over night. Wheat may come back even as far as the 1.16 level of the old May option" (which was equal to the 1.14 level of the September option).

He soon found a broker on the ground floor, went in and placed an order to buy 20M bushels "at the market," giving him the name of his broker at New York. He had waited a while, when the clerk came and handed him a slip which showed that he had bought 10M September wheat at $97\frac{1}{2}$ but for the other two he had to pay $97\frac{5}{8}$.

He soon left the place, took a walk through the "Loop," the business center of the City. "Just about as much turmoil, running and racing to get places as there is in New York," he remarked. When he came back, his suitcase and trunk were at his room. It was hot in Chicago. 101° it was yesterday, so the paper said. "But I left New York for cooler places. Of this heat I've had enough in New York. Such hot weather should help ripen grains as well as give the farmers a chance to harvest. One would think such favorable weather would drop grain prices! But I have it that they are bound to rise, weather or no weather. Two weeks ago they said that the first car of this year's crop had arrived at Chicago on June 11th from Oklahoma. It found takers immediately, because of its quality. I don't blame them," thought George, "while it could be had at 90 cents."

He had spied a big fan in his room which made his stay quite comfortable. He began to work with his stamps for a while, but had to give up the idea on account of the fan. Discus throwers of Greece would mix with whales of New Foundland, Victorias became mixed with the Chinese dragons. He just packed everything back into his trunk, took a walk with the set purpose to make a reservation for a berth next morning to continue his journey.

CHAPTER VII

GEORGE WOLLSTEN CONTINUES TRADING IN THE WEST

George Reaches San Francisco

A few days later – the holidays were over – we find George emerging from the Ferry Building at San Francisco. He looked like a "Greenhorn" at the maze of trolleys that circled around in front of him. He was greatly surprised that within four years a large city had again been built over the damage done by the destructive fire of April 18, 1906. Building still was going on at many places. The temperature was much cooler here, but through the mountains it had been very hot. Breathing was easier. He engaged a room at a hotel, but soon made a decision to look for a more permanent place, possibly with some family.

On the 5th Saturn had been crossed by Mercury; that was at the time while he had crossed the great salt beds of Utah. "Since Jupiter had turned the trend downwards last May, I have to expect Saturn will turn the trend upwards now," he said.

He bought a paper at Kearny and Third and saw that wheat had made a gap upwards to run an additional two and a quarter cents. It had closed on Saturday at 98⅝.

"My results should turn out favorable all over," he remarked. "I left New York with Mercury at freezing, I mean 0°, Saturn being passed by Mercury wheat runs up fast. At the same time I am at a new place which I intend to make my home. I see things run pretty much my way, provided I do not overstep or take too many chances . . . I will have to follow what I have learned and mastered. I will have to take one wrung of the ladder after the other."

At the hotel desk they informed him that a broker's office was in the building. They just were ready to close for the day, but allowed him to have a glance at the Board. The quotations of the newspaper had been correct. The next few hours he used to walk through the City's streets, had an evening meal at some restaurant which was followed by a good night's rest after the long journey.

George was out bright and early the next morning. He went to the broker. Grains had opened there at 7:30, against 10:30 at New York. He found markets opened strong, receded a little, then made new highs. "That's all I wanted to see" he said. "I am going to look for a place to get settled down." Equipped with a newspaper he boarded a trolley. After a while he decided to get off. It said "Lyon Street." "That name sounds good to me; grains may be only bullish, but they can be leonic at times, as when they come up, from 90 for example, cross 100 and keep going. He walked slowly into a street that led uphill. The houses appeared of the two-family type whose apartments extended from the street deeply into the lots. Many of them had six or seven rooms. He noticed signs "Rooms for rent, furnished or unfurnished." "I'll try one to find out. He who don't try, can't find out." He rang the bell of the third house. A lady, about 40 years of age, answered the door bell. "I see you have a room for rent. Can I look at it?" He walked into a nicely laid out apartment, moderately but neatly furnished. Everything was clean. The way led through a spacious front room with a piano, followed by the dining room that opened into a long hall. One of the side doors led to the kitchen. Beyond were several bedrooms. He was shown to the last room that contained just what he wanted: a big table and built-in book shelves and – a view that made him gasp. "You have a beautiful view over the sand dunes from here or what are these hills?" "These are real sand dunes. The ocean is beyond. You can see the Cliff House in the distance too," said the lady. "I am a stranger around here, just arrived from New York. I work at home quite a bit, usually rather late nights to do some research, but I make no noise whatever. Have you a telephone? I need one," said George. "You may have one put in in a few days," answered the lady. "Is there a chance to have meals with you? I am fed up eating out three times a day. I am satisfied with any good home cooked food. Just say yes, I like this room; you appear to be an excellent cook. I can get my baggage from down town immediately and get settled down. There is a lot of work awaiting me." Mrs Nancy Branche was delighted to have a chance to rent her room. For months she had been trying to rent, but nobody even looked at it. Her husband, an Alsatian, had bought the house about a year ago. The payments on it had been a little high for their income. They had quite some expense fitting it up. The spare room had been intended as a study for their only daughter, Gusty, who had just graduated from Junior College. Last Winter illness kept Mr Branche at home. He used to sell imported delicacies for an Importing House. His trade would first send orders directly, but other salesmen were elbowing in to take away orders here and there. In short, the little family was pretty hard up, the reason for attempting to rent out a room.

Madame Branche had sized up George. He had appeared to her a desirable roomer, but about meals – of that she would not approve. Their table had been very meager. At times they would have but toast and milk for supper, leaving an odd lamb chop for father. Besides, she had no idea what to charge for such service. George could readily see how anxious she was to have the room rented and yet something was wrong; he couldn't think what. In order to give her a chance to think matters over he went to the window to admire the scenery. "Is it always as clear as to-day?" he asked, to change the subject. "We have more fog mornings than we had over in the Mission district," she said, "but by eleven it's usually gone." She never thought that fog might prevent the man from taking the room. Since no other answer was forthcoming, George said to her, "I am going to rent the room anyhow, whether you give me something to eat or not. I'll simply eat out. How much is it?" "Four dollars a week, too much? Mr?" she asked inquiringly, "or three-fifty," she added quickly. "Wollsten is my name, George Wollsten," he said. "I will pay you five dollars a week with an option to get meals later on, after you know me a little. I want a home life, if I can get one," he added. "You know, my sister-in-law up state, I mean in New York State, has spoiled me. I lived there with my brother and sister-in-law for a while, but the town was a small place of only 2,000 people. I was too far away from business. Here are $22.00 to cover one month's rent in advance for the room. By that time you can tell me about the meals."

George marked down the street and number. "Mrs Branche, isn't it?" he said. He had seen the name at the doorbell.

An hour later George was installed in his new place, "the Castle" as he called it, from which he could see the open spaces and work at the same time. Now he was away from heat. While down town he ordered a telephone to be installed.

Tickers had not reached as far as San Francisco at that time. Everything was done by telegraph. Board boys, equipped with ear phones, dragged wires along with them so that they could listen to the ticks of the telegraph that was in a corner through which quotations came from the East. Price quotations would come in batches. For a while there were all rail prices, then grains, followed by prices for industrials, then cotton and so on.

The Family Branche

In the evening Mrs Branche knocked at George's door, telling him that she would like to introduce her family members. George came with her to the dining room. There was father Branche, a man of about 45 and Gusty, their daughter, sitting at the dinner table. Probably the situation about the new roomer had been fully discussed, also about his desire to have meals with the family. Gusty made a little curtsy, then resumed her place, while the father, a man grown up in the selling game, asked him to join them with a cup of coffee, because they just had finished dinner. In less than an hour George knew the whole list of specialties sold by Jacques Branche, where they came from, their brands and labels. He learned of Edam Cheese, of Lingue di Passero, of Kieler Sprotten as well as of Paté de Foie gras, as much as he needed.

"Your various Antipasti have created an enormous appetite in me, that you have to excuse me for an hour. I am going to eat something somewhere," said George. The long conversation had given him an opportunity to size up the girl. Whenever he had the chance he would attempt to get her into the conversation to get acquainted with her. Gusty was a pleasant, happy sort of a girl.

Suddenly George brought up his nerve and simply asked the parents whether they would allow Gusty to come with him to find a suitable place to eat, since "I am a complete stranger in this town." I haven't had anything to eat since 2 o'clock except two cookies which I found in my suitcase. I surely will bring her back safely within an hour."

After the speech George did not dare to even glance at Gusty to see what her reaction would be. Father Branche consented, of course, saying he never thought of that, and to Gusty, "Bring Mr Wollsten down to Tait's. They have good food." Gusty quickly disappeared to get ready, while mother Branche was happy.

She had come from Luxembourg. The people of the little country which is squeezed between France, Belgium and Germany speak a German slang that nobody can understand except themselves. Only in the southernmost part around the Capital City of Luxembourg do they speak French. She had taught Gusty that language while father Branche had taught her quite a bit of French that helped in school.

Within five minutes Gusty was ready. George had gone to his room to fetch his hat. Mother Branche said laughingly as they left, "Be sure, don't lose each other, else you might not find the way back in the dark."

Dinner at Tait's

The young couple walked spryly down towards the trolley station. "Miss Gusty," said George, "you do me a great favor to take me some place to eat. I am starved. When I found the room this morning I never dreamed that your mother had such a lovely daughter." She had not said a word. "How could I guess it?" he continued, "Maybe this is the reason why she did not want to let me have meals at your house." They boarded a Geary car that brought them down town. The conversation had drifted to his trip from New York across the country. Gusty had never been there. "Did you not like New York?" she said. "One way I liked it, the other way I did not. I could make money there, but I never had an opportunity to get acquainted with a charming young lady, such as . . . Miss Gusty," he answered. "This is Van Ness Ave," said Gusty, "one of the big cross streets, just a few blocks further we get off. You watch; when you see Jones Street then one block further." "I will do as you want me to, Miss Gusty, and report as soon as I see the sign. You know, New York was an awful place compared to San Francisco! I can see that now, at least with me it was so. There were too many people in New York. Here, I have now a little 'Castle,' that's what I said to myself to-day at your home without knowing that a sweet little lady lived there too," said George. "Here we are now," said Gusty. "Let's get off before we have to walk back. They walked down to Tait's, an old, well known place. It was worth the extra twenty minutes' ride. Without making inquiry of Miss Gusty, George ordered everything for two. He had a feeling as if she might say "No, thanks." That was out, as far as he was concerned.

Gusty had never been out alone with anyone except with some girls. She had immediately taken a liking to George as soon as he had spoken a few words at the table. Intuition, so natural for boys and girls, assisted her. Besides, Saturn was favorably inclined at that time, unknown to her, of course.

Saturn – Stock Movements

"Even the scytheman can smile at times," thought George. But he smiles usually at Grain traders, whereas Stock traders do not seem to have too much luck with him," he added. As it was, grains had risen sharply since mid-June, while stocks rallied only for 10 days and declined again after July 4th contrary to the movements of grains. Saturn was against stocks at this time.

Even the scytheman can smile at times. But he smiles usually at Grain traders.

George had noticed this as he checked previous years, that every time when stocks did not follow grains, especially in secondary movements, after an important top had been made and the secondary rise would occur such as the June rise of 1910. If, instead of continuing with grains upwards, stocks quieten down, drift sidewise or slightly lower, then something is wrong. After all, grains are but a part of the general economic structure, whereas stocks represent the complete economy, that is, all the factors of our economic life.

We may have a bumper grain crop, while the boll weevil may eat up the cotton down south. The one commodity would decline, the other would rise on that account. Anyone can understand this, whether he knows something about Jupiter and Saturn or not.

These thoughts ran swiftly through his brain while he enjoyed the grand meal and the company of a pleasant girl. Gusty felt herself in grand state. After a while they returned home. The parents still were sitting at the table. He thanked all three for the favor and retired to his room.

Wheat Movement May–July 1910

He had work to do. The charts had to be entered, the Jiggle line had to be brought up to date.

He was just sizing up the situation:

"From the high of May 9th, 1910, which was at 1.16¼, wheat had dropped to 88⅜ or 27⅞ points in a little more than one month.

If I consider the flop-over from June 4th to 7th, it had actually dropped 30⅜ points. I remember having seen at other periods such 30⅜ points movements. They seem to represent one unit of a decline or of a rise, in case they occur upwards. Therefore, this low of 88½ should form an important resistance level for quite some time. We can come back to it, of course, after this present rise is over.

"In the top area we had been in the 1.10–1.14 range nearly all Spring with two sharp peaks at 1.16. I doubt if we will get much above 1.10 this time.

"On the way down from May 9th two gaps had been made, one at 1.07½, the other at 1.05. Near the end we had the necessary downward 'Exhaustion Gap' over Decoration Day between 94 and 93¼.

"Such gaps of a major decline are usually closed when the trend reverses, like nature covers everything with growth again after the ploughman has cut his furrows in his fields. The furrows should represent the declines.

"One of those gaps has been closed to-day, the one at 1.05. I will wait for the last gap to be closed, the one at 1.07½ and sell when it is closed. The strength at the time of closing such a gap should last for a couple of days anyhow, because traders are prone to begin buying at those places."

The descent had been on the 71° angle. "I see that the present rise is also running pretty well along that same angle, only upwards, but the whole structure looks somewhat weaker here compared to the picture that had been produced on the declining side last May.

"We have nearly passed through half of the 6″ ellipse when I set it into the low of 88⅜ and let the major axis run through the 71° angle. The centre of the 6″ ellipse will be reached on July 9th at 1.05. The next crossing of Jupiter is due on August 6th. Ah," he said, "that is where the end of the ellipse comes which is set in the low of 88⅜ and

We have nearly passed through half of the 6″ ellipse.

which has been set into the 71° upwards! So, we could rise until August 6th to make top when Jupiter crosses, but – that would produce new highs, which is not possible from other indications that I use.

"If only I could improve that 'jiggle line' just a little bit! That thing kicks over sometimes too soon, sometimes too late. It tries to fool me, yet, there is something to that line. Nobody can talk me out of that!"

Final Adjustment of "Jiggle Line" to 54–33

He got busy trying another combination of adding those numbers. This time he used for the advances 5 units and in the second column 4 units. On the declining side he left things as they had been: for the first column 3 units, for the second 2 units. It was 3 a.m. before he had reworked the line from January to the present day.

"Still kinks," he said next afternoon when he continued his work. "That minus side may need a raise of one notch because, whenever we have two days of decline in succession followed by a sidewise movement of a few days, that line kicks over for want of weight. The numbers disappear too fast." He raised the declining side from the 3–2 units up to 3–3 units, so that each column of the minus side had three units.

By midnight the line was refigured and plotted on the chart, as shown for the period of early April to July 1910 in the big wheat chart of 1910–1911 at the end of the book.

He looked at and compared the wheat movements above. The line had kicked over on May 8–9 when its value was very high. It had kicked over on June 2–3, when its value was way down in the minus side. True, there was a kick-up for two or three days in the middle of May, but from checking past periods during the next few days he noticed that if they do happen, they usually are important top days on which or during which additional commitments should be made.

It even happened in past cycles that the line would rush straight up with price advancing rapidly, then the line would turn down, but the price itself would hold firm around top levels and even begin a new rise, provided the line did fall precipitously. When the "jiggle line" was just about ready to turn up for a last short kick, grain prices would rise very sharply yet to new highs and then make top. The reason for such action he found was hidden in the values that dropped out each day.

When the "jiggle line" was just about ready to turn, grain prices would rise.

Phenomena Found in the "Jiggle Line"

He soon found out that he could even figure a day ahead already how the line would have to look the following day.

He knew the closing price of the day and assumed this price to be the high of the next day, as if the market would have just one sale. Then he figured the imaginary advance as well as decline to that closing number on a strip of extra paper. That way he could judge direction for each successive day in a rough and ready way.

George further noticed that each segment of the "jiggle line" had different sizes, beginning with small on either end, increasing up to the middle and decreasing gradually again until it would turn around. From such mechanical, normal increase and decrease and from figuring every day the estimated value point for the next day, based on the closing price, much advantage was gained. He could have made some quick short commitments of a day or two, had he wanted to. But he said, "I rather trade for church steeples than blades of grass."

Figuring every day based on the closing price, much advantage was gained.

His "Polish Ellipse" had to be set into the line Marked C for the low of July 1st. While it had but a very narrow margin left to crawl up in, he decided to hold his commitments until his "Polish Ellipse" would be broken. It had become one of his most valuable indicators.

The new 54–33 series was now developed back over a period of 10 years to see how the patterns repeated and where flaws or trouble had developed, if any.

Several weeks had now passed since the job was completed. He discovered that even the "jiggle line" ran inside of ellipses. He found that the length of the "jiggle line" up or down was quite often of the same length as the actual wheat performance, in spite of the fact that they had no relation to each other, since the one was based on price, the other merely on the differentials of advances and declines; not only that, but its construction had rather complicated proportions.

About all this George was not too much surprised. Ellipses and planets, jiggle lines and "Polish Ellipse" had become his flesh and blood. What did he care whether it rained or snowed, whether the crop reports were bullish or bearish, whether they shipped the first car of wheat on June 11th or by the end of August . . . "Those things may be used by others if they care to. I use what gives results!" he said.

Ellipses and planets, jiggle lines and "Polish Ellipse" had become his flesh and blood.

Personal Applications of Rules

"Since everything moves in ellipses, grain trends and 'jiggle lines,' planets or what have we, I myself must also be moving upwards at the 71° angle. Each next thing turns out better than the previous," he continued.

"My low had been made the day I landed in New York. The first rise occurred at Upper Red Hook. The next rise happened when I began to trade grains, followed by a gap up when I decided to go to San Francisco. There is still another gap due to come before I reach a top in my personal ellipse, whose length of course is different from that of markets. I need a wife, that's going to be the next gap up! I think Gusty would be my ideal, if I can win her. That would crown my success," he mused.

It gradually became a habit with the young folks. Gusty had to bring George for dinner from now on. Various places had been chosen by her. They became more and more friendly. In a short time she would take care of the "jiggle chart." They would admire his stamps and have Saturday afternoon outings.

Such close friendship developed which brought them to a point where they discovered, at least George did, that life does not consist only in trading grains and gathering profits, but that a companion was necessary who would share his success.

Reasons for Selling on July 21st, 1910

George sold his wheat on July 21st and went short at the same time for these reasons:

(1) The jiggle line had bent over.

(2) The "Polish Ellipse" had been crossed which had been set into the low of July 1st with its line marked C.

(3) Wheat had made three gaps upwards: on June 20th, over the holidays and on July 15th, a fourth gap made had been closed.

(4) Whereas from June 13th to July 1st the movement had trailed up on the left side of the 71° angle, after the holidays it had run up below that angle and the distance from the low of June 13th to July 1st was just one half of the entire distance up to July 17th.

(5) July 21st the 9″ ellipse, when set into the low of June 13th along the 71°, had just reached its centre place.

(6) The Mercury line connecting Saturn and Jupiter was on that day just exactly at half, a place which had often caused a change of trend.

(7) Wheat prices had reached the area from last January to May 9th from which level the big decline had started.

(8) A 20 cents advance in a little more than one month with but one reaction amounting to four cents or over put the market technically in a weak condition.

George had pointed out to Gusty these details one after the other, concluding with, "That's why it's time to make hay while the Sun shines" – and, taking her around the waist, be pressed a long sweet kiss to her lips. "I love you, dear," he told her as she looked with bewilderment in his eyes, but had responded to it subconsciously. She herself had quietly had a flame glowing for a few weeks or longer. She had noticed George's occasionally "planned movements" to reach for a pencil, to help her put dots in the charts, in fact, many other things she had noticed that went slightly beyond strict etiquette.

Mother Branche would bring milk or coffee around ten o'clock, telling Gusty that it was time for her to retire. Even Pa Branche had to peep once in a while through the door to find out how the charts were progressing. They all had long begun to like George.

Plans of Marriage for November 5th, 1910

Time kept marching on. George had seen that on November 5th of that year Jupiter would again be crossed by Mercury. "That's the day when we will get married," he told Gusty one day during late September. "Let's go and ask the folks their permission! They can't say no more than 'no.' This plan had been decided upon as they sat at dinner in a restaurant down town.

When they came home that evening, George, without taking off his coat, said to Mrs Branche: "I am sorry," he began, "I don't think I can use the room very much longer." Mrs Branche turned pale. Like thunder and lightning thoughts went through the poor woman's body. "That brat, I knew something would happen: it must have happened. Why else would George move? Everything was alright when they left. That is why she disappeared so fast to her room," she thought. Her hopes to ease matters to be able to hold the house, the possibility of a match – everything she felt was exploded. Pa Branche, sitting at the table, also looked rather amazed at the sudden turn of events. "What happened, Mr Wollsten?" he asked. "Why would you want to leave us and move when it took three months to make you feel at home?" "I am getting lonesome back in my 'Castle,'" said George. "I have decided to get married on November 5th," he said. "That's news, at least good news for you," answered Pa Branche. "Who is the lucky girl who inveigled you to take such a step?" They could only think that some Eastern belle of whom they had no knowledge had sufficiently made up her mind to cause him to leave. They knew he made a lot of money since he had come here. Why should he bother any longer with them?

Mr Branche imagined Gusty weeping and crying in her room with all hopes shattered that she might become Mrs Wollsten. How could Wollsten – but that was all over now.

"When do you intend to leave?" said Mrs Branche, swallowing a few times to be able to withhold her tears. "As soon as I shall have your permission and that of Mr Branche," said George with a hard face. (Grete would have said: "That's him all over.")

"Now we know you are kidding," said Mrs Branche, as his face turned into a broad smile. "You just wanted to scare us. You just can't leave us like that. Gusty would faint, please don't say such things anymore." "She knows all about it and is as happy about it as myself. With your permission we would want to become engaged and get married, that's why I can't use your room any longer . . ." Gusty came running from her room to George to embrace him while the parents gave their blessing.

"So that's what you two have been planning during your dinner trips, instead of eating your meals and coming back to the charts. You have been plotting other things aside of grain prices," said Pa Branche.

"Do you recall, Ma, how we had planned years ago and nobody knew of it?" "But 25 years ago is not to-day," interrupted Ma. "Pa," said George, "you better take lessons from us to learn all about 'repeating Cycles' before it is too late." Gusty had to withstand several hearty kisses, Ma Branche received a few; even Pa was not overlooked. He had his pasted to the cheeks in "French fashion."

"Let's have a little party at some Night Club to celebrate," said George. "I'll treat you at the Portola to coffee and cake." "Go away, I had of that just a while ago," answered Pa. "You must do better than that; you can't fool us a second time with your serious face."

George and Gusty Get Married

November 5th was the big Day. Mr and Mrs George Wollsten had just been married. Pa and Ma saw them off at the train on their honeymoon.

They had intended to see the country at the same time. First they stopped for a week at old Monterey, then at Santa Barbara and continued their trip leisurely through the south. By Christmas Eve they had reached Upper Red Hook. Grete and Jim had been informed, of course, of George's marriage to a girl from San Francisco. They had received a few post cards, but for five weeks or more the mail had stopped.

Their baby, Jim Jr., had arrived early in September, just about the time George and Gusty had made plans to become engaged.

Grete and Jim were very happy. Their couple had quickly become accustomed to the place. The new house was finished just a week ago and furnished with new furniture. The old abode was taken over by the help. It had received a coat of paint inside and out. The new house had even a spare room all neatly furnished, just in case "His Grace" would arrive unannounced.

Christmas Eve at Upper Red Hook

The reunion on Christmas Eve was a happy one. Gusty was delighted to get acquainted with her in-laws. Quite some time was consumed in admiring the nephew in his crib. "You two are next," said Grete.

Jim was on edge to show George around before it grew dark. "You two girls keep on entertaining Junior, while we go out to make the round before it gets dark," said George. "The apples are all in the barn; it is packed full this time. They keep very nicely. I had two men besides the couple to pick them and assort them. Paul worked the grading machine. When shall I sell them?" said Jim on the way. "I would say to offer them early in March," said George, "because they are not very late varieties." The chicken yard and coops had to be gone over. The chicks had become chickens. Many had already been laying small eggs since September. While they were walking around, George told Jim to exercise his purchase option by Lincoln's Birth Day. I will give you $3,000 – to pay off the biggest slice so that in a year or two the place will be clear and another headache off my mind," said George. "Your mind? What about mine? Don't you think I made no money this past year? I had figured to do the very same thing." "But," said George, "I made you take the option, so I will also see that you exercise it. Then one of us is settled. How do you find my little wife?" "She is a little beauty," said Jim. "Where did you discover her?" "She is my Western Queen," said George. "How is yours, I mean your Western Queen? How much honey did her swarm produce?" and so they kept on talking, both happy to be together again. The two girls felt the same way. They chatted as if they had known each other for many years. Gusty had to inspect the little shoes, panties and other things of baby's. When the men came back all three were sitting on the floor amid baby clothes and diapers. They had been so engulfed in conversation that they had not even missed them.

Happy holidays were had by them. George and Gusty had brought gifts for all; even a case of wine had been ordered from Dingle's before they came down. The couple had not been forgotten. They also participated in the celebrations.

Analysis on August 2nd, 1910 of Wheat

How did George fare with his trading after he had shorted wheat on July 21st, 1910?

His special attention focused on August 6th, the day when

Saturn was crossed by Mercury to see how it responded He had noticed that just a few days prior, that was on August 2nd, the 6" ellipse had been abandoned which continued the upmove that had started on the 13th of June. The C line of the "Polish Ellipse" was also abandoned at the 1.06–1.07 level. All this was bearish in itself. He had already laid a 6″ ellipse downward from the actual top of July 17th 1910. Wheat had sagged ever since. No rally of 4 cents or more had developed. He had laid the 6″ ellipse down into the 71° angle and had noticed that on August 2nd the price walked away from this angle; besides, the "Jiggle line" had reached into minus by that time and had started to kick up on the 30th of July.

He laid the 6″ ellipse down into the 71° angle.

This was his analysis of that period:

Indications for decline

(a) "Polish Ellipse" uptrend of July 4th had been abandoned.

(b) 6″ Ellipse set upwards into June 13th had been abandoned.

(c) Spring 1910 area had been well penetrated but rapid retreat had then resulted.

(d) The pattern in the "Jiggle line" showed that this turn-up corresponded to the short line up made May 13th to 16th.

The corresponding points of the "jiggle line" were:

CORRESPONDING POINTS OF "JIGGLE LINE"

April 12	June 24
April 18	July 7
April 26	July 11
April 29	July 15
May 9	July 20
May 13	July 30
May 16	August 6* (due)

"From these four indications I can see positively that the crossing of Mercury over Jupiter will have to become bearish."

The 123° Angle Within the Ellipse

While he played around with his 6″ ellipse the evening of August 4th he made again a discovery that proved important. He had found that if he laid the ellipse as is shown in Figure VI.1 through the top of July 9th and through the top of July 17th, an angle of 123° was formed inside of the ellipse that passed through the top of July 17th and through the low of August 2nd.

That way the end of the ellipse would fall to November 5th 1910.

George immediately scratched the lines of this 123° into the 6" ellipse, so important it appeared to him.

"Aha," he said, "that trend leads back to the low of June! We'll go down for 90 days."

"That trend leads back to the low of June! We'll go down for 90 days."

General Rules on Bull and Bear Movements

Another deduction he was able to make right there and then, in spite of the fact that the pattern had not even developed yet: There are bull moves, slow and wearisome, which never seem to come to an end, such as the ones from August 25th 1909 to May 9th. When they end, a regular burst follows.

There are bull moves, fast and furious, such as the one from June 13th to July 17th. These bring about a slow but steady sag of prices until finally, after several months, a low is made.

"Of course," he said, "these latter deductions cannot be used for practical trading purposes, but I just keep them in mind so that I do not get impatient when such long wearisome moves develop."

Switching Wheat Options

He had switched the options on August 2nd 1910 on his chart from September into May. The September price of $1.00 he now had marked as $1.10. The ten cents was the difference in both options on August 2nd.

As soon as an option had been pretty well run through and approached the time to become "Cash Wheat," he switched prices of the chart into a later option. From September option he switched to May, then again into September. The rye he had plotted in July and December options, plotting July option again early in November. However, there was no particular reason why he plotted rye in those options. Any one option might have been used, as long as the switches were made right.

George could not allow any "unnatural" holes in his charts. For example, it would have hurt his analysis if he had raised his price level on August 2nd 1910 from the September option's price of $1.00 up to $1.10 just because he now used the May option. It would have given him an unnatural gap. The May $1.10 price had to be plotted at the $1.00 price with the chart re-numbered.

May wheat indicated therefore 96 by November 5th. He now ignored September wheat completely. As far as he was concerned, May wheat was the only option traded on the Board, until by the next March he would switch into September option again and forget the May option.

August 5th, 1910 More Wheat Shorted

On August 5th he shorted some more wheat at 1.13¼ which put him short 5 contracts all told.

It was top. As prices gradually moved away from this level, George took it easy since another "star" had entered his life that needed attention.

On November 1st 1910 the 6″ ellipse with its 123° angle had been completed. There were still 4 days to go to the day of the change expected on November 5th. Since on his wedding day his mind was occupied with other matters, he covered his shorts and bought long on the 4th. He had obtained 94¼, making close to $4,000 – on the decline.

It had been a decline without any excitements.

George had another ellipse laid into the high of July 17th 1910 for a long time, the 9″ ellipse which pointed to late December, when Mercury was due at 0° and shortly thereafter was to cross Saturn again on December 29th 1910.

During their honeymoon they kept charts faithfully. Gusty had become his right hand and chart keeper as well, of which she was very proud.

Visit to New York December 29th, 1910

After the holidays they paid a visit to New York to visit Mr Holten. They also went to see Mr Mayer who was still old Mr Mayer, who kept watching from his "Judge's dais" the goings on in markets. He was still a sort of a shepherd to the traders who ate the prices as they came forth from under the wheel like sheep eat blades of grass. So much depended on the very next number that tried to emerge! That next number might stop one out; it might put one in. It was an "eagle's watch."

Grains did not look any too good just then. It was the 29th of December. The 22nd had been a top with Mercury at 0° and wheat had declined ever since, until Saturn would kick it up again. Lopez whispered to George, "They are liable to fall out of bed here." "Yes, they have all the earmarks of falling out of bed, haven't they?" said George, but within he thought, "The same old gang; they never will learn that when things look real bad an upmove is without – without them."

On Hedging

"I might take a hedge to protect myself," said Lopez. "What do you mean, 'a hedge'?" asked George.

"What do you mean, 'a hedge'?" asked George.

Lopez explained: "If I have a long position in wheat and the trend runs against my commitment, but I am not too sure of the situation, then I take a hedge, that is a commitment in some other month for the opposite side (if I am long I go short in another option), and release it as soon as I notice things appear to go my way again. Big traders do that quite often, especially when a wicked move occurs beyond all expectations against what they thought would be the trend. No use letting a house get afire and just look and see what happens. Another way would be to just jump out of the position, but that would upset a trader too much."

"Thanks, Lopez," said George, "that's a new one to consider."

At Naples, Fla.

George and Gusty decided in the afternoon to take a short vacation down to Naples, Fla.

On the way George sized up the "Hedge-idea" and concluded that it is a swell idea in case something does go sour with his commitments. "Supposing," he said to Gusty, "our planets act stubborn, but our commitments have been made, then in such a case we take on a commitment just contrary to what we have in another option. It actually puts us into neutral, until we can see clear in which way the trend continues. As soon as we recognize the trend we drop either one of the commitments and are then again on one side." "It surely is a protection," said Gusty, "because when the unexpected happens we must not lose our head, but simply get into neutral with a hedge. No use hoping, waiting, asking, rechecking, but use a hedge. The cost is just one commission."

They had reached the little village on New Year's Eve. The nearest broker's office at Fort Myers was some 40 miles north.

Half-way Points Between Saturn and Jupiter

Aside of his specific rules, he had noticed that the first week or ten days of January with the very few exceptions were strong with advancing prices. He told Gusty of that, who retorted that it might be due to the various New Year's resolutions made by the public to begin the year bullish and end it the other way. George had shown

Gusty how to figure half-way points, saying, "Don't count like a school girl from December 29th to February 2nd: 3 days in December, 31 in January and 2 in February, gives 36, divide by two is 18. Add 18 to December 29th gives January 15th, but say Mercury crosses Saturn at 35° and Jupiter at 213°. The difference is 178°. Divide by 2 is 89°. Add this value to Saturn's crossing at 35° is 124°. Look in the Almanac when Mercury passes 124°. On that day is the half distance." Gusty followed instructions and found the point to be between January 12th and 13th 1911.

By mid-January, the day of the half-way point between Saturn and Jupiter, wheat had risen 7 points.

The 6″ ellipse set into the low of November had just reached half its length. The price actually reached the centre of the ellipse on January 12th.

"We will sell out and short at the close of January 12th and see what happens," suggested Gusty. "Right. I shall order the first medal for you this evening," he said jokingly, "in the form of a Potato Pancake which you shall have for dinner."

CHAPTER VIII

ADVANCED TRADING OF GRAINS AND STOCKS

Imagine that Mercury represents the Sun. It acts like the Sun, too, that old hole in the sky of which Descartes speaks in his "Discours sur la Methode." "What do you mean by 'hole in the sky?' Isn't the Sun a fiery ball as we are taught in schools which is watched so eagerly by astronomers when it makes eclipses? They travel half-way around the globe to observe the fiery flares protruding from its mass. This fiery ball they say gives us life and heat and all that, doesn't it?" said Gusty. 'From work I have done for more than a year I have quite different ideas about actions in the Universe," said George.

"See here," taking a magnifying glass. "Give me your hand; I will show how I think the Sun works." They went towards the window to stand in the hot Florida Sun. "All the active forces of the Universe, planets, fixed stars, the Milky Way, seem to me to be just small little balls like our earth. They are carried through space in well defined order. Scientists have found that they are subject often to small irregularities. They all move around a focus." He held the magnifying glass at a distance over her hand. A small whitish yellow spot appeared. "That's the way we did when kids, to light a piece of newspaper without a match," said George. "Ow, ow," cried Gusty, jerking her hand away, "you are purposely hurting me, dear. Is that all the love you have left for me after eight weeks of happiness?"

"Let's go to the beach," she said. "You keep your hole in the sky. Tell me of it in the evening when that hole does not shine."

They went to gather a bag full of sea shells of all colors and sizes. "We will send them to baby Jim to play with," said Gusty. They took in a swim and returned in good time to have their dinner, including some potato pancakes which George had not forgotten.

In the evening they concentrated once more on that January 12th date. They calculated once more the half-way point to be sure. They laid the ellipse carefully and found the center hit automatically on January 12th 1911 and the price was to become 1.02½.

"Now I tell you, dear what we shall do," said George. "After the top is made on January 12th we can decline once more to the lows of June and November of last year." He drew a dotted "trend line" from the June low 1910 via the November low 1910, extending it into Spring of 1911. Let us now assume that 1.02½ will be made and if I lay the 71° angle downwards, it hits this dotted trend line by February 2nd. The price would then be about 90½. We know that on February 2nd Mercury reaches Jupiter! However, we have to consider something else that is of importance."

The Horse-Whip

Major declines always develop in a form that looks like a horse whip. "Note," he said, "the word consists of two parts: first comes the horse, then the whip. The whip sort of waves down until the thin end fades out into a narrow string. George showed her various past patterns. "I am certain that we are in such a whip ever since early February of 1910. He pointed at the odd windings made by wheat's movement thus far. "That calls for a quiet market after a while, one that will have calm and narrow waves. With our three planets alone it is impossible to see the horse-whip. This horse and its whip is part of a much bigger cycle which we shall try to locate in due time. Hidden within the horse and the whip are the smaller swings caused by our three planets."

Major declines always develop in a form that looks like a horse-whip.

Squaring the Circle

While he searched around in his suitcase for some notations made on this subject he came across an envelope marked: "Squaring the circle." "I don't think I ever showed you how to square the circle," he said. "Don't get silly now," said Gusty, "all mathematic books say it is impossible to square the circle. I have learned that much in school." "Oh yeah," retorted George. "Many things are known to a few people. You read some books on markets published for the benefit of traders and find out what they dish up. If a book writer does not know certain things, that does not mean somebody else is in the same boat. Just read what good old Searle's had to say in the foreword of his Koran translation of which I have a copy dated 1796 that those heathens had to be gradually taught and converted over to a better religion. Read what commentators say about old man Paracelsus! They call him a drunkard, an idiot who just by luck was able to cure diseases which doctors of his age pronounced incurable. He had cured kings and princes and people of the lowest class, provided their actual predestined span of life had not been exhausted. The same thing is true with squaring the circle. I came on it some time ago. I have to go over the situation quickly, else I won't be able to explain it to you, doubting Thomas."

All mathematic books say it is impossible to square the circle.

"Notes about how to square the circle, found on January 22 1910 while searching for effect of Sun's movement through Zodiac upon price fluctuations of Wheat," was the heading of his papers.

He handed Gusty the drawing the way he had produced it (see Figure VIII.1). "How and what actually caused me to get to it I do not remember," he said. "Instead of running degrees in a straight line I put them around in a circle. This inner circle was the beginning. The Sun proper I imagined to be in the centre. At the same time I was trying to practice with zodiacal signs, such as Aries, Taurus etc., and used for each 30° one of those signs in their

FIGURE VIII.1

Original Pattern Used to Discover the Squaring of the Circle

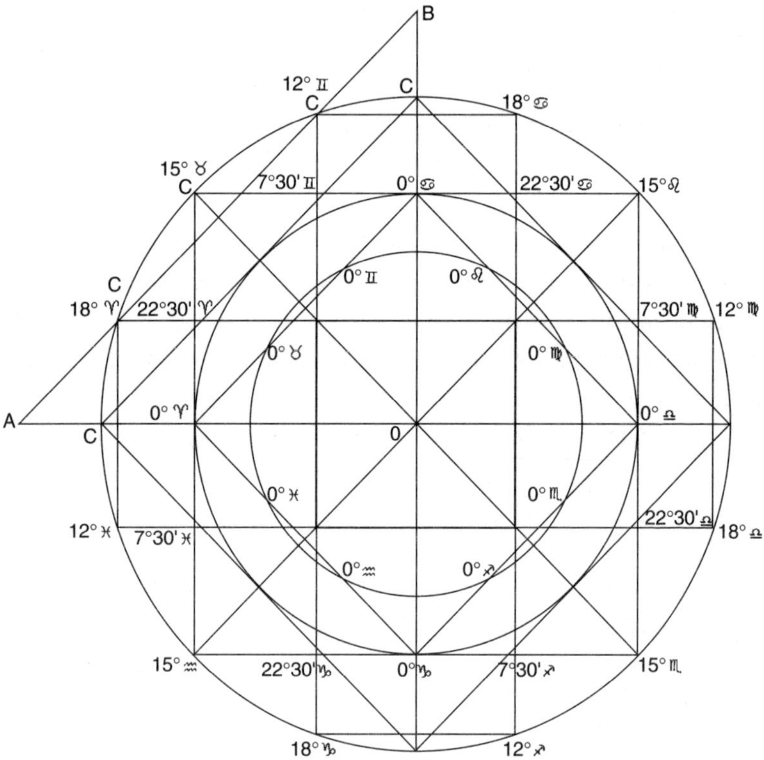

proper sequence. I was searching for divisions that would show changes of trend in smaller cycles with the help of the Sun only.

"I figured: In one certain year the inner circle would give changes of trend. The next year the middle circle would supply such changes and the third year the outer circle would supply them. You can see that the values which I marked there are proper divisions of any one circle, but they are grouped differently in each of their circles. Some show 30°, others 22° 30′, others 18° of the various signs. But all that may be too deep for you at present. Suffice to say that one of the sides of those squares you see drawn in this picture is the square root of its circle through which it runs. And, it's the outer with the outer! if . . . you allow for a . . ." "For what?" asked Gusty. "Mathematicians don't allow for anything. Just look at logarithmic Tables and note how they give the logs in 7 decimals with proportional parts to boot and supply those values from 0° 0′ 1″ clear up to 89° 59′ 59″ plus 1" for sin. cos, tang and ctg." "We do our things in a rough and ready way. You see how rough our ellipses are. When we lay the 71° angle, we might draw the line at a whole degree off. Not even Mercury works accurately himself. I told you that he missed at times a whole day or even two when he gets to 0°. Wheat is not any too accurate with its prices. Look at November 4th last year! It went two full points beyond the ellipse then. The bath tub had sprung a leak there . . .

"But in this case I shall try to show you a little more accuracy than usual, because 'this is scientific' and not just a commitment in grains. And, furthermore I am not explaining this for any 's-eye-end-ist's nor for any echo-numb-ist's* who don't seem to be able to hit market movements so very well either, but, that's another horse, just like this squaring of the circle is one of ours."

"Let's finish now that 'if-stuff' on which you have asked for an allowance, before we forget it. You broaden out too far. What or how much shall I allow you so that the outer line's length shall be the root of this outermost circle?" "You allow me to use a couple of foci, half a degree each, not more. Too much asked?"

"A circle has but one focus, which is in the centre," said Gusty, unless you want to put two dots into one hole. You only have two foci in an ellipse, that is if you put equal pressure on both sides of a circle . . ." "How many sides has a circle?" asked George to keep her in confusion.

*The purpose of spelling the words "scientists" and "economists" as above is to show underlying relationship of meaning such as was done with the word "if" on page 133.

"All we have to do," said George seriously, "is to lower the line ½ degree so that instead of passing through 18° Aries and through 12° Gemini (he pointed at those two places on the drawing), we have to draw the line through 17° 30′ Aries and through 12° 30′ Gemini. Then the length of this line, that is, the side of this square is exactly the square root of the same circle." Gusty had to try it immediately.

Practical Rules on Trading Found Therefrom

"That reminds me," continued George, "I have found something else of importance in case we decide some time to trade stocks. These stocks like to make swings whose length is 17½ points, also double that much, that is 35 points. The smaller swings extend just half of that or 8¾ points and the very small swings amount to 4⅜ points. The horse-whip idea can be incorporated in those movements also," he added. "In bull markets such moves may amount to as much as 70 points, that is 4 times those 17½. Not only that, but when we have a little more time I shall show you that stocks themselves like to use these numbers to make tops or bottoms there, such as at 17½, at 52½, at 70 etc. But to judge right one has to have complete daily charts over a period of several years to see whether they use the full unit of 17½ or whether they prefer its fractions, that is 21⅞, 26¼, 30⅝ and the multiples thereof."

I shall show you that stocks themselves like to use these numbers to make tops or bottoms.

"I always thought it takes a lot of money to make more, but I can see now that instead of a wad of bills it takes something else besides . . . I think you know enough now to make money," she added. "Who – me?" said George. "I am just beginning with my research. The things I found so far are just roughly mined stones from a quarry. We shall soon begin to delve into Ovid, Cicero, into Paracelsus – that drunkard, into Swedenborg, too."

"Just remember for the present that AB is the root of circle Occc in this drawing."

Gusty found that AB measured 4. 8″ . The radius of the outer circle was 2.7".

Area of a circle is $r^2\pi$.
$2.7 \times 2.7 \times 3.14 = 22.84$.

Log. 22.84. "Get the log Tables!" They found one in the old Geometry book. Log. 22.84 = 1.358696: ½ of it is 0.679348 or 4.78.

While Gusty did the figuring George made another drawing for her which demonstrated the squaring of the circle in a simple way. We note on the picture reproduced (Figure VIII.2) that he simply drew inside of a right angle that was set with its angle into a circle two new angles that were drawn 17° 30′ inward.

Therefore angle GOC was 17° 30′; so was angle FOD. He connected point C with point D and extended the line on both ends, which gave him point E on AO and point F on FO.

The distance EF was the root of the square whose contents or area was the same as that of the circle whose radius was GO or CO. So the shifting of which he had spoken referred to 17° 30′ being used instead of 18°.

The proof he made by construction:

Area of Circle $r^2\pi$.

Given: r=2.5″

log r =	0.3979400
then area is log	0.3979400
	0.3979400
log π	0.497149
	1.2930298:2 = 0.645149
	= 4.431

He measured the distance between E and F and found it to be 4.43″.

"Why did you not continue to use this idea further to develop cycles? There had been many other similar discoveries I ran across

FIGURE VIII.2
Short and Quick Construction to Square the Circle
(Length of EF is Square Root of Circle with Radius OG)

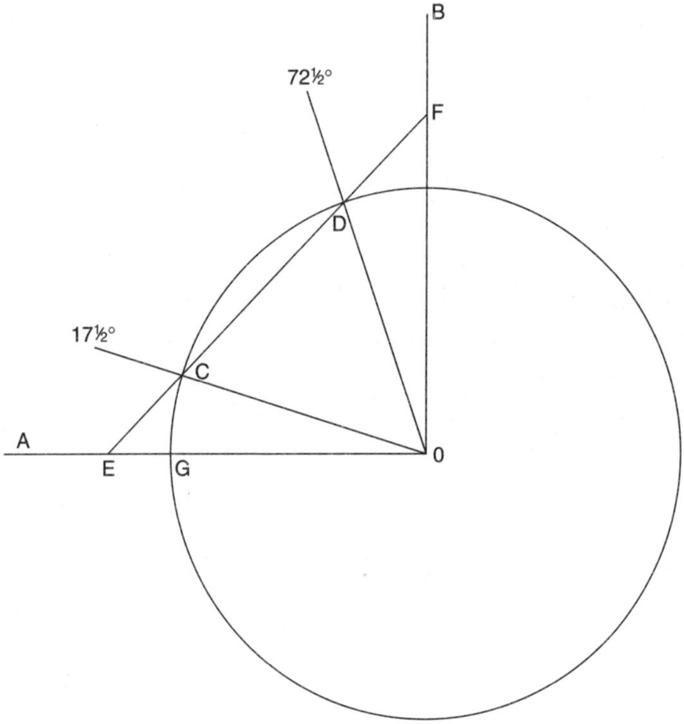

which had tried to put me off the track, away from Jupiter and Saturn that would have led me into caves which contain nothing but dragons, behemoths and poisonous asps. They give false and misleading omens and auguries. To tease they may work for a while, but would land in a dead-end road. Virgil and Xenophon have spoke of them, how beautiful they look, how they lead to destruction. I had my medicine last March and April when they began to beguile me for a while. That is why I put them together with arsenic and vitriol. Some other day I will tell you the rest about that hole in the sky," he said, "about that fiery ball. We pack now. Tomorrow we go back to New York. I have something else planned in my mind. How about spending 2 points of our profit and run over to Europe? The market can decline all by itself after the 12th."

As sure as George's rough and ready tools indicated a top at 1.02½ for January 12th, so it came. May wheat hit even 1.02⅝. They had turned around at 1.02 so as not to try for the last eighth and get greedy.

Recognizing Adam & Eve and the Baby in Patterns

While George worked on the wheat chart at the St. Andrews, where they had taken quarters, he noticed that the decline from May 9th to November 4th had amounted to 30⅝ points.

"Those things can't be seen by people. It has to do with the squaring of the circle because 30⅝ is one of those fraction points I had found. How can chartists see that, when they run one option at a time and, when it ends, start with another wherever its price might begin? What a farce! Dogmatic. They let each option run singly. They never think of marrying them by binding them together. He could now see his Adam from August 15th 1909 to March 31, 1909 marrying his Eve on June 13th 1909, that is Eve proper started on July 17th, 1909. The result of the happy union was a baby born to them on November 4th 1909. It was but a tiny, weeny tot, 70 days long, extending to January 12th 1911. He scrutinized the movement from March 31st to April 20th 1910, then up to May 9th and down to June 7th, saying, "what an odd pattern that is . . ."

It has to do with the squaring of the circle.

"That baby has to be kept in the cradle for a while," he mused. It was born on January 12th 1911. No man after he is born walks erect – at least not those born of "Mother Nature."

Shifting of Ellipses

However, in his present analysis of the wheat pattern he did not like the idea that Mr Adam as a man was tall and measured 9 inches, whereas little Eve would be but 6 inches in length. That can't be, he said. Normal couples have about the same size. I am just wondering, he continued thinking. Babies are carried in the womb and not at the toe. Eve may not be finished in the pattern." He had set a long time ago his 9" ellipse into the high of July 17. 1910 and had seen its lower end stick out like a sore toe on January 5th 1911. He glanced across at the place where he had put an arrow and said: "It's the baby's fault. I have to shift the 9″ ellipse over to the January 12th place to get my next bottom." He then discovered that this January 12th top was exactly in the centre of the shifted 9″ ellipse and the low was shown for early April 1911.

This price was also 17½ points below the January 12th high, the same as the November 4th low was 8¾ points below the January 12th high.

They went to Europe for two months and came back as the bottom was made. The pattern from March 1st to April 3, 1911 indicated the foot of Eve including the big toe.

Before children can walk they have to learn first how to creep. Wheat had to learn to do the very same thing for 9″ in time. The creeping lasted until October 22, 1911.

"We had to make hay while the Sun shone," said George one day in July. "We cannot make any money in this market for a while unless we begin to chisel and that is out! We just simply have to hold positions until that baby has learned to creep and only then will it start to walk, but," he added cautiously, "it isn't far for a baby to fall, in case it does fall. It is not big enough to fall deep and then it gets up quickly and tries to run . . ."

Sepp Muller and Holten at a Party

Sepp Muller had come into his mind again. George asked him to come over for a little party. Holten was not forgotten. After a good dinner Europe was discussed, also California, even the market was touched upon. "You are a lucky boy," said Sepp. "A year in the market and knocked out a trip to Europe already, while I am still in the planning stage. You tell me a stock, I shall buy it. What do you say?"' "I trade for the present only in wheat, something which Mother Nature produces out of the ground." "I do not trade in dynamite," retorted Muller, "where one can burst in less than a week because it always does what nobody expects. Wheat, you mean, you trade in wheat?" "Just that," said George. "No thanks, I won't have any. I want something substantial, something that has a factory standing. A hail storm may knock wheat down 30 cents and laugh at you. Frost can do the same thing the other way. I know what I am talking about. I saw it with my own eyes." Sepp Muller was all steamed up against grains.

Mr Holten remained the quiet onlooker. He had his moderate salary. He tried to help the immigrants. Yet, he could size up the vast difference between his two friends, the one and the other. As soon as the one made just a step beyond, the "Sword of Damocles" (the Most Heinous) was in action with "no trespassing or else." The other also had the same sword hanging over him, but to him it was visible. He was able to go "with the sword," that is to watch it. He never did extend his operations beyond a proper margin. Many times he had placed stop loss orders, just in case Damocles tried the sword, in case his calculations would not accord with realities. In that way he never could get bitten by the serpent for 30 points. He was quick to change his mind, if necessary, yet never became excited. He had learned to stay away from the real dynamite.

Shortly thereafter Gusty and George left to return to San Francisco by way of Upper Red Hook. Grete and Jim were to be taken along to visit San Francisco to have their honeymoon somewhat belated. The couple was to take charge of the place until their return. George had laid this plan ahead of time. "Baby Jim must be able to walk by now," added Gusty, "so he won't be too much of a burden. You remember, they wrote us that he was able to creep already quite a while ago . . ." This discussion had occurred on May 3rd 1911 because on the 4th Jupiter was crossed by Mercury and that was the day George had selected to leave. George had worked up a $2000 profit again, but since he considered wheat was just learning how to crawl, he did not take it.

The Western Bees Sting Jim

They had arrived at Upper Red Hook as planned. While they walked up to the farm they met Grete. "How is everybody, how is baby Jim, how is Jim?" they asked. "Baby is fine, but Jim is in bed," said Grete. "What ails him?" asked George. "His Western Queen with an assistant gave him a sting two days ago, one on the nose, another near the eye. That one is shut and his nose, you have to look at it yourself! What those Western Queens can do to a man!" Grete was excited. "I don't mean you, Gusty dear," she said, "I retract it all." Gusty had no way of knowing anything about the bee hives which Jim had bought; one of them was occupied by that queen supposedly originating from the West. Jim had been changing a frame in one of the hives without using a veil and besides he had opened it without a smoke torch. Apparently they had resented such intrusion. All he knew was that a few began to chase him immediately before he had even been able to lift the lid by more than two inches. He dropped it as fast as it would come loose of his hand and began to run with all his might. They could fly faster. He had three or four stings. Two were not bad, but the others made up for it.

Poor Jim, he was lying there, bandaged all over his face! He had to laugh for shame that something like this should happen to him. That confounded George had to come back just when he thought him to be out in California or somewhere. Gusty, what would she think of her brother-in-law now, a little bee to knock out big Jim! George guessed what went on in Jim's mind. To console him he said, "Those things happen in Wall Street and in the Pit every day."

This accident helped to get Grete and Jim out to the Coast. "Those critters will be after you for quite a while," said George. "I wouldn't doubt that a minute," answered Jim. "How do they treat Robert and Paula?" said George. "They seem to get along fine with them. It was Robert who changed the frames after they had chased me away," said Jim.

After a week's stay Gusty and George had succeeded in convincing them to come along with the baby and leave the couple in charge of the farm. The latter were delighted to be able to show their employers that they were worthy of the trust.

To Santa Cruz, California

In due course we find the whole family including Ma and Pa Branche in a house rented for the summer in the Santa Cruz mountains, some 50 miles south of San Francisco. They had a wonderful time.

However, George and Gusty did not just merely idle away their time, but began to approach a subject that had been planned for some time, the Stock Market and its intricacies.

The Assortment of Stocks

This is what went through George's head for some time: "The Stock Market is composed of an assortment of stocks that represented shares of Corporations whose activities spread all over the country. Their interests were various. Iron and Steel manufacture, Leather and Bread, Rubber and Dry Goods, Railroads and Gas Companies aside of many others were behind those stocks. Common sense told him that Iron and Bread were not the same, neither had the gas used for cooking anything to do with a railroad, or with the manufacture of hot water bottles. Consequently, he concluded, we have to do with a perfect assortment of vegetables or of flowers which require different seasons to grow, different soils, and they have different uses. A woolen mill stock cannot possibly run in harmony with the stock of an Electric Company.

"Stocks run in broad swings very nearly alike. To find out the big trend we can use the Dow Jones Averages which I believe are fine for this purpose. But, when it comes to individual stocks, we may have to select them by groups and make an average that way taking 10 or 15 of related stocks. Else, we have to treat one stock at one time and follow it the way I have done with May–September Wheat.

"First of all we need the past performance of a stock for several years back, the further back the better."

Some time past he had plotted U.S. Steel back to the time it was first traded in March 1901. He found that his ellipses fitted nicely into the patterns. He discovered that the 17½ points movements and its fractional components worked well. The "Jiggle line" as well as the "Polish Ellipse" could be applied with great accuracy. Only the planets, Saturn, Jupiter and Mercury, refused to work as safely as they did with wheat.

He found that his ellipses fitted nicely into the patterns.

George then tried to apply his rules to cotton and found that all the mechanical rules could be applied with good results, but as far as the three planets were concerned, they could be upside down and cotton would not act on them. "I may have to use other planets for cotton on the same principle though, as I did for wheat, but not just now," he said. The same applied to hides, cotton seed oil, sugar, cocoa and other commodities as he put them to the test.

He said to Gusty, "What chance has a trader who trades in stocks and in cotton and in wheat all at the same time?" "Isn't one enough?" said Gusty.

Then they went to the beach.

Wheat 1909–1911

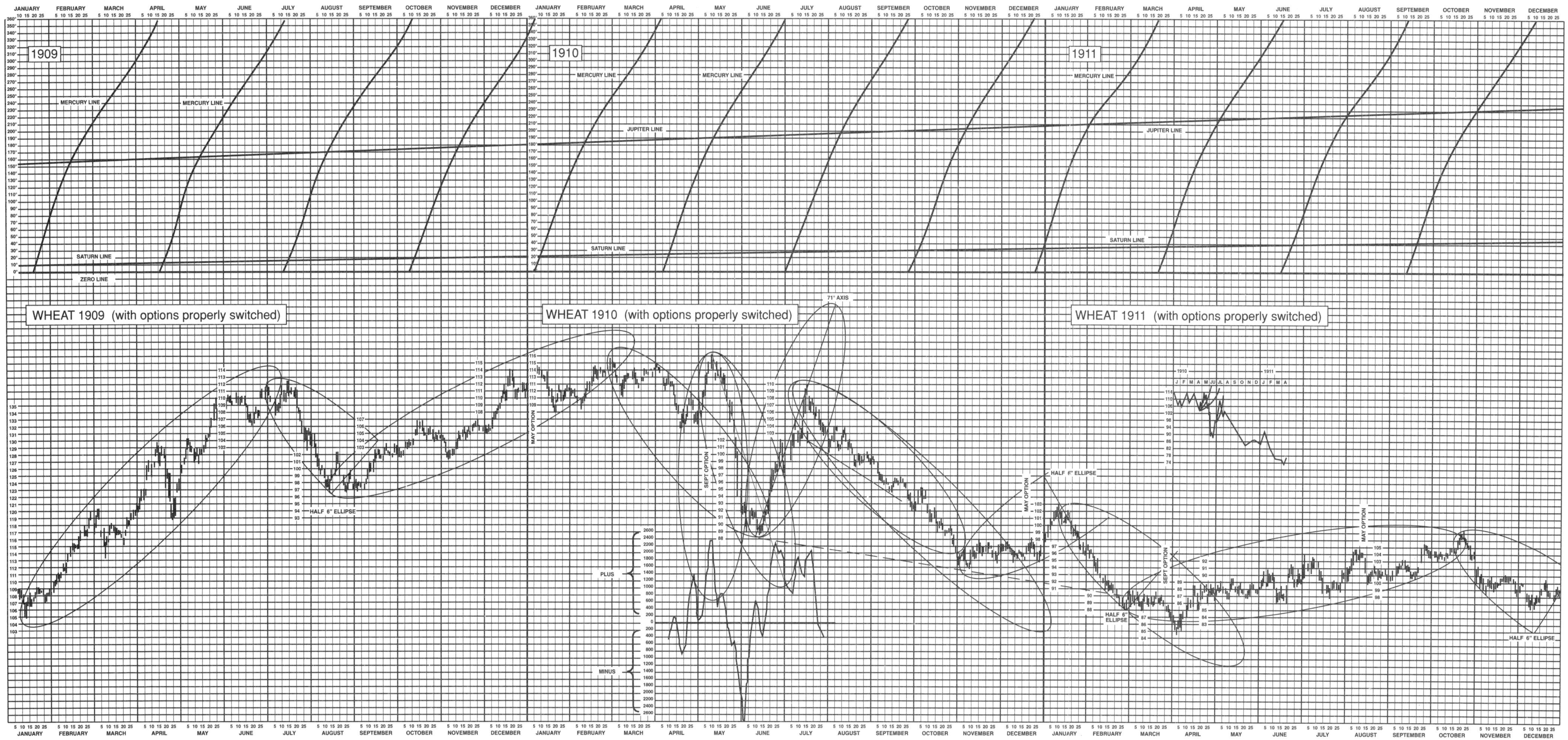

APPENDIX

Planetary Positions, 1943–1947

It should be remembered that the Mercury curve has always a pattern which is similar to all previous ones. Therefore, when you know the 0° positions (same as 360°), you can readily draw the entire line by transferring the previous on transparent paper. The Saturn and Jupiter lines are nearly straight, always slanting upwards. The scale to plot is 10° for each square.

Here are the positions:

Table of Jupiter's movement

January	1, 1943	109° 21′	
July	1, 1943	124° 7′	
January	1, 1944	139° 1′	
July	1, 1944	153° 0′	
January	1, 1945	167° 8′	(use as a straight line)
July	1, 1945	180° 53′	Yearly Advance
January	1, 1946	194° 47′	About 28°
July	1, 1946	208° 28′	
January	1, 1947	222° 27′	

Table of Saturn's movement

January	1, 1943	70° 9′	
July	1, 1943	76° 51′	
January	1, 1944	83° 43′	
July	1, 1944	90° 28′	
January	1, 1945	97° 25′	(use as a straight line)
July	1, 1945	104° 10′	Yearly Advance
January	1, 1946	110° 59′	About 13½°
July	1, 1946	117° 42′	
January	1, 1947	124° 30′	

Mercury at 0°		Mercury at 180°	
January 4,	1943	February 5–6,	1943
April 2,	1943	May 4–5,	1943
June 28–29,	1943	July 31–Aug. 1,	1943
September 24–25,	1943	October 27–28,	1943
December 21–22,	1943	January 23–24,	1944
March 18–19,	1944	April 20–21,	1944
June 14–15,	1944	July 17–18,	1944
September 10–11,	1944	October 13–14,	1944
December 7–8,	1944	January 9,	1945
March 5–6,	1945	April 7,	1945
June 1–2,	1945	July 4,	1945
August 28,	1945	September 30,	1945
November 24–25,	1945	December 27,	1945
February 20,	1946	March 25,	1946
May 19,	1946	June 21,	1946
August 15,	1946	September 17,	1946
November 11,	1946	December 14,	1946

Plot in curve of pattern given in Wheat Chart. The crossings will appear immediately; also the halfway points must be figured.

The Crossing of the Critical Points:

1944	1945	1946
Saturn Jan. 5–6	Jupiter Jan. 6	Mercury 0° Feb. 20
Jupiter Jan. 17	Mercury Mar. 6	Saturn Mar. 11–12
Mercury 0° Mar. 18	Saturn Mar. 23	Jupiter Mar. 31
Saturn April 3	Jupiter April 5	Mercury 0° May 19
Jupiter April 13	Mercury 0° June 1	Saturn June 8
Mercury 0° June 14	Saturn June 19	Jupiter June 29
Saturn June 29–30	Jupiter July 3	Mercury 0° Aug. 15
Jupiter July 12	Mercury 0° Aug. 28	Saturn Sept. 9
Mercury 0° Sept. 10	Saturn Sept. 16	Jupiter Sept. 27
Saturn Sept. 26	Jupiter Oct. 2	Mercury 0° Nov. 11
Jupiter Oct. 9	Mercury 0° Nov. 24	Saturn Dec. 2
Mercury 0° Dec. 7–8	Saturn Dec. 12–13	Jupiter Dec. 26
	Jupiter Dec. 31	

Sample of the 5–4:3–3 Computation

Table of the 5–4:3–3 Computations used by George Wollsten for the test period of April 8, to August 1, 1910 (see chart "Wheat 1909–1911" between pages 220 and 221) using the HIGH of each trading day:

	Price	advance	5	4	decline	3	(to plot) 3 difference of 4 & last 3	
April								
1	1.15,2	0			0			
2	1.14,6	0			50			
3	1.14,6	0	50		0	50		
6	1.13,1	0	75		162	212		
7	1.12,3	0	0		75	237	500	
8	1.13,1	75	75	200	0	237	675	–475
9	1.14,0	87	162	312	0	75	550	–237
11	1.12,5	0	162	400	137	137	450	–50
12	1.12,4	0	163	562	12	150	362	+200
13	1.12,2	0	162	650	25	175	462	+187
14	1.10,5	0	87	575	163	200	525	+50
15	1.09,3	0	0	412	125	313	687	–275
16	1.09,0	0	0	250	37	325	837	–587
18	1.07,3	0	0	87	162	325	963	–887
19	1.08,1	75	75	75	0	200	850	–775
20	1.06,7	0	75	150	125	287	812	–662
21	1.08,0	112	187	337	0	125	612	–275
22	1.09,1	113	325	662	0	125	537	+137
23	1.09,7	75	400	987	0	0	250	+737
25	1.10,5	62	387	1300	0	0	125	+1175
26	1.09,7	0	387	1500	75	75	75	+1425
27	1.07,5	0	250	1425	225	300	375	+1050
28	1.08,0	37	175	1200	0	300	675	+525
29	1.08,1	13	113	925	0	225	825	+100
30	1.08,5	50	100	638	0	0	525	+112
May								
2	1.08,2	0	100	487	37	37	262	+225
3	1.11,0	275	375	687	0	37	75	+612
4	1.11,3	37	375	950	0	37	112	+837
5	1.13,2	187	550	1400	0	0	75	+1325
6	1.13,5	37	537	1637	0	0	37	+1600
7	1.15,2	163	700	2162	0	0	0	+2162
9	1.16,2	100	575	2362	0	0	0	+2362

	Price	advance	5	4	decline	3	3	(to plot) difference of 4 & last 3
May								
10	1.15,4	0	487	2300	75	75	75	+2225
11	1.12,2	0	300	2062	325	400	475	+1587
12	1.13,5	137	400	1762	0	400	875	+887
13	1.15,1	150	387	1575	0	325	1125	+450
14	1.14,0	0	287	1375	112	112	837	+538
16	1.14,4	50	337	1412	0	112	550	+862
17	1.13,0	0	337	1350	150	262	487	+863
18	1.13,4	50	250	1212	0	150	525	+687
19	1.13,4	0	100	1025	0	150	562	+463
20	1.11,5	0	100	787	187	187	487	+300
21	1.11,2	0	50	500	37	225	562	–62
23	1.09,6	0	50	300	150	375	787	–487
24	1.09,4	0	0	200	25	212	812	–612
25	1.10,2	75	75	175	0	175	762	–587
26	1,07,0	0	75	200	325	350	737	–537
27	1.04,4	0	75	225	250	575	1100	–875
28	1.02,4	0	75	300	200	775	1700	–1400
		Switch option; the old 1.02 equals now 1.00						
31	93,2	0	75	300	725	1175	2525	–2225
June								
1	92,3	0	0	225	87	1012	2962	–2737
2	93,1	75	75	225	0	812	3000	–2775
3	91,3	0	75	225	175	262	2087	–1862
4	90,4	0	75	225	87	262	1337	–1112
6	92,0	150	225	450	0	262	687	–237
7	92,3	37	262	637	0	87	612	+25
8	91,6	0	187	750	62	62	412	+337
9	91,6	0	187	862	0	62	212	+650
10	91,7	12	200	837	0	62	187	+650
12	90,6	0	50	625	112	112	237	+388
13	89,7	0	12	450	87	200	375	+75
14	89,7	0	12	275	0	200	512	–237
15	90,2	37	50	125	0	87	487	–362
16	91,2	100	137	212	0	0	287	–75
17	92,0	75	212	412	0	0	87	+325
18	92,6	75	287	687	0	0	0	+687
20	94,4	175	462	1100	0	0	0	+1100
21	97,2	275	700	1662	0	0	0	+1662
22	97,0	0	600	2050	25	25	25	+2025
23	96,6	0	525	2287	20	50	75	+2212
24	99,1	237	687	2512	0	50	125	+2387
25	98,6	0	512	2325	37	62	162	+2163

	Price	advance	5	4	decline	3	(to plot) 3 difference of 4 & last 3	
June								
27	1.00,4	175	412	2137	0	37	150	+1987
28	1.02,2	175	587	2200	0	37	137	+2063
29	1.01,6	0	587	2100	50	50	125	+1975
30	99,4	0	350	1937	225	275	362	+1575
July								
1	98,5	0	350	1875	87	312	637	+1238
6	1.01,7	337	512	1800	0	312	900	+900
7	1.02,0	12	350	1562	0	87	712	+850
8	1.02,2	25	375	1587	0	0	400	+1187
9	1.05,0	275	650	1887	0	0	87	+1800
11	1.03,4	0	650	2025	150	150	150	+1875
12	1.03,1	0	312	1987	37	187	337	+1650
13	1.03,6	63	363	1975	0	187	525	+1450
14	1.04,6	100	438	1762	0	37	412	+1350
15	1.07,6	300	462	1575	0	0	225	+1350
16	1.09,1	137	600	1863	0	0	37	+1837
17	1.10,0	87	687	2188	0	0	0	+2188
19	1.09,0	0	625	2375	100	100	100	+2275
20	1.07,4	0	525	2437	150	250	350	+2087
21	1.08,1	62	287	2125	0	250	600	+1525
22	1.07,3	0	150	1587	75	225	725	+862
23	1.06,0	0	62	1025	137	212	687	+338
24	1.06,6	75	137	637	0	212	650	–12
26	1.06,3	0	137	487	37	175	600	–112
27	1.04,7	0	75	412	150	187	575	–162
28	1.04,5	0	75	425	25	212	575	–150
29	1.04,4	0	75	262	12	187	587	–325
30	1.04,0	0	0	225	50	87	487	–262
August								
1	1.03,6	0	0	150	25	87	362	–212

Wheat, Daily High and Low Range Charted for 1908–1911

Daily Highest and Lowest Prices – May Wheat Futures – Chicago Board of Trade

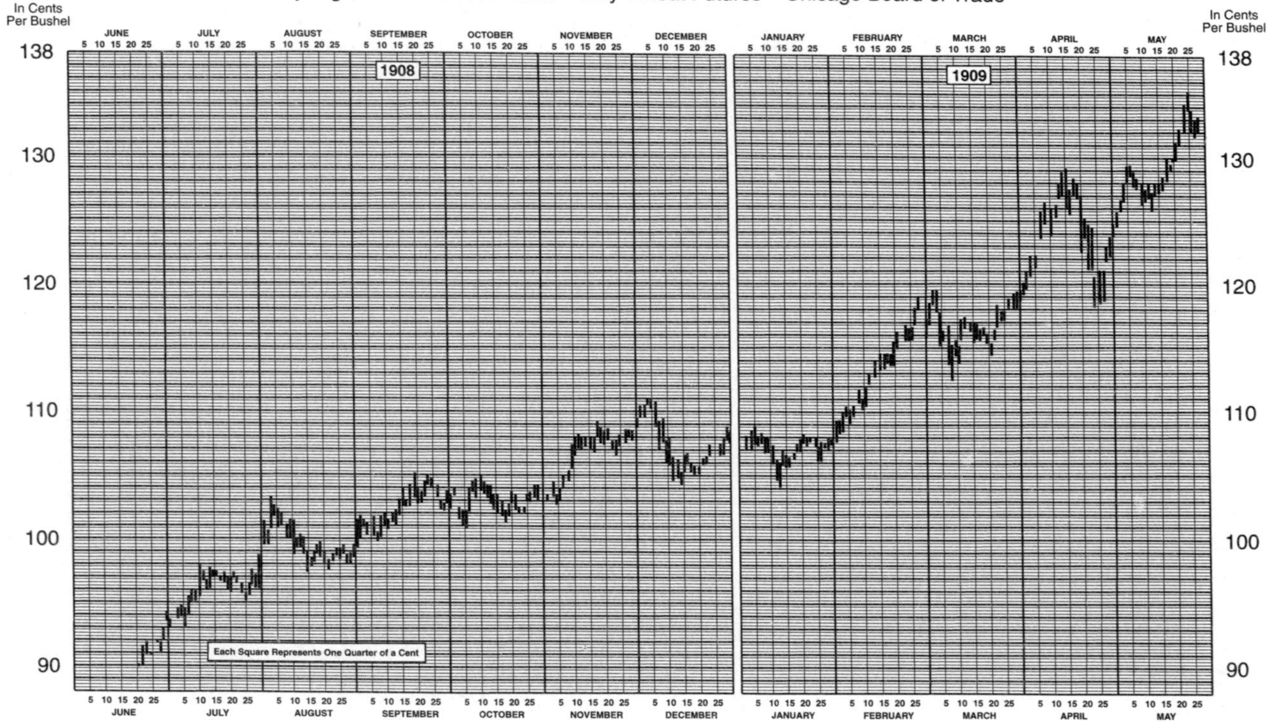

• MAY 1909 •

Daily Highest and Lowest Prices – July Wheat Futures – Chicago Board of Trade

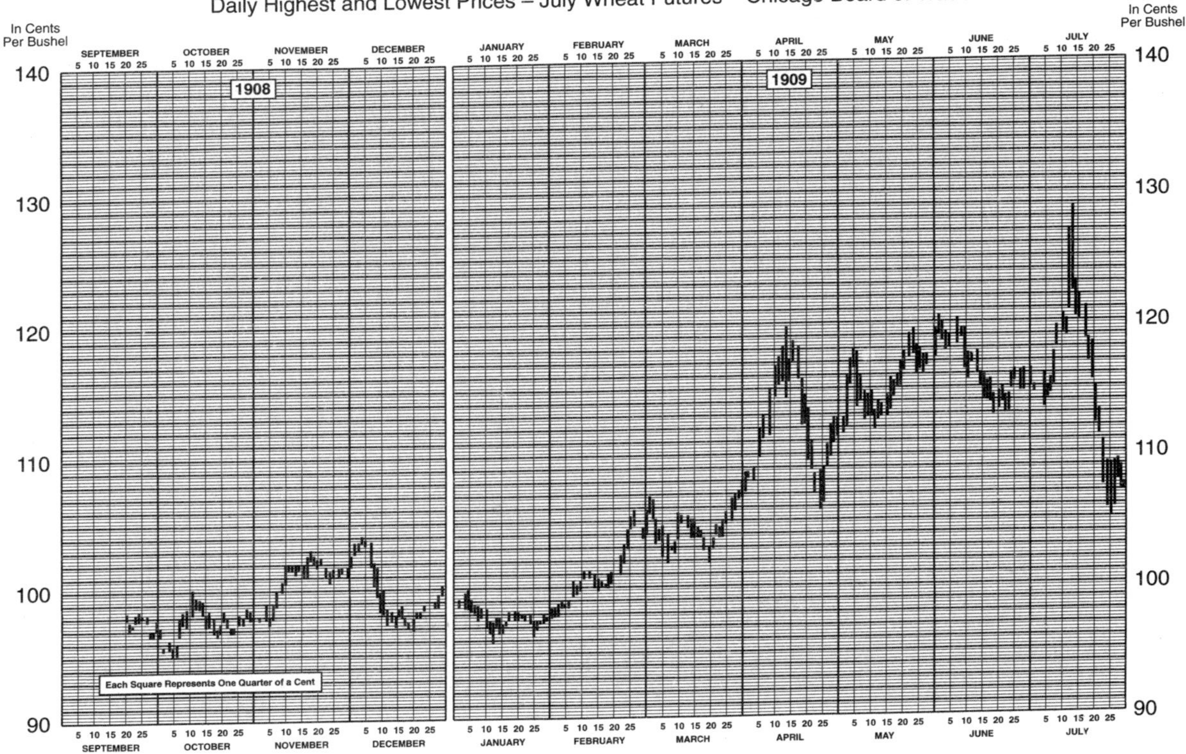

• JULY 1909 •

Daily Highest and Lowest Prices – September Wheat Futures – Chicago Board of Trade

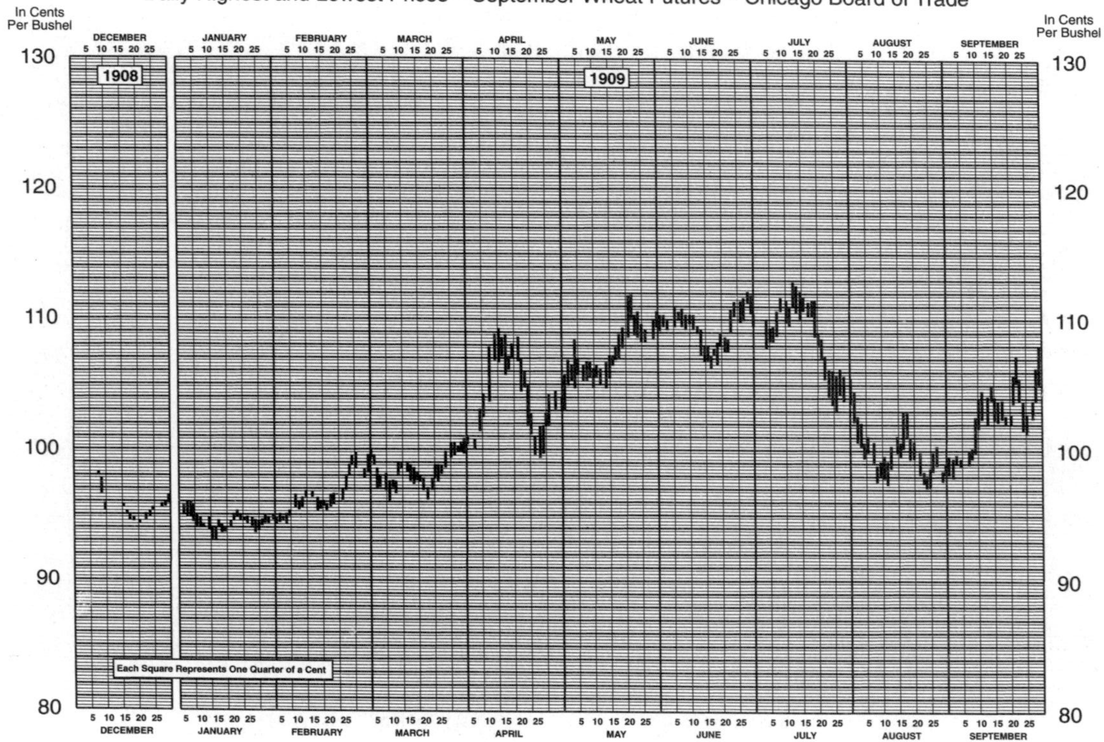

• SEPTEMBER 1909 •

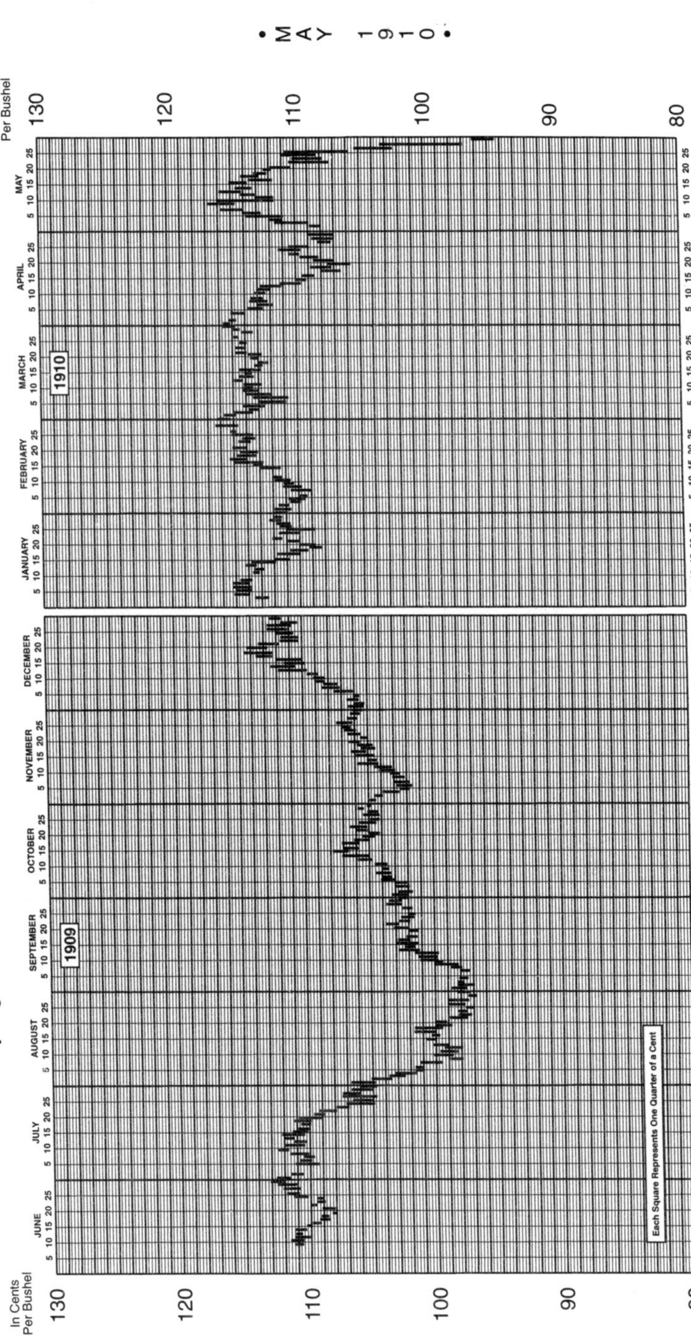

Daily Highest and Lowest Prices – May Wheat Futures – Chicago Board of Trade

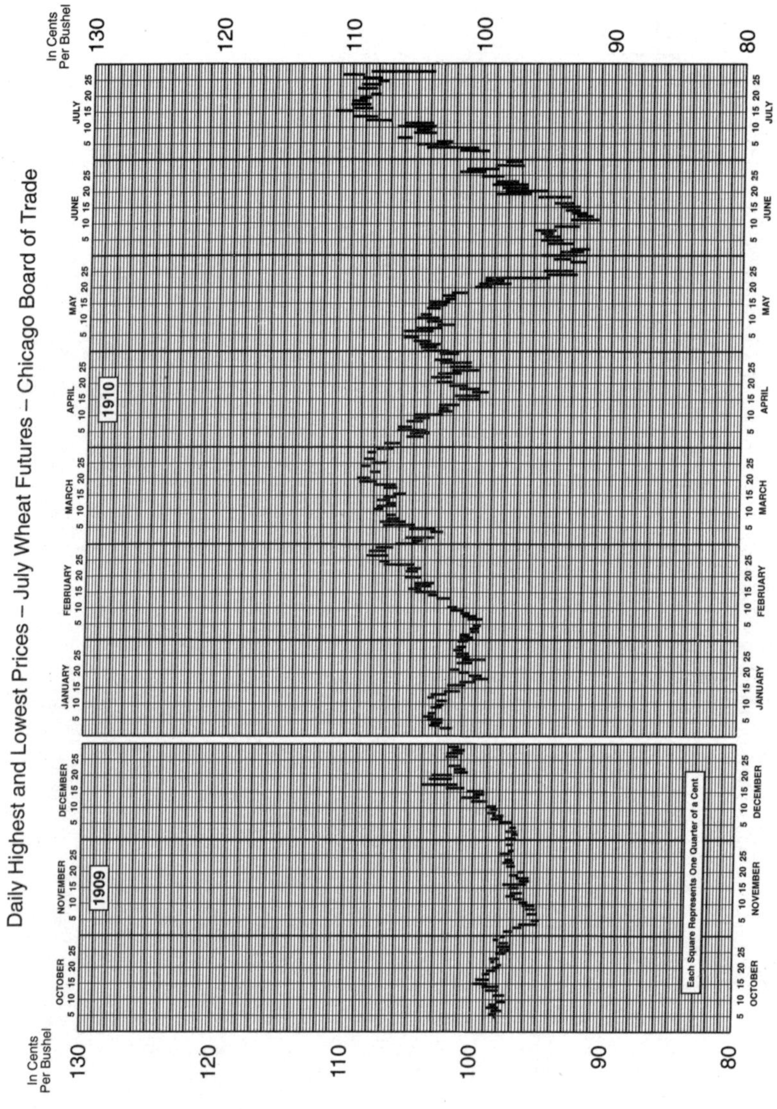
Daily Highest and Lowest Prices – July Wheat Futures – Chicago Board of Trade
In Cents Per Bushel
130
120
110
100
90
80
1909
1910
OCTOBER
NOVEMBER
DECEMBER
JANUARY
FEBRUARY
MARCH
APRIL
MAY
JUNE
JULY
5 10 15 20 25
Each Square Represents One Quarter of a Cent

• SEPTEMBER 1910 •

Daily Highest and Lowest Prices – September Wheat Futures – Chicago Board of Trade

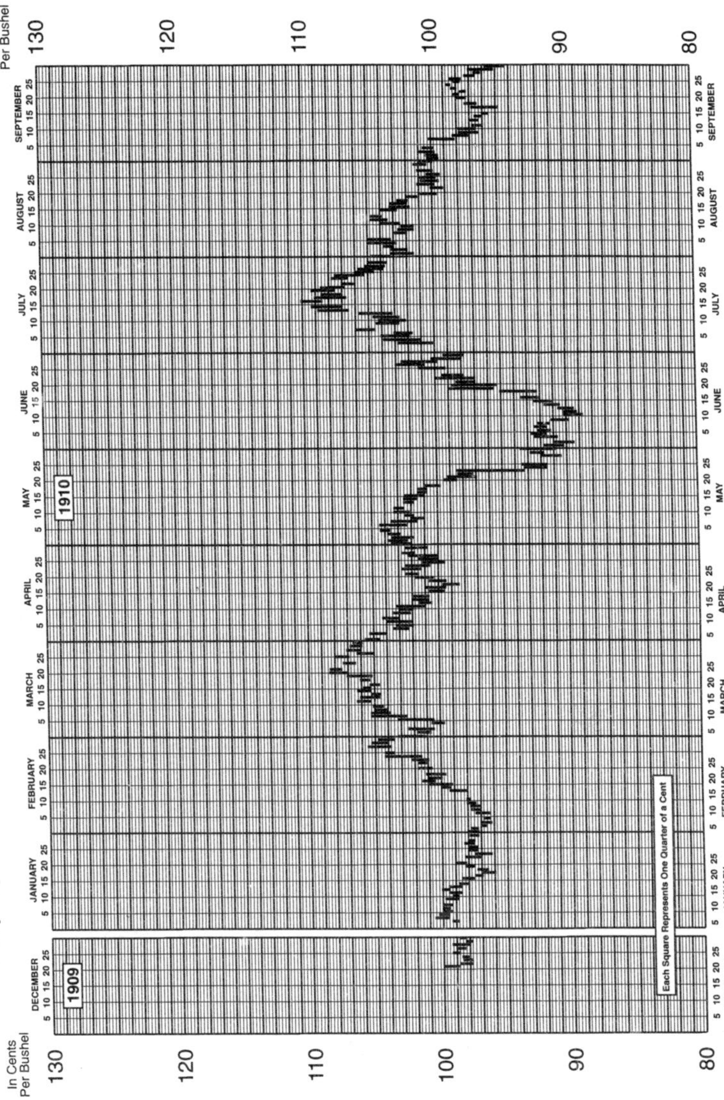

Daily Highest and Lowest Prices – May Wheat Futures – Chicago Board of Trade

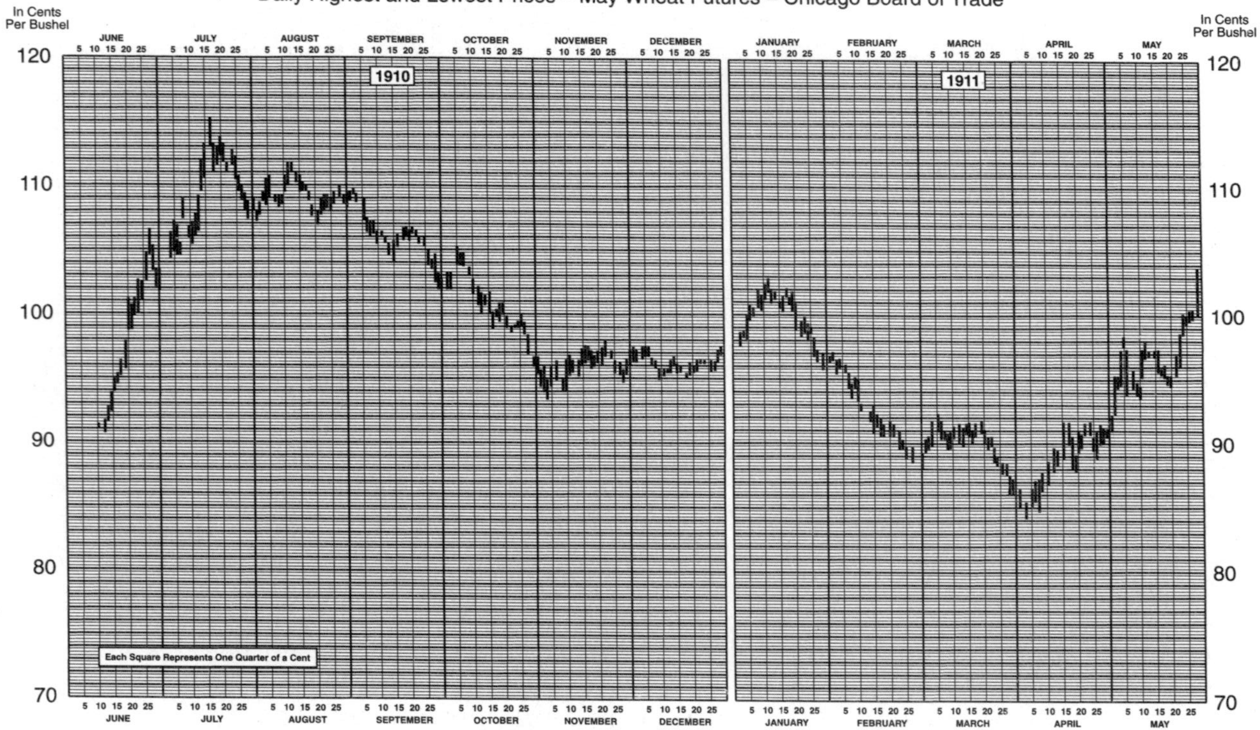

• MAY 1911 •

Daily Highest and Lowest Prices – July Wheat Futures – Chicago Board of Trade

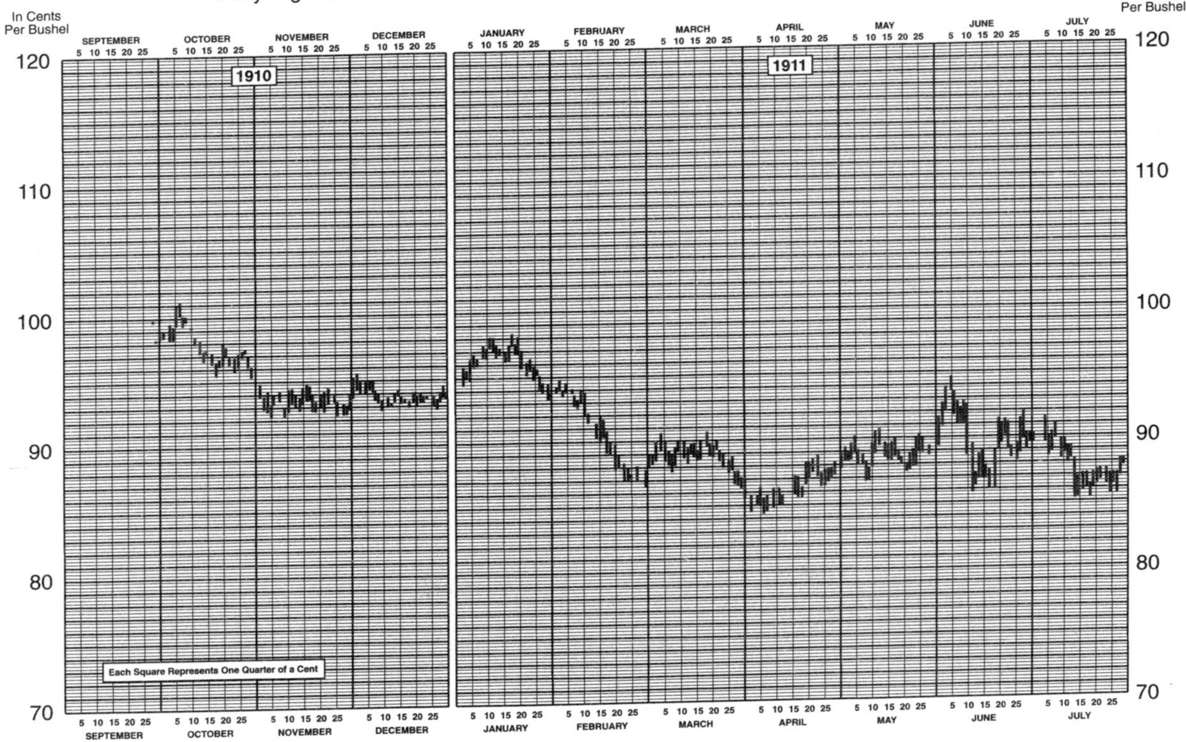

Daily Highest and Lowest Prices – September Wheat Futures – Chicago Board of Trade

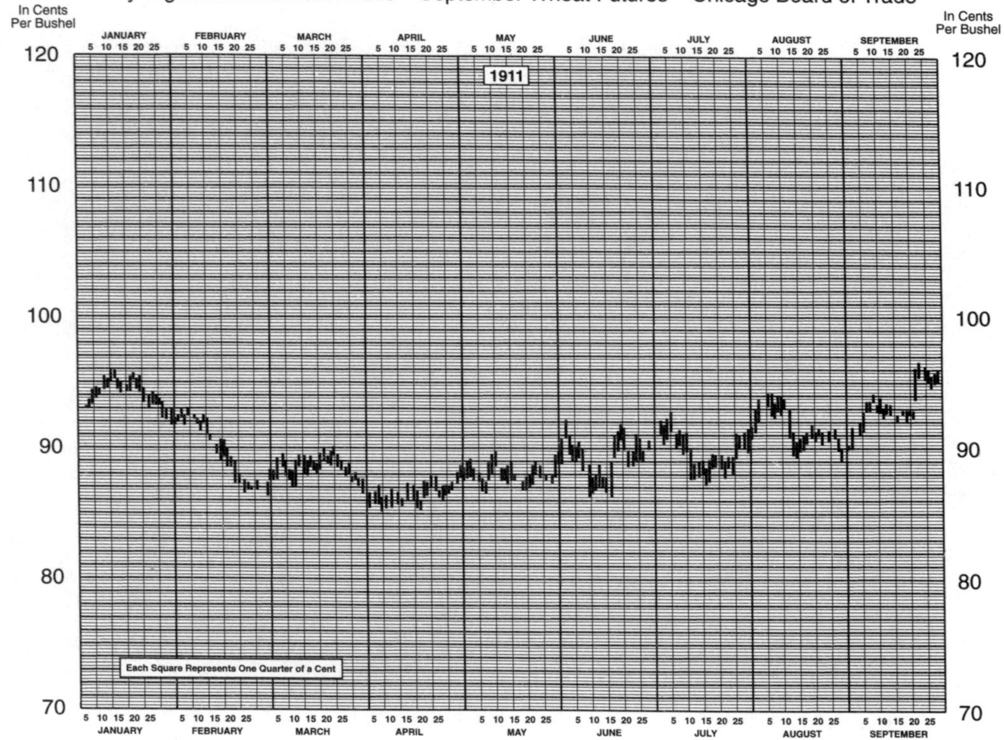

INDEX